FRONTISPIECE: Multi-sensor reconnaissance and military aircraft are typified by the six designs pictured here:

A. The U-2 high-altitude research plane manufactured by Lockheed Aircraft Corporation.

B. Lockheed's YF-12A (SR-71), a fighter-interceptor that is the probable successor to the U-2. This interceptor is capable of flying faster than 2,000 miles per hour and has an operating ceiling of around 80,000 feet.

C. The RF-4C "Phantom," a tactical all-weather reconnaissance fighter manufactured by McDonnell Aircraft Corporation.

D. The RA-5C high-performance fighter-type aircraft manufactured by North American Aviation, Inc.

E. The F-111 variable-sweep-wing fighter manufactured for both the U.S. Air Force and the U.S. Navy by the Fort Worth Division of General Dynamics Corporation. In this illustration, the wings are tucked back near the 72.5-degree sweep position for supersonic flight.

F. U.S. Air Force Republic RF-84F photo reconnaissance aircraft on low-altitude mission.

INTERPRETATION OF AERIAL PHOTOGRAPHS

Second Edition

T. Eugene Avery, Ph.D.
School of Forestry
Northern Arizona University
Flagstaff, Arizona

Burgess Publishing Company

426 South Sixth Street • Minneapolis, Minn. 55415

DEDICATION

TO

PHILIP R. WHEELER

Preface

The scope of this second edition has been broadened to encompass a wider span of photographic interpretation applications. All of the materials included in the 13 chapters of the first edition are covered in only nine chapters of this volume. Of the last seven chapters, six contain information that was not generally treated in the 1962 edition.

New subject matter includes chapters on remote-sensing techniques, agricultural and land-use patterns, landforms and physiographic features, engineering applications, urban-industrial patterns, and air intelligence and military target analysis. A glossary of common photogrammetric terms has been included at the end of the book.

Whereas the earlier version contained 70 references to current literature, a total of 249 have been listed here. For quick reference, these articles are classed according to subject matter and placed at the end of each chapter. The number of black-and-white illustrations has been increased from 130 to more than 250, and a special insert of color aerial photographs has been included. Twelve suggested exercises for student use or self-instruction have been incorporated into Chapters 1 through 8, which deal with basic techniques. In essence, this volume retains the features of the first edition, but it contains a large proportion of additional information.

I am indebted to the many cooperators who supplied illustrations for this new edition. Most of the new line drawings were prepared by Professor Dennis M. Richter, Wisconsin State University at Whitewater. The U.S. Department of Defense deserves a special acknowledgment for providing unclassified military and target photographs for Chapter 15. Special thanks are also expressed to my wife, Marianna, for assistance in proofreading, and to my secretary, Miss Dorothy Hanke, for typing the final manuscript.

Finally, a word of appreciation and gratitude to the many readers who expressed their satisfaction with the earlier version of this book. It is my hope that this volume will be even more valuable to aerial photo interpreters of varied backgrounds.

T. Eugene Avery

Table of Contents

CHAPTER 11 – FORESTRY USES OF AERIAL PHOTOGRAPHS

CHAPTER 12 – LANDFORMS AND PHYSIOGRAPHIC FEATURES

CHAPTER 13 – ENGINEERING APPLICATIONS

INTERPRETATION OF
AERIAL PHOTOGRAPHS

CHAPTER 1

Introduction to Photography and Photogrammetry

History of Photography

An understanding of the photographic process is essential for a full comprehension of photogrammetry and aerial photo interpretation. The origin of photography has been traced back to 1839 when Louis J. M. Daguerre of Paris invented a positive-image process for making portraits. The daguerreotype method utilized metal film plates that had been light-sensitized with a layer of silver iodide. The early day camera was often no more than a light-tight box with a pinhole or simple glass plate comprising the lens. After a picture was taken, the photographic plate was removed from the camera, exposed to fumes of mercury, and then heated to produce a direct-positive image. These positive images, of course, could not be duplicated.

A few years after Daguerre's technique had been developed, an Englishman, William H. Fox-Talbot, introduced the negative-positive process that continues in use today. The early 1840's also witnessed a reduction in camera exposure time from several minutes to a few seconds. This was made possible by the development of new lenses and the discovery of the superior light sensitivity of photographic plates coated with silver chloride, and later, silver bromide. For all practical purposes, the photographic techniques devised by Fox-Talbot remained basically unchanged for more than 100 years.

The Simple Camera

The design and function of a camera is not unlike that of the human eye. Each consists of an enclosed chamber with a lens at one end and a light-sensitive film (retina) at the other. The lens gathers light rays reflected from given objects and transmits them in an orderly fashion back to the light-sensitive area. A shutter assembly serves to regulate the amount and duration of light reaching the film when making an exposure *(Figure 1-1)*.

When a camera is focused at infinity, the distance from lens to film is known as the focal length, and the area in which the film is held flat during an exposure is referred to as the focal plane. Shutters may be positioned behind the lens, between elements of the lens, or in the focal plane immediately in front of the film. Operation of a focal plane shutter is analogous to drawing a slitted curtain across the area where the film is positioned. Intensity and length of exposure can be changed by varying the width of the curtain slit and the tension of a spring-driven roller. Between-the-lens shutters are commonly characterized by a series of overlapping metal "leaves" that are rapidly opened and closed by an intricate gear chain *(Figure 1-2)*. The diameter of the lens opening (effective aperture) can be varied by adjustment of a second set of thin, metal blades which comprise the iris diaphragm.

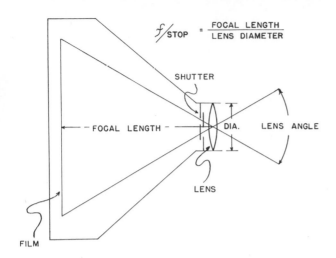

$$f/\text{STOP} = \frac{\text{FOCAL LENGTH}}{\text{LENS DIAMETER}}$$

FIGURE 1-1. Nomenclature of a simple camera.

FIGURE 1-2. Camera lens with between-the-lens shutter. Note shutter speed and f/stop settings. Courtesy of Calumet Manufacturing Co.

Relative Apertures

The ratio of the camera focal length to the diameter of the lens opening is known as the "f/stop," an expression used to designate the relative aperture setting or "speed" of a lens system. For example, a camera with a focal length of 2 inches and a lens diameter of $1/2$ inch at full aperture would have an f/4 lens. If the aperture were 1 inch instead of $1/2$ inch, the lens rating would be f/2; conversely, a $1/4$-inch aperture with a 2-inch focal length would result in a lens rating of f/8. Thus the smaller the f/rating, the "faster" the lens, i.e., the more light is admitted through the lens opening.

While the focal length of a camera is normally fixed, the iris diaphragm can be used to regulate the effective aperture, with accompanying changes in f/stop values. When an f/4 lens is "stopped down" to f/8, it simply indicates that the effective *diameter* of the lens opening has been cut in half. More explicitly, the *area* of the lens opening is only one-fourth as large. Similarly, a lens setting of f/16 admits only one-fourth as much light as a setting of f/8, and only one-sixteenth as much as a setting of f/4. Use of this lens rating system furnishes a uniform standard for making film exposures with any camera under varying light conditions. The more commonly used aperture settings and corresponding shutter-speed ratios are as follows:

Relative aperture or f/stop	**Larger lens openings** — — — — — — **Smaller lens openings**										
	f/2	2.8	4	5.6	8	11	16	22	32	45	64
Index no. for shutter-speed	**Faster speeds** — — — — — — — — — — **Slower speeds**										
	1	2	4	8	16	32	64	128	256	512	1024

These relationships are well known to most camera enthusiasts. Simply stated, changes in aperture settings must be accompanied by adjustments of shutter-speeds if a constant exposure is desired. For instance, a lens setting of 1/100 second at f/4 admits the same amount of light as a setting of 1/25 at f/8 or 1/400 at f/2. These paired relationships comprise the basis for "light value systems" featured on many cameras; when the iris diaphragm is coupled with the shutter-speed selector, a change in either value results in an automatic adjustment of the other.

Camera Viewing Angles

The angle of view encompassed by a camera lens is a function of the focal length and the diagonal measure of the film negative. When these two distances are approximately equal, the angle is roughly 45 to 50 degrees, and the lens is referred to as "normal angle." The distinction between normal and wide lens angles is somewhat arbitrary. For aerial cameras, lens angles up to 75 degrees are considered normal; those with angles of 75 to 100 degrees are termed wide-angle, and those that exceed 100 degrees are designated as ultra-wide. As will be seen later, the choice of a proper camera focal length and lens angle is of prime importance in planning photographic surveys.

Lenses may vary from a single curved piece of glass to multi-element, distortion-free designs that are little short of optical perfection. A thorough evaluation of camera lenses is beyond the scope of this volume, but it should be noted that lens quality is the major factor to be considered in the purchase or use of any camera.

Photographic Film

Photographic film is ordinarily composed of a cellulose acetate base[1] or support that has been coated on one side with a light-sensitive layer known as the emulsion. On the other side of the film base is the anti-halation backing, a light-absorbing dye that prevents the formation of halos around bright images. A simplified film cross-section is illustrated in *Figure 1-3*. The prime ingredient in the film emulsion is metallic silver, generally in the form of silver bromide crystals suspended in a gelatin vehicle. During the split second when the camera shutter is open, light reaches the emulsion and a latent image of the scene viewed is recorded on the film. This image is made visible to the human eye by subsequent processes of film development and printing.

Emulsions for photographic films possess varying degrees of sensitivity to light waves, and knowledge of a particular film's "speed" is essential to obtain a correct exposure. "Slow" films may require bright sunshine or artificial light for proper exposure, while "faster" films permit good pictures under minimal light conditions. A disadvantage of high-speed film, however, is that resultant negatives and prints are apt to be excessively grainy, i.e., coarsely textured.

In the United States, the American Standards Association rates each film emulsion on a relative scale of light sensitivity. The A. S. A. exposure index, as it is called, provides a uniform classification system that can be applied easily under changing light intensities.

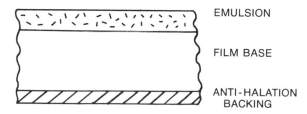

FIGURE 1-3. Cross-section of photographic film.

EMULSION

FILM BASE

ANTI-HALATION BACKING

---

[1] Aerial films are also available on low-shrink, polyester film bases.

Black-and-white films most commonly used have exposure ratings of 50 to 300, although extremes may range from around 8 to 1,000. The larger the A. S. A. rating, the greater the sensitivity of the emulsion. Many black-and-white aerial films are rated at 80 to 200, and such speeds provide a reasonable latitude of exposure with a minimum of graininess.

When a roll of exposed film is removed from a camera, it must be protected from light, extremes of temperature, and humidity until it is processed. Briefly, the step-by-step dark-room procedure in the production of a film negative is as follows:

1. **Developing:** Immersion of film in a chemical solution to produce the photographic image recorded during exposure. Image highlights take the form of heavy metallic silver deposits; medium tones are characterized by lighter silver deposits. Negative tones are the reverse of those on a positive print.

2. **Short-stop:** Immersion of film in dilute acetic acid to stop the developing reaction.

3. **Fixing:** Removal of unaffected silver salts from the emulsion.

4. **Washing:** Agitation in running water to remove all processing chemicals.

5. **Drying:** Film hung on clips and dried by natural air circulation or placed in special film-drying ovens.

Positive prints are produced by a series of steps similar to those followed in film development. A sheet of sensitized photographic paper is placed over the negative and "exposed" by light from underneath. The exposed paper is then subjected to a developing solution, followed by a short-stop bath, fixing, washing and drying. If a hard, high-gloss photographic surface is desired, the print is dried on heated stainless steel rollers or platens, a process known as ferrotyping.

Kodak Bimat Process

As reported by Tarkington (1965), the Kodak Bimat process is a new method that utilizes a special film-like material. When this "film" is brought into face-contact with an exposed negative material, it completely develops and fixes the negative image, and at the same time produces a positive image in the processing film. Both the processing film with its positive image and the negative film with its negative image are immediately usable. Two outstanding advantages are evident for this new process:

1. Free liquids are eliminated from photographic processing.

2. A positive image is simultaneously obtained with the developed and fixed negative without the necessity of the usual printing step and additional processing step.

The Bimat process is especially suitable for tactical aerial reconnaissance, because in-flight processing is easily accomplished without free solutions being involved. By the time the aircraft returns to base, processing can already be completed, and a positive image is available for study immediately upon landing.

Larger reconnaissance aircraft can accommodate the dual Bimat transfer film method in which the positive image is available almost immediately for on-the-spot interpretation while the plane is still in the air. Thus, films can be examined to determine whether the information originally sought has been successfully recorded. If not, more photographs can be made while the aircraft is over the target area, assuring a successful mission. Equipment for this process has been designed by Eastman Kodak Company under U.S. Air Force contract. The Bimat process is diagrammatically illustrated by *Figures 1-4* and *1-5*.

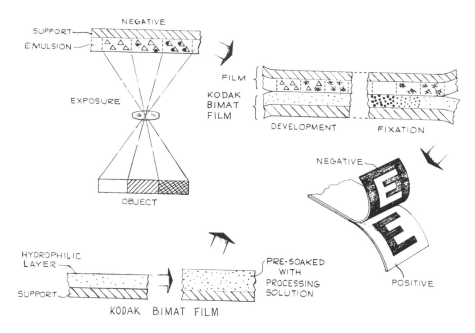

FIGURE 1-4. Kodak Bimat film is soaked in a developer containing a silver halide solvent. The film is then placed in intimate contact with the exposed, light-sensitive material and the solution immediately begins to diffuse into the negative emulsion layer. Exposed negative grains begin to develop, and unexposed grains start to dissolve in the silver halide solvent. As the process continues, some of the dissolved silver halide diffuses to the processing film where it is reduced to silver on the nuclei present and forms a positive image. Courtesy of Eastman Kodak Co.

FIGURE 1-5. The Kodak Bimat "wind-up process." The presoaked processing film is laminated to the exposed, light-sensitive film by winding the two together on a single spool. The two are kept in contact for the proper length of time, which depends on the type of film. Since the process is self-limiting, the films can remain in contact for a considerable time before they are unwound and separated, provided they are not allowed to dry while in contact. The outstanding advantage of this mode of operation is that it accommodates varying rates of film transport through the camera. Courtesy of Eastman Kodak Co.

The Development of Photogrammetry

Photogrammetry is defined as the science of obtaining reliable measurements of objects from their photographic images. The word "photogrammetry" is derived from three Greek roots meaning "light-writing-measurement." Odd as it may seem, aerial photographs and photogrammetric principles were employed in mapping and military reconnaissance before the Wright brothers' first historic flight in 1903. In the early 1850's, Aimé Laussedat, a French Army Engineer, conducted a series of experiments with aerial photographs taken from kites and captive balloons. Although the work was later abandoned without notable success, Laussedat has often been referred to as the *father of photogrammetry*.

Captive-balloon photography *(Figure 1-6)* proved highly utilitarian during the American Civil War when General McClellan employed this innovation to make photo-maps of Confederate positions in Virginia. During the period from 1890 to 1910, new techniques in terrestrial photogrammetry were devised, and the U.S. Geological Survey used a panoramic camera for contour mapping in Alaska. The military significance of aerial photography and photo interpretation was brought sharply into focus by World War I and the development of airplanes for military use. In the early 1920's, government agencies began to utilize aerial photography in map compilation, and several private aerial survey firms were founded; some of these pioneer corporations are still flourishing today.

FIGURE 1-6. This 1860 picture of Boston Harbor, made by J. W. Black, was one of the first aerial photographs taken in the United States. The exposure was made from a captive balloon at an altitude of 1,200 feet. Courtesy of Ansco, General Aniline and Film Corp.

Prior to the first World War, many of the airphotos used in mapping were oblique views, i.e., exposures made with the camera aimed at an angle to the vertical *(Figure 1-7)*. In the ensuing years, however, emphasis was shifted toward greater use of stereoscopic coverage with vertical photography. The 1930's saw the formation of the Agricultural Adjustment Administration[2] in the U.S. Department of Agriculture and the beginning of this agency's extensive photographic coverage of farm and range lands. The Geological Survey began to rely more heavily on aerial photographs in topographical surveying, and the creation of the Tennessee Valley Authority gave new impetus to an expanding program of federal mapping. During this same period, the U.S. Forest Service demonstrated the feasibility of using airphotos for timber type-mapping on the national forests.

The Development of Photo Interpretation

Photo interpretation may be defined as the identification of objects on airphotos and the determination of their meaning or significance. The art of photo interpretation was a little-known skill in America prior to 1939 and the advent of World War II. Within the next 5 or 6 years, however, countless tactical military decisions were based on aerial reconnaissance missions. The British were foremost in the development of photo intelligence systems, and their superiority was highly significant in the early detection of German V-2 rocket-launching sites along the coast of France. A most interesting history of British photo intelligence has been written by Constance Babington-Smith (1957).

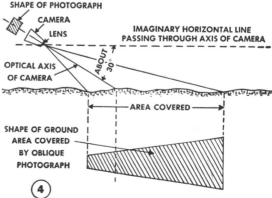

FIGURE 1-7. Orientation of aerial camera for vertical and oblique photography. Courtesy of U.S. Department of the Army.

---

[2]Presently known as the Agricultural Stabilization and Conservation Service (ASCS).

During the past twenty years, civilian uses of photogrammetric techniques have multiplied at a phenomenal rate. Aerial photographs are now employed on such diversified projects as real estate zoning, highway route location, mineral exploration, archeological excavations, automobile traffic control, assessment of underwater marine life, and tracking of guided missiles. In this same period, equally significant technological advances have been made in aircraft, aerial cameras, and optical systems *(Figures 1-8, 1-9, 1-10).*

How Aerial Photographs Are Used

As an illustration of the many problem situations in which aerial photographs might be involved, the following applications were extracted from a listing compiled by the American Society of Photogrammetry:

Aeronautical engineering	Land classification
Agronomy	Mapping and surveying
Appraisals of land resources	Military target analysis
Archeology	Mineralogy
Astronomy	Mosaics
Beach protection	Natural resources inventories
Biology	Oceanography
Boundary delineation	Police protection
Charting of water depths	Production and marketing
Control surveys	Range management
Crop yield predictions	Real estate zoning
Disease and insect detection	Recreation planning
Drainage studies	Relief model construction
Ecology	Reservoir capacities
Engineering structures	River currents and tides
Erosion problems	Satellite tracking
Fire protection	Sociological studies
Fish migrations	Soil surveys and trafficability
Flight planning	Space exploration
Flood control	Stockpile inventories
Food production	Taxation of land
Forestry	Traffic control
Frost damage	Transportation studies
Geography	Triangulation networks
Geology	Urban area analyses
Glacial studies	Valuations of property
Highway planning	Watershed management
Hydrology	Wildlife management
Irrigation planning	Zoology

In military parlance, the collection and evaluation of photo intelligence data is now standard operating procedure. This fact was again demonstrated by the revelation of the U-2 flights over the U.S.S.R. in 1960 and the discovery of missile-launching sites in Cuba during 1962. Much national attention is centered on sending men and instruments to the moon, the planets, and to way-stations in outer space. The science of photogrammetry is contributing to these explorations — and the sky is no longer the limit!

FIGURE 1-8. Low oblique aerial view (horizon not shown) of Grant's Tomb, New York. Courtesy of Abrams Aerial Survey Corp.

FIGURE 1-9. High oblique aerial view (horizon included) from upper New York State. Courtesy of Aero Service Division of Litton Industries.

FIGURE 1-10. The potential of modern optical systems is revealed by this vertical photograph of Philadelphia, taken with a Wild RC-9 aerial camera from an altitude of 36,000 feet. Scale is 1:122,000 or about two miles per inch. Courtesy of Aero Service Division of Litton Industries.

American Society of Photogrammetry

The principal functions of the American Society of Photogrammetry are the advancement of photogrammetry through research, the free exchange of ideas, and the dissemination of technical knowledge to present and potential users of photogrammetric methods. Founded in 1934, the Society now has about 4,500 members in the United States and foreign countries. Membership is not limited to one or two technical disciplines; instead, the Society attempts to encourage interest among a wide diversity of professional groups. Included are photogrammetric and civil engineers, foresters, geologists, geographers, cartographers, soil scientists, and military personnel. A special grade of membership is also open to college students with an interest in photogrammetry and photo interpretation.

The Society's official journal, *Photogrammetric Engineering,* is received monthly by all members. Also, a national technical meeting is held jointly with the American Congress on Surveying and Mapping in Washington, D. C., each year. Exhibits of new photogrammetric equipment are among the principal attractions at these meetings. Several outstanding technical books have been published by the American Society of Photogrammetry. One of these, the *Manual of Photographic Interpretation* (1960), represents one of the most comprehensive volumes ever compiled on this subject. Information on Society membership and publications may be obtained from:

American Society of Photogrammetry

105 North Virginia Avenue

Falls Church, Virginia 22046

In Canada, photogrammetric activities are coordinated by the Canadian Institute of Surveying and the Interdepartmental Committee on Aerial Survey. These groups have periodically sponsored special international symposia on aerial surveying and photo interpretation.

Photogrammetric Training

During World War II, several private aerial surveying corporations taught courses in airphoto interpretation and mapping to Army, Navy, and Marine Corps personnel. All branches of the U.S. Armed Forces and most colleges and universities now offer formal courses in photogrammetry or photo interpretation. In most instances, college instruction is at elementary or intermediate levels, and courses are commonly found in departments of forestry, geology, geography, and civil engineering. Offerings in advanced work are generally oriented toward civil engineering and metrical photogrammetry rather than photo interpretation. Only a small number of American universities offer graduate studies leading to the doctoral degree in photogrammetry or photo interpretation.

On an international basis, one of the widely recognized seats of photogrammetric training is the International Institute for Aerial Survey and Earth Sciences at Delft, The Netherlands. A bulletin from this Institute contains the following statement of aims:

"A successful and efficient utilization of a country's natural and human resources requires investigations of a various nature: geological, geomorphological, ecological, and soil surveys are as necessary as agricultural, economic and sociological investigations. All these investigations should be carried out in such a way, that an overall integrated picture of the area under survey is obtained, offering a basis for well-supported decisions on planning and execution of development projects. This calls for a systematic organization of integrated surveys, in which all pertinent aspects should find their proper place.

"To provide for the need of training in the particular problems of such integrated surveys, UNESCO and ITC (the International Institute for Aerial Survey and Earth Sciences, Delft, The Netherlands) have agreed to cooperate in organizing courses on integrated surveys.

"Three different types of courses are given:

1. Advanced courses, of 4 or 7 months duration, designed for specialists, who have already sufficient experience within their own field, but who wish to concentrate on the subject of integrated surveys, including an introduction to the survey problems of related disciplines;

2. Standard courses of 12 to 18 months duration for a full training in aerial photo-interpretation as applied to natural resources inventory combined with an advanced training in selected subjects of integrated surveys;

3. Orientation courses of one month duration for administrators and civil servants, associated with the planning and organization of integrated surveys for development projects."

A prospectus of these courses will be sent on request to:

ITC-UNESCO Centre for Integrated Surveys

3, Kanaalweg

Delft, The Netherlands

Photogrammetria, the official journal of the International Society of Photogrammetry, is edited and published under the auspices of the ITC-UNESCO Centre. This technical journal is issued six times each year.

References

Abrams, Talbert.
   1944. *Essentials of Aerial Surveying and Photo Interpretation.* McGraw-Hill Book Co., New York, N.Y., 289 pp., illus.

American Society of Photogrammetry.
   1963. What about a career in photogrammetry? Falls Church, Va., 24 pp., illus.

_____.
   1960. *Manual of Photographic Interpretation.* Banta Publishing Co., Menasha, Wis., 868 pp., illus.

Anonymous.
   1966. Abstracts of current and recent air photo research projects. The Center for Aerial Photographic Studies, Cornell Univ., Ithaca, N.Y., 31 pp.

Babington-Smith, Constance.
   1957. *Air Spy:* The story of British photo intelligence in World War II. Ballentine Books, Inc. (Harper and Bros.), N.Y., 190 pp., illus.

Coleman, Charles G.
   1960. Recent trends in photographic interpretation. Photogram. Engineering 26: 755-763, illus.

Colwell, Robert N.
   1964. Aerial photography—a valuable sensor for the scientist. American Scientist 52:17-49, illus.

Eliel, Leon T.
   1959. One hundred years of photogrammetry. Photogram. Engineering 25:359-363.

Larmore, Lewis.
   1965. *Introduction to Photographic Principles,* 2nd ed. Dover Publications, Inc., New York, N.Y., 229 pp., illus.

Livingston, Robert G.
   1964. A history of military mapping camera development. Photogram. Engineering 30:97-110, illus.

McNair, Arthur J.
   1957. Education in photogrammetry. Photogram. Engineering 23:508-512.

Sewell, Eldon D.
   1957. Fifty years of aerial photography, beginning in 1880. Photogram. Engineering 23:835-850, illus.

Tarkington, Raife G.
   1965. The Kodak Bimat process. Eastman Kodak Co., Rochester, N.Y. Pamphlet P-63, 11 pp., illus.

U.S. Department of the Army.
   1944. Map reading. Field Manual 21-26. Government Printing Office, Washington, D.C., 141 pp., illus.

EXERCISE 1 — General Photography

1. What would be the "speed" of a lens having a focal length of 70 mm. and a lens diameter of 20 mm.

   at full aperture?_____

2. If a correct exposure can be made with a shutter speed of $1/100$ second at f/8, what f/stop would you use at $1/200$ second? What shutter speed would be required with an aperture setting of f/16?

   a._____ b._____

3. If a correct exposure combination for a film is 4 seconds at f/64, what is the required f/stop for a

   $1/4$-second exposure?_____

4. What would be the focal length (in millimeters) of a "normal angle" lens having a negative format of $2\frac{1}{4}$ by $2\frac{1}{4}$ inches? What would it be for a negative format of 9 by 9 inches?

   a._____ b._____

5. Refer to any standard text on photography and explain what is meant by:

   a. Depth of field:

   b. Hyperfocal distance:

   c. How are these items affected by changes in relative apertures?

6. List 3 commercially available films and their corresponding A.S.A. exposure ratings. What are the recommended shutter speeds and f/stops for these films under conditions of bright sunlight and strong shadows?

Name of film	A.S.A. rating	Shutter speed	f/stop

CHAPTER 2

Orientation and Study
of Aerial Photographs

Principles of Object Recognition

Most persons have little difficulty in recognizing features pictured on oblique photographs, for such views appear relatively "normal" to the human eye. On the other hand, a vertical or near-vertical view from an altitude of several thousand feet can be quite confusing, particularly for individuals who have never ridden in an airplane *(Figure 2-1)*. An experienced aerial photo interpreter exercises *mental acuity* as well as *visual perception,* and consciously or unconsciously must evaluate several factors in identifying features on vertical photographs. Prominent among these are:

Shape: This characteristic alone may serve to identify some objects. Examples include a highway "cloverleaf" intersection, an airfield, or a football stadium.

Size: Both relative and absolute sizes are important. Thus a super-highway will not be confused with a rural road, or a small residence with an apartment building. Size, of course, is a function of the photographic scale.

Photographic tone: Objects of different color have different qualities of light reflectance and, therefore, register in varying shades or tones on a photograph. Obvious examples include quartz sand versus dark topsoil, cultivated versus fallow fields, or coniferous versus broad-leaved tree crowns.

Pattern: If the spatial arrangement of trees in an orchard is compared with that of natural vegetation, a contrast in patterns will be evident. As another example, a pattern produced by contour plowing might reveal information on topography, type of soil, or the nature of the crop being cultivated.

Shadow: A truly vertical photograph of a tall smokestack or an isolated oil derrick might present a difficult identification problem, except for the characteristic shadows cast by these objects. By the same token, shadows may also be offensive to the interpreter by obscuring ground detail, e.g., shadows alongside tall buildings or beneath dense canopies of vegetation.

Topographic location: Relative elevation, including drainage features, can be an important clue in predicting soil conditions or the probability of encountering a particular vegetative association. The natural occurrence of willow trees on floodplains or river sandbars supplies a good example.

Texture: The degree of coarseness or smoothness exhibited by photo images can be a useful key to identification. Texture, just as object size, is directly correlated with photo scale. Contrast the texture of grass with that of a corn field, or saplings with large, overmature trees.

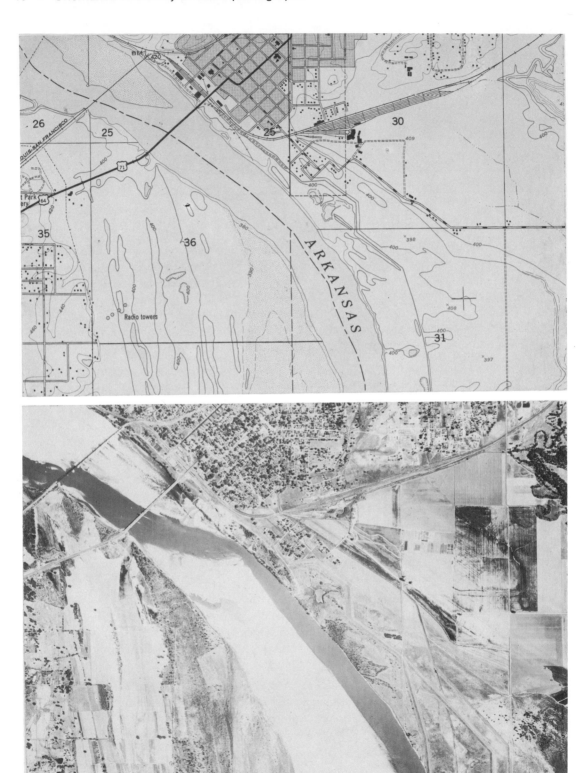

FIGURE 2-1. Portion of topographic map and aerial photograph of Fort Smith, Arkansas. Courtesy of U.S. Geological Survey and U.S. Department of Agriculture.

Checklist of Typical Features

In the identification of unfamiliar features on vertical photographs, it has been found that the power of suggestion is often beneficial to beginning interpreters. Accordingly, the following checklist has been prepared to illustrate the kinds of features commonly encountered in the study of aerial photographs. The groupings according to ten general categories are somewhat arbitrary; therefore, a given feature might logically be assigned to more than one of the classifications shown.

Forests and Natural Vegetation
Coniferous forests
Hardwood forests
Mixed coniferous and hardwood forests
Forest plantations

Agricultural Features
Cultivated crops (e.g., corn)
Contour plowing or terraced cropland
Irrigated crops (specify type)
Orchards (specify type)
Vineyards
Improved pastures
Fences or hedgerows
Barns or silos
Baled hay or shocked wheat
Livestock or wild game
Greenhouses
Nurseries
Abandoned or fallow fields

Mining and Excavation
Strip-mining (e.g., coal)
Placer-mining (e.g., gold)
Open-pit mining (e.g., copper)
Sand and gravel excavations
Rock quarries
Oil drilling and development
Channel dredging
Land-clearing operations

Water and Natural Shoreline Features
Shorelines and beaches
Coastal bays and inlets
Swamps or marshes
Floodplains or deltas
Permanent rivers or streams
Inland lakes or ponds
Sand bars or mud flats
Limesinks or potholes

Physiographic and Geologic Features
Active glaciers
Cirques or cliffs
Eskers or drumlins
Talus slopes and alluvial fans
Gully erosion
Sheet erosion
Volcanic lava flows or cones
Rock outcrops
Hogbacks
Anticlines and synclines
Faults and dikes

Urban-Residential Patterns
Apartment houses
Mobile homes
Garages
Schools (specify type)
Churches and cemeteries
Parks or playgrounds
Statues or monuments
Civic or recreational centers
Shopping centers
Downtown business districts
Gas stations
Automobile sales
Mobile home sales
Motels or hotels
Drive-in theaters
Country clubs
Swimming pools
Golf courses
Tennis courts
Football fields
Other athletic fields
Race tracks
Auto junkyards
Prisons
County rest homes
Hospitals

Industrial and Utility Features
Electrical power plants
Electrical power substations
Steel towers for electrical lines
Cleared rights-of-way
Buried pipelines
Sewage disposal plants
Water purification plants
Petroleum or chemical industries
Petroleum products storage tanks
Sawmills and lumber yards
Pulp and paper mills
Furniture manufacturing
Automobile manufacturing
Steel or other metal industries
Cement block manufacturing
Ready-mixed concrete plants
Stockyards or meat-packing plants

Transportation and Communication Features
Four-lane, divided highway
Three-lane, paved highway
Two-lane paved highway
Graded, nonsurfaced road
Woods road or Jeep trail
Traffic circles and interchanges
Overpass-underpass
Railroad
Railroad terminal
Bus terminal
Trucking terminal

Airports
Radio or TV transmission tower
Radar antenna
Railroad coal dumping spur
Boat docks and piers

Engineering Structures
Dams (describe type of material)
Bridges (describe type of material)
Road cuts and fills
Levees
Athletic stadium
Fire lookout tower
Water tanks
Canals or drainage ditches
Reservoirs
Ferry landing

Military and Defense Installations
Post headquarters
Barracks and residences
Temporary encampments
Ammunition dump
Rifle or artillery range
Tanks
Warships
Shipyards and drydocks
Missile test sites
Operational missile base
Airfields and planes
Radar installations

Three-Dimensional Photography

In many instances, it is entirely feasible to use single, vertical photographs for the recognition or classification of specific features. The principal disadvantage of the technique, however, is that only two dimensions (length and width) of most objects can be perceived. This is the equivalent of using only one eye, a practice referred to as *monocular vision*. The all-important third dimension of depth perception is provided only when objects are viewed with *both eyes*. Here, the converging lines-of-sight from each eye are transmitted to the brain, and the result is *binocular* or *stereoscopic vision*.

A quick comparison of "one-eyed" versus stereoscopic vision can be obtained by viewing a distant object, first with a telescope and then with binoculars having equal magnification. A second example is the "coin-on-a-table" trick. If one eye is covered and only the coin's *edge* is seen from the level of the table top, it becomes quite difficult to place the forefinger directly on top of the coin. With both eyes open, the difficulty vanishes.

While almost everyone possesses and automatically employs stereoscopic vision, there have been a number of fairly successful business enterprises based on the somewhat startling effects of exaggerated three-dimensional pictures. In the early 1900's, the stereopticon or "periscope" was almost a standard fixture in American parlors. This instrument, shown in *Figure 2-2,* was used to view paired photographs that had been taken from slightly different camera positions. The stereopticon allowed each eye to see only one print, thus creating the illusion of depth for the viewer. A paired photo-view of the Rock of Gibraltar is shown in *Figure 2-3.* Although the corresponding images are rather widely separated, persons experienced in stereo-viewing may be able to see this scene three-dimensionally without the aid of special instruments.

Three-dimensional motion pictures were popular for brief periods during the 1930's and again in the early 1950's. Two cameras were used to photograph each scene; both views were then projected on theater screens through polarized or red and blue-green lenses. Each patron was issued a pair of viewing spectacles to provide "fusion" of the projected images into a three-dimensional picture. Today, the emphasis on wider and wider movie projection screens is partially an attempt to create an illusion of depth without the necessity of two film projectors and special eyeglasses for the audience.

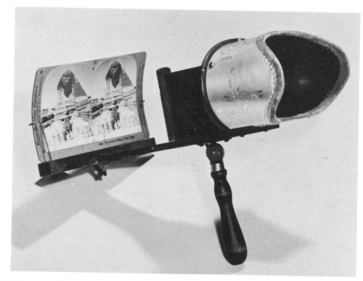

FIGURE 2-2. Old-fashioned parlor stereoscope. Note stereo-pair of the Sphinx. Courtesy of Keystone View Co.

FIGURE 2-3. Example of paired photographs that produce a three-dimensional picture when viewed through a parlor stereoscope. View shows the Rock of Gibraltar at the southern tip of Spain. Courtesy of Keystone View Co.

FIGURE 2-4. Stereo-camera for making three-dimensional color slides. Courtesy of Eastman Kodak Co.

Stereo-photography has also enjoyed periodic revivals of popularity among camera hobbyists. A few years ago, 35-mm. stereo-cameras with dual lens systems were marketed by several leading camera manufacturers *(Figure 2-4)*. The decline of interest in three-dimensional color slides may be partially attributed to the fact that (1) hand viewers can be used by only one person at a time, and (2) audience projection equipment is quite expensive by comparison with that required for conventional color slides.

When objects greater than 1,500 to 2,000 feet away are viewed by unaided eyes, the special ability of depth perception is essentially lost. At such distances, lines-of-sight from each eye converge very little; in fact, they are practically parallel when the eyes are focused at infinity. If the human eye base (interpupillary distance) were increased from the normal 2.5 or 2.6 inches, the perception of depth could be greatly increased. In a manner of speaking, this feat can be accomplished through aerial photography. From an airplane in level flight, overlapping camera exposures are made at intervals of several thousand feet. When any two successive prints are viewed through a simple stereoscope, each eye "occupies" one of the widely separated camera stations. This "stretching" of the human eye base results in a greatly exaggerated three-dimensional photograph for study and interpretation *(Figures 2-5, 2-6)*.

Photo Interpretation Equipment

Equipment essential to one interpreter may be of limited value to another, but anyone who uses aerial photographs regularly will probably find that this list closely approximates his minimum needs. If purchased with discretion, necessary items can be obtained for less than $250.

Lens stereoscope, folding pocket type

Stereometer or parallax bar for measuring object heights

Engineer's scale, graduated to 0.02 inch

Drafting instruments, drawing ink, triangles, and protractor

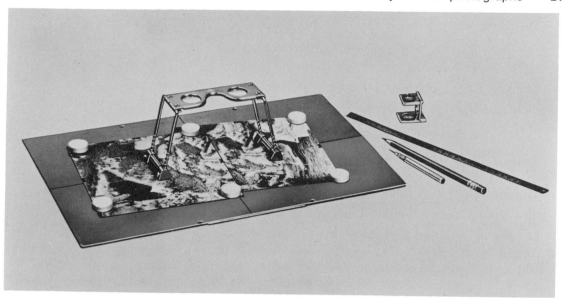

FIGURE 2-5. Pocket-type lens stereoscope for viewing overlapping pairs of aerial photographs. Stereoscope and prints are held firmly to portable steel table by magnets. Courtesy of Carl Zeiss, Inc., New York.

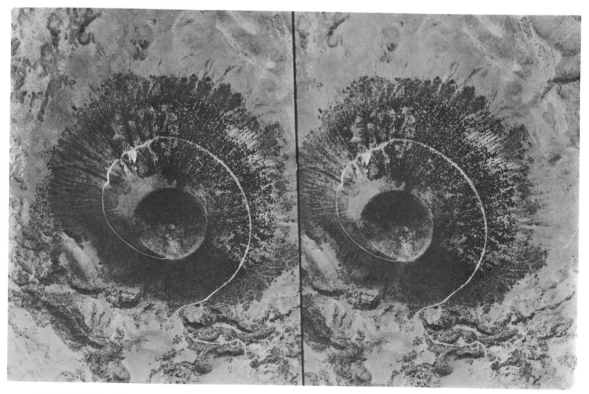

FIGURE 2-6. Stereogram of an extinct volcanic cone, Mt. Capulin, New Mexico. Scale is about 1,667 feet per inch. Courtesy of U.S. Department of Agriculture.

Drop-bow pen and pencil set

Fountain pen for use with drawing ink

China-marking pencils or water-soluble inks

Tracing paper, vellum, drafting tape, and lens-cleaning tissue

Carbon tetrachloride and cotton swabs for cleaning photos

Needles for point-picking

Proportional dividers

Magnetic or spring clipboard for holding stereo-pairs

Illuminated tracing table or fluorescent desk lamp

Dot grids or polar planimeter for area measurements

Several of the items listed may be improvised. A good tracing table can be built by installing several fluorescent tubes in a desk drawer. The top is then covered with double-weight frosted or "flashed-opal" glass. An elaborate version of this design is pictured in *Figure 2-7.* To eliminate the need for fastening down stereo-pairs with drafting tape, an efficient holder can be made with a few ordinary magnets and a sheet of steel measuring about 11 by 16 inches. Another design, shown in *Figure 2-8,* enables the viewer to see the "hidden area" of the overlap by turning the edges of the photographs downward into a central slot.

A price list of photo measuring scales and dot grids may be obtained by addressing the Division of Engineering, Forest Service, U.S. Department of Agriculture, Washington, D.C., 20250. Individuals with extensive interpretation and mapping duties may find it desirable to acquire more specialized equipment, such as a mirror stereoscope, vertical sketch-master, reflecting projector, or stereo-plotting devices. Functions of these items are detailed in chapters that follow.

Types of Stereoscopes

The function of a stereoscope is to deflect normally converging lines-of-sight, so that each eye views a different photographic image. Parlor stereoscopes accomplished this by the placement of a thin prism before each eye. Ordinarily, no magnification was involved, but the result was a sharply defined, if occasionally distorted, three-dimensional picture.

Instruments used now for three-dimensional study of aerial photographs fall into two general groups, viz., lens stereoscopes and mirror or reflecting stereoscopes. Lens stereoscopes utilize a pair of simple magnifying glasses to keep the eyes working independently and their lines-of-sight approximately parallel. Photographs are viewed at a distance roughly equal to the focal length of the lenses, i.e., the height of the instrument legs. Most lens stereoscopes have a magnifying power of two to three diameters. They are inexpensive, relatively durable, and can be quickly folded for field use or storage. The Zeiss lens stereoscope pictured in *Figure 2-5* has a fixed interpupillary distance of 65 millimeters and 2.8X lenses; the Abrams lens stereoscope *(Figure 2-8)* features adjustable interpupillary settings and 2X lenses. Other suitable makes are also available.

The primary drawback to lens-type stereoscopes is that only one-third to one-half of a standard print overlap can be studied stereoscopically at one time. However, the low cost and portability of such devices ensure their continued popularity among photo interpreters.

Reflecting stereoscopes provide a view of the entire overlap zone through a system of prisms or first-surface mirrors that effectively increase the interpupillary distance from

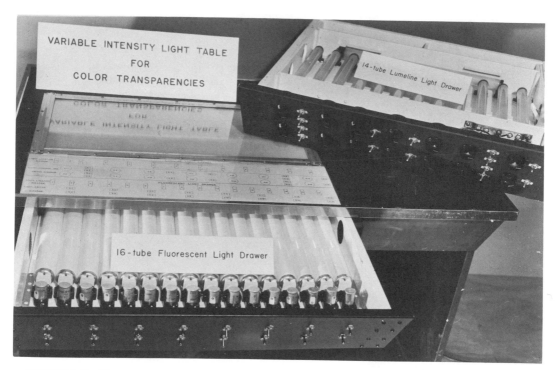

FIGURE 2-7. Illuminated table for photographic study. Lights can be controlled individually by toggle switches. Courtesy of U.S. Forest Service Remote Sensing Project, Berkeley, California.

FIGURE 2-8. Slotted clipboard for viewing the ''hidden area'' of overlapping prints with a lens stereoscope. The area indicated by arrows cannot be stereoscopically studied when prints are lapped as in Figure 2-5.

about 2.5 inches to 6 or 8 inches. Most basic models afford no magnification, but 3X to 8X binocular attachments are available at an added cost. The greater the enlargement, however, the smaller the field of view.

Reflecting stereoscopes, being specialized instruments, are produced in a variety of designs and price ranges. Two types are illustrated here. *Figure 2-9* shows the Wild folding mirror stereoscope. Optional accessories include 3X or 8X binoculars and a parallax bar for measuring differences in elevation. The Old Delft scanning stereoscope, pictured in *Figure 2-10,* permits viewing of the entire overlap of 9- by 9-inch photographs without movement of either the instrument or the prints. The field of view can be moved in both

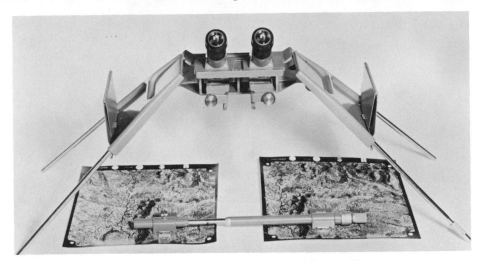

FIGURE 2-9. Mirror stereoscope with inclined magnifying binoculars. Positioned on the photographs is a stereometer for measuring object heights. Courtesy of Wild Heerbrugg Instruments, Inc.

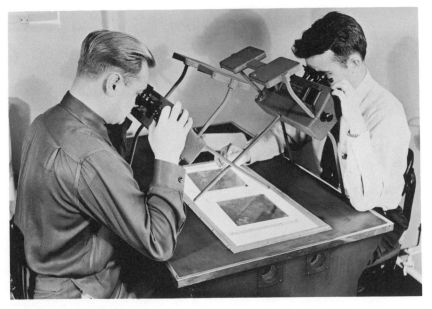

FIGURE 2-10. Tandem arrangement of two Old Delft scanning stereoscopes over a light table. Such setups permit both interpreters to study the same stereoscopic image simultaneously. Courtesy of U.S. Forest Service Remote Sensing Project, Berkeley, California.

X and Y directions by rotating knobs on opposite sides of the eyepieces. In addition, two magnifications (1.5X and 4.5X) are available for interpretation.

Stereoscopic lenses, prisms, and other optics should be protected from dust or corrosion and cleaned only with optical lens tissue. Mirror stereoscopes, vertical sketchmasters, and other devices having first-surface mirrors also require delicate handling. As these mirrors are silvered on the reflecting surface, they are easily corroded by fingerprints or perspiration. In many instances, these sensitive surfaces may be safely cleaned with a soft cotton swab moistened in carbon tetrachloride or household ammonia.

Stereo-Viewing without Instruments

Persons with normal vision and eyes of equal strength can often develop a facility for stereoscopic vision without the necessity of special aids or devices. With practice, some individuals can learn to keep lines-of-sight from each eye parallel and still bring images into focus. Practice in stereoscopic fusion is aided by such tricks as the "sausage" exercise sketched in *Figure 2-11*. The eyes are focused on a distant object as the forefingers are brought slowly into the line of vision. The farther apart the fingers when the "sausage" begins to form, the more nearly parallel are the lines-of-sight.

Another means of "forcing" each eye to see a different image is to place a card upright between left and right-hand views of a stereo-pair such as that shown in *Figure 2-6*. In practice, most persons easily master the art of keeping the lines-of-sight parallel; the primary difficulty is that of maintaining this condition while bringing the two different images into focus. In the case of the three-dimensional motion pictures discussed earlier, stereoscopic fusion was assisted by the use of polarized spectacles (*vectograph* principle), or by viewing images projected in complementary colors through eyeglasses having lenses of the opposite complementary colors (*anaglyph* principle). Stereoscopic prints based on these two concepts can be constructed for specialized illustrations, and instruments such as the Kelsh plotter utilize the anaglyph principle to create a three-dimensional model for contour mapping.

Preparing Photographs for Stereo-Viewing

Photographic flights are planned so that prints will overlap about 60 percent of their width in the line of flight and about 30 percent between flight strips. For effective stereo-viewing, prints must be trimmed to the nominal 9 by 9-inch size, preserving the four fiducial marks at the midpoints of each edge. Then the principal point or optical center of the photograph is located by aligning opposite sets of fiducial marks with a straightedge. A light cross is drawn at the photo center and a fine needle hole picked at the intersection.

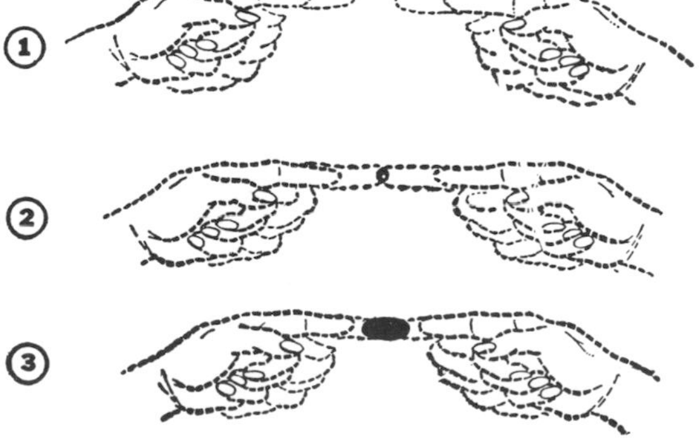

FIGURE 2-11. The "sausage" exercise is a helpful technique for developing the facility of stereoscopic vision with unaided eyes. Courtesy of U. S. Department of the Army.

Next is the location of conjugate principal points on each photograph, i.e., the points that correspond to principal points of adjacent photos.[1] The lens stereoscope is adjusted to the proper interpupillary distance, and the first two photographs from a given flight line are arranged so that gross features overlap. Image shadows should be toward the observer; if they fall away from the viewer, there is a tendency to see relief in reverse. One photograph is clipped down, and the adjacent photograph is moved in the direction of the line of flight until corresponding images on each print are about 2.2 inches apart. The lens stereoscope is placed over the prints *parallel to the line of flight* so that the left-hand lens is over the left photograph and the right-hand lens is over the same image on the right-hand photograph. The area directly under each lens should then appear as a three-dimensional picture.

The movable photograph should next be fastened down. While viewing the three-dimensional picture, the observer places a needle on the unmarked print until it appears to fall precisely in the hole picked for the PP. This locates the CPP, although a monocular check should be made before the print is permanently marked. This procedure is repeated for all photographs; each will then have one PP and two CPP's, except that prints falling at the ends of the flight lines will have only one CPP. When all points have been verified, they should be marked with an inked circle having a diameter of 0.2 inch.

Flight lines are located on each print by aligning the PP's and CPP's. The edges of the aligned circles should be connected with a finely inked line. Because of lateral shifting of the photographic aircraft in flight, a straight line will rarely pass through the PP and *both* CPP's on a given print *(Figure 2-12)*. The photo base length for each stereo-overlap is determined by averaging the distance between the PP and CPP on one photograph with the corresponding distance on an overlapping print. This value should be measured to the nearest 0.02 inch and recorded on the back of each overlap. There will be two average base lengths for each print, i.e., one for each set of overlapping flight lines.

Aligning Prints for Stereoscopic Study

Stereoscopic study is beneficial to individuals having eyes of approximately equal strength and will not induce eyestrain or headaches if the photographs are aligned properly at all times. A print is selected and clipped down with shadows toward the viewer. The adjacent photograph is placed with its CPP about 2.2 inches from the corresponding PP on the first photograph. With flight lines superimposed, the second photograph is positioned and clipped down. The stereoscope is placed with its long axis parallel to the flight line and with the lenses over corresponding photo images. In this way, an overlapping strip 2.2 inches wide and 9 inches long can be viewed by moving the stereoscope up and down the overlap area *(Figure 2-13)*.

With the photos still clipped down, the prints can be flipped into reverse position with the opposite photo on top. This presents another area of the overlap for stereo-viewing. To study the narrow strip between, the edge of one print must be curled upward or downward and the stereoscope moved parallel to the flight line until the "hidden area" comes into view.

---

[1] In subsequent discussions, the letters "PP" and "CPP" refer to the principal point and conjugate principal point, respectively.

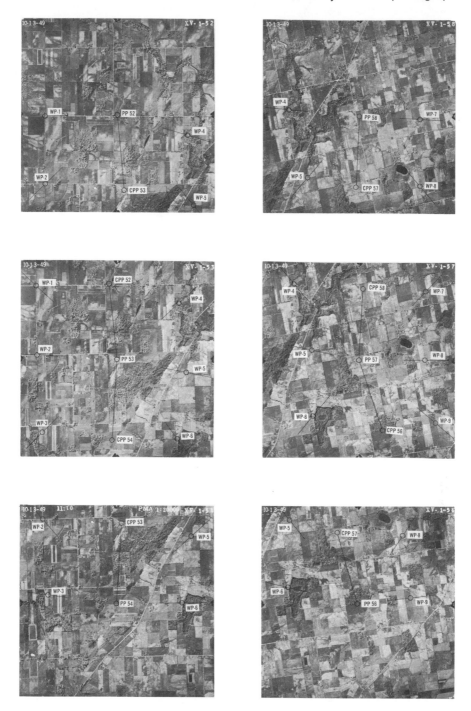

FIGURE 2-12. Stereo-triplets from adjacent flight lines, reduced from 9 by 9-inch contact prints. Shown from left to right across the top edge of print 54 is the date of photography (10-13-49), time of day (11:10), fiducial mark (center), agency (PMA), scale or RF (1:20,000), project symbol (XV), film roll number (1), and exposure number (54). Print 54 is the last exposure in its flight line, as evidenced by the time of day stamp. Note location of principal points (PP), conjugate principal points (CPP), and connecting flight lines. Radial lines drawn through wing points (WP) are used in map compilation and control as discussed in later chapters. Courtesy of U.S. Department of Agriculture.

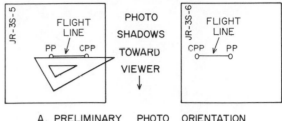

A. PRELIMINARY PHOTO ORIENTATION

FIGURE 2-13. Method of aligning 9 by 9-inch contact prints for viewing with a lens stereoscope.

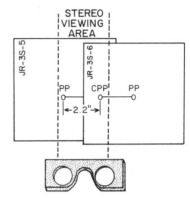

B. FINAL PHOTO ALIGNMENT

Proper Use of the Stereoscope

Beginning photo interpreters should be especially careful to cultivate proper stereoscopic viewing habits. Some of the more important rules to be observed are as follows:

1. Make certain that the photographs are properly aligned at all times, preferably with shadows falling toward the viewer.
2. Be careful to keep the eye base and the long axis of the stereoscope parallel to the flight line at all times.
3. Maintain an even, glare-free illumination on the prints or transparencies being studied and arrange for a comfortable sitting position.
4. Keep the stereoscope lenses clean, properly focused, and separated to the correct interpupillary distance. For most individuals, interpupillary distance is about 62 to 64 millimeters.
5. At the beginning, do not attempt to use the stereoscope more than 30 minutes out of any given one-hour period.

Special Problems Affecting Stereo-Vision

Interpreters that have difficulty in mastering the use of the stereoscope should be cognizant of the following factors that may affect stereo-vision:

1. A person's eyes may be of unequal strength. If one normally wears eyeglasses for reading and closeup work, they should also be worn when using the stereoscope.
2. Poor photographic illumination, misaligned prints, or uncomfortable viewing positions may result in eye fatigue.
3. Illness or severe emotional stress may create sensations of dizziness when using a stereoscope.

4. An erroneous reversal of left and right prints will often cause a pseudoscopic view, i.e., topography will appear reversed. A similar image may be created if shadows fall away from the observer rather than toward the viewer as recommended.

5. Objects that change positions between exposures (i.e., automobiles, trains, boats) cannot be viewed stereoscopically.

6. In areas of steep topography, scale differences of adjacent photographs may make it difficult to obtain a three-dimensional image.

7. Dark shadows or clouds may prohibit stereoscopic study by obliterating detail on one photograph.

8. Individuals who have continued difficulties in using the stereoscope should not attempt to master the art of stereoscopic vision with unaided eyes.

Care of Aerial Photographs

In using and handling aerial photographs, special care must be exercised to protect the emulsion surface. Exposure to direct sunlight or excessive moisture should be avoided, and prints should not be marked upon when damp. Drafting tape should be removed by pulling slowly toward the edge of the print; otherwise, the emulsion may be peeled off. As long as the surface is free from cracks, photographs may be cleaned with carbon tetrachloride or a damp sponge. Prints subjected to heat, even that produced by a desk lamp, have a natural tendency to curl. For this reason, aerial photographs should always be stored flat and under a moderate amount of pressure.

References

American Optical Company.
 1957. *A-O, H-R-R Pseudoisochromatic Plates,* 2nd ed. Buffalo, N.Y., 15 pp.

Anson, Abraham.
 1959. Significant findings of a stereoscopic acuity study. Photogram. Engineering 25:607-611, illus.

Campbell, C. J.
 1964. Compact field kit for aerial photographic interpretation. Jour. Forestry 62:266-267, illus.

Carow, John.
 1954. The University of Michigan photointerpreters scale. School of Natural Resources, Ann Arbor. Michigan Forestry Note 6, 2 pp., illus.

Chase, Clarence D., and Spurr, S. H.
 1955. Photo-interpretation aids. U.S. Forest Serv., Lake States Forest Expt. Sta., Misc. Rpt. 38, 13 pp.

Colwell, Robert N.
 1955. Some uses of three-dimensional models for illustrating photogrammetric principles. Photogram. Engineering 21: 491-510, illus.

Meyer, Merle P., and Amundsen, Odd.
 1962. A transparent aerial photo scale for measuring distance between any conjugate points. Photogram. Engineering 28:478-479, illus.

Moessner, Karl E.
 1954. A simple test for stereoscopic perception. U.S. Forest Serv., Central States Forest Expt. Sta., Tech. Paper 144, 14 pp., illus.

Olson, Charles E., Jr.
 1960. Elements of photographic interpretation common to several sensors. Photogram. Engineering 26:651-656, illus.

Rabben, Ellis L.
 1955. The eyes have it. Photogram. Engineering 21:573-578.

Seymour, Thomas D.
 1957. The interpretation of unidentified information — a basic concept. Photogram. Engineering 23:115-121.

Sims, W. G., and Hall, Norman.
 1956. The testing of candidates for training as airphoto interpreters. Forestry and Timber Bureau, Commonwealth of Australia, Canberra, A.C.T., 12 pp., illus.

Thayer, T. P.
 1963. The magnifying single-prism stereoscope, a new field instrument. Jour. Forestry 61:389-390, illus.

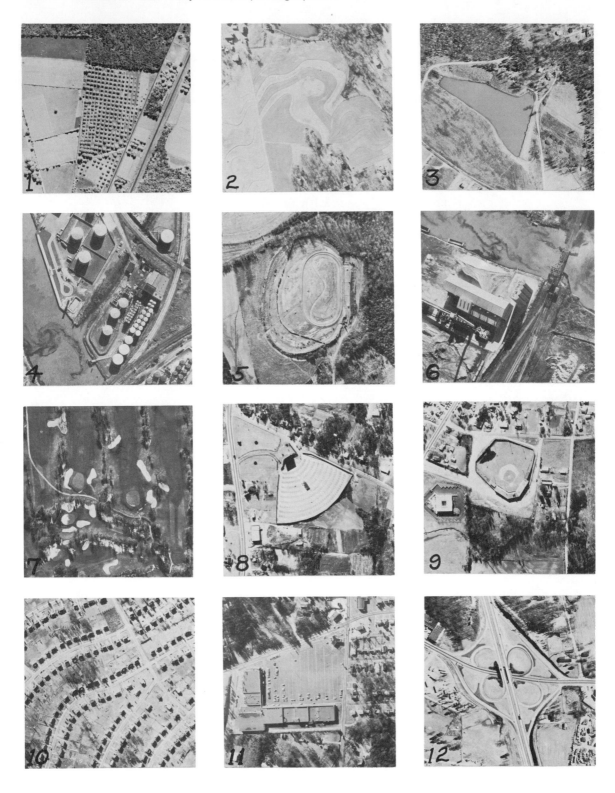

FIGURE 2-14. Cut-out views from vertical aerial photographs. Courtesy of Abrams Aerial Survey Corp.

EXERCISE 2 — Photo Identifications and Stereoscopic Acuity

1. A map and aerial photograph covering part of Fort Smith, Arkansas, is shown in *Figure 2-1*. Locate and number the following features on both map and photograph:

1. Railroad bridge	7. Business district
2. Highway bridge	8. Residential area
3. River sandbars	9. Woodland
4. Overpass	10. Cultivated field
5. Railroad trains	11. River levees
6. Roundhouse	12. Small ponds

2. Study the 12 cutouts from aerial photographs in *Figure 2-14* and write your identifications below. Describe *all* of the prominent features pictured:

1. _____

2. _____

3. _____

4. _____

5. _____

6. _____

7. _____

8. _____

9. _____

10. _____

11. _____

12. _____

3. Position a lens stereoscope over the Zeiss stereoscopic vision test chart shown in *Figure 2-15*. Then rank the details within rings 1, 2, 3, and 6, 7, 8 in height order (highest = 1, second highest = 2, and so on).

1. ( ) Triangle
   ( ) Square
   ( ) Point
   ( ) Marginal ring

2. ( ) Flanking mountains
   ( ) Marginal ring
   ( ) Spotting mark and central mountain

3. ( ) Square
   ( ) Cross
   ( ) Marginal ring
   ( ) Circle, lower left
   ( ) Circle, upper center

6. ( ) Circle, lower right
   ( ) Circle, upper left
   ( ) Circle, lower left
   ( ) Marginal ring
   ( ) Circle, upper right

7. ( ) Black circle
   ( ) Black triangle
   ( ) Flag with ball (black)
   ( ) White triangle
   ( ) Marginal ring
   ( ) Tower with cross and ring
   ( ) White rectangle
   ( ) Black rectangle
   ( ) Double cross with arrowhead

8. ( ) Marginal ring
   ( ) Steeple and the two triangles

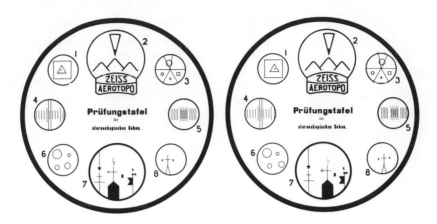

FIGURE 2-15. Stereoscopic vision test chart. Courtesy of Carl Zeiss, Inc., New York.

4. Position a lens stereoscope over the hidden word stereograms shown in *Figure 2-16*. What words appear in the three views?

Top view_____

Middle view_____

Bottom view_____

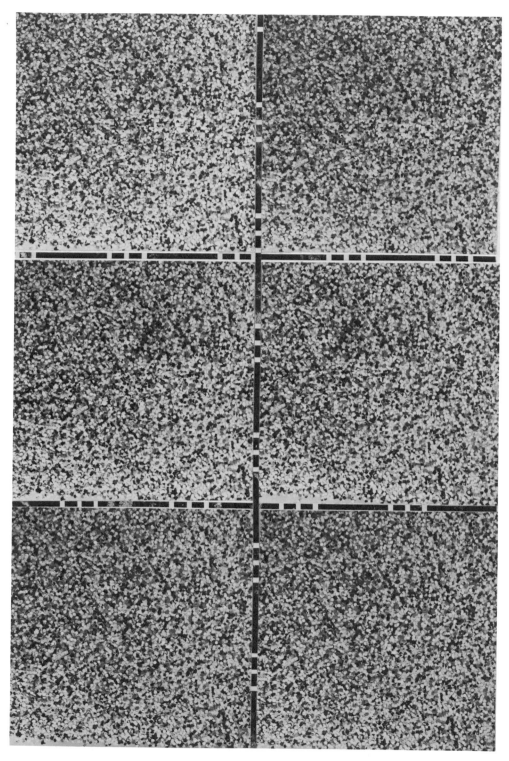

FIGURE 2-16. Hidden word stereoscopic test developed by Sims and Hall (1956).

EXERCISE 3—Airphoto Nomenclature and Stereoscopic Study

1. Obtain four or more overlapping aerial photographs of your local area. At least two flight lines should be represented. Write your name on the back of each print. Following previous instructions, trim each print, locate principal points (PP) and conjugate principal points (CPP). Double-check to verify precise location; points picked incorrectly will appear to "float" or "sink" with respect to surrounding terrain. When available, a set of older prints should be used for practice in point-picking.

2. With a drop-bow pen, circle each PP and CPP. Ink flight lines and record average photo base length for each overlap as directed; these values will be used later in computing object heights from

   parallax measurements. P values:_____

   _____

3. Arrange prints in mosaic fashion and observe direction of flight lines and orientation of shadows. If time of day is not shown, estimate the time of day: (early morning) (midday) (late afternoon). Obtain the exact time and record on first and last prints in each flight line.

   Time of day_____

4. Recheck photo nomenclature in *Figure 2-12* and record the following data for your own prints:

   a. Date(s) of photography_____

   b. Organization for which photos were originally flown_____

   _____

   c. Project symbol, film roll, and exposure numbers_____

   _____

   d. Film-filter combination used_____

   _____

   e. Approximate scale of photography_____feet per inch

   f. Camera focal length (if shown on prints)_____inches

   g. Average ground elevation of local area_____feet above sea level

5. Arrange prints in mosaic fashion and measure:

   a. Average forward overlap_____percent

   b. Average sidelap_____percent

6. Obtain a reliable map of the local area, such as a U.S. Geological Survey quadrangle sheet. With an engineer's scale and protractor, measure:

   a. Compass bearing of flight line 1_____degrees

   b. Compass bearing of flight line 2_____degrees

   c. Was the intended flight course north-south or east-west?_____

7. Check print alignment in each flight line.[2] The combination of "crab" and "drift" should not exceed 10 percent of the print width for any three consecutive photographs. Record as a percent of print width affected:

Line 1_____percent   Line 2_____percent

8. Inspect all of your photographs closely and determine whether any of the following "defects" appear. Write print numbers opposite the applicable description.

Excessively long shadows_____

Shadows fuzzy due to overcast sky_____

Poor tonal contrast_____

Print detail blurred, especially in corners_____

Chemical streaks or stains_____

Emulsion scratches or cracks_____

Clouds or cloud shadows_____

Smoke or smog (industrial areas)_____

Excessive snow cover on ground_____

Floodwaters obscuring ground detail_____

Inadequate or incorrect print titling_____

Forward overlap excessive (over 65 percent)_____

Forward overlap deficient (less than 50 percent)_____

Sidelap excessive (over 45 percent)_____

Sidelap deficient (less than 15 percent)_____

Improper print alignment_____

Tilted photographs (check ends of flight lines)_____

---

[2] If crosswinds are encountered during flight, the airplane may be blown off course, causing a defect known as drift. The pilot can avoid this by heading the airplane slightly into the wind. If the photographer does not adjust his camera to counteract this condition, a skewed or crabbed photograph results. Excessive drift or crab may reduce overlap to an undesirable level.

9. On a 10 by 10-inch sheet of transparent cellulose acetate or heavy vellum, draft a point-designator grid such as that pictured in *Figure 2-17*. For 9 by 9-inch contact prints, each small square will be ½ inch on a side. Set up your own prints for stereoscopic study with the point-designator grid carefully taped over the right-hand print so that grid midpoints are aligned with the four photo fiducial marks. Then refer to the checklist of typical features and write down (by grid location) as many items as you can identify. Following the name of each feature, indicate a level of confidence for the identification, i.e., *Positive, Probable,* or *Possible*. Tabulate information as follows:

Print number under grid_____   Locality_____

Grid location	Feature identified	Confidence level

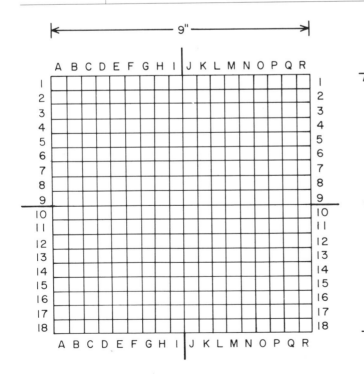

FIGURE 2-17. A point-designator grid for use as an overlay on 9 by 9-inch contact prints.

CHAPTER 3

Geometry of the Aerial Photograph

Photographic Scale

As illustrated in *Figure 3-1,* the scale of a vertical aerial photograph is a function of the focal length of the camera lens and the height from which the exposure is made. The vertical aerial photograph presents a true record of angles, but measures of horizontal distances are subject to wide variation because of changes in ground elevations or flight altitudes. The nominal scale (as 1:15,840) is representative only of the datum, an imaginary horizontal plane passing through a specified elevation above mean sea level. To make accurate measurements of distance, area, or height, it is therefore necessary to compute the *exact* photographic scale.

Aerial cameras in common use have focal lengths of 6, 8.25, or 12 inches (0.5, 0.6875, or 1.0 ft). Knowledge of the focal length used, along with the altitude of the photographic aircraft, makes it possible to determine the representative fraction (RF) or natural scale:

$$RF = \frac{\text{Camera focal length (ft.)}}{\text{Altitude above ground datum (ft.)}}$$

For example, with a camera focal length of six inches, a flight altitude of 6,500 feet above mean sea level (MSL) and an average ground elevation of 1,500 feet, the representative fraction would be computed as follows:

$$RF = \frac{0.5 \text{ ft.}}{6,500 \text{ ft.} - 1,500 \text{ ft.}} = \frac{0.5}{5,000} = \frac{1}{10,000} \text{ or } 1:10,000$$

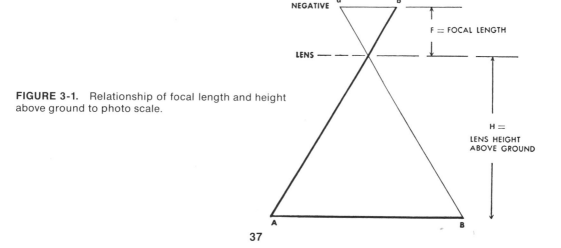

FIGURE 3-1. Relationship of focal length and height above ground to photo scale.

Another application of this relationship might require determination of the flight altitude that must be maintained to obtain a specified photographic scale. Again assuming a focal length of six inches, a specified scale of 1:12,000, and an average ground elevation of 2,000 feet, the flight altitude above MSL would be:

$$\frac{1}{12,000} = \frac{0.5 \text{ ft.}}{X - 2,000 \text{ ft.}}; \; X - 2,000 = 6,000;$$

and X (altitude) = 8,000 feet above MSL.

It must be remembered, of course, that the computed scale of 1:12,000 will be precisely obtained *only* as long as the land surface is uniformly 2,000 feet above sea level. If the elevation decreases, the photographic scales will be smaller; conversely, if higher topographic features are encountered, photo scales will be increased, because the land will have "moved closer" to the camera *(Figure 3-2)*.

While the foregoing method of deriving photo scale is theoretically sound, it often happens that either camera focal length or flight altitude is unknown to the interpreter. In such cases, scales may be determined by this proportion:

$$\text{RF} = \frac{\text{Photographic distance between two points (ft.)}}{\text{Ground or map distance between same points (ft.)}}$$

In applying this technique, the two points selected should be diametrically opposed in such a way that a line connecting them passes near the principal point (PP). If the points are approximately equidistant from the PP, the effect of photographic tilt[1] upon the scale measurement will be minimized. Features selected must also be chosen for easy recognition and measurement on map or ground. As a result, scale checks are commonly made along highways, rights-of-way, railroads, or section lines *(Figure 3-3)*. In most instances, it is not essential to calculate the scale of every photograph in a flight line. Where the topog-

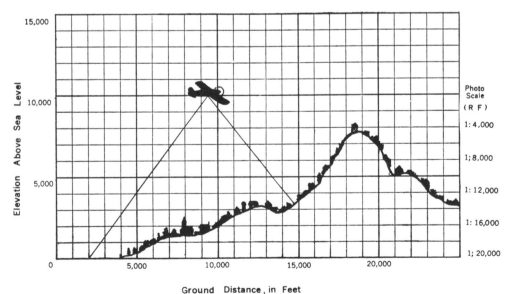

FIGURE 3-2. Scales of vertical photographs change constantly with variations in land elevation. A six-inch camera focal length is assumed here. From Rogers (1948).

---

[1]If the camera lens-axis is not perpendicular to the ground at the moment of film exposure, the result is a tilted or nonvertical photograph.

raphy is relatively steep, measurements may be made on every third or fourth print; in flat terrain, even fewer checks are required.

Table 3-1 lists conversion factors for the range of photographic scales most commonly available to interpreters in North America. Comparisons of identical photographic images at different scales are illustrated in *Figure 3-4*. A problem exercise at the end of the chapter suggests methods of determining the scales of these stereograms.

FIGURE 3-3. Determination of photo scale from a U.S. Geological Survey Map. Map scale is 1:24,000 or 2,000 feet per inch. Map distance between points "X" and "Y" is 2.00 inches, or 4,000 feet on the ground. Photo distance is 4.80 inches. Thus the photo scale is 4.80 ÷ 4,000 × 12, or 1:10,000. Photograph courtesy of Abrams Aerial Survey Corp.

TABLE 3-1. Scale conversions for vertical aerial photographs[1]

Representative fraction (scale)	Feet per inch	Chains per inch	Inches per mile	Acres per square inch	Square miles per square inch
(1)	(2)	(3)	(4)	(5)	(6)
1: 7,920	660.00	10.00	8.00	10.00	0.0156
1: 8,000	666.67	10.10	7.92	10.20	0.0159
1: 8,400	700.00	10.61	7.54	11.25	0.0176
1: 9,000	750.00	11.36	7.04	12.91	0.0202
1: 9,600	800.00	12.12	6.60	14.69	0.0230
1:10,000	833.33	12.63	6.34	15.94	0.0249
1:10,800	900.00	13.64	5.87	18.60	0.0291
1:12,000	1,000.00	15.15	5.28	22.96	0.0359
1:13,200	1,100.00	16.67	4.80	27.78	0.0434
1:14,400	1,200.00	18.18	4.40	33.06	0.0517
1:15,000	1,250.00	18.94	4.22	35.87	0.0560
1:15,600	1,300.00	19.70	4.06	38.80	0.0606
1:15,840	1,320.00	20.00	4.00	40.00	0.0625
1:16,000	1,333.33	20.20	3.96	40.81	0.0638
1:16,800	1,400.00	21.21	3.77	45.00	0.0703
1:18,000	1,500.00	22.73	3.52	51.65	0.0807
1:19,200	1,600.00	24.24	3.30	58.77	0.0918
1:20,000	1,666.67	25.25	3.17	63.77	0.0996
1:20,400	1,700.00	25.76	3.11	66.34	0.1037
1:21,120	1,760.00	26.67	3.00	71.11	0.1111
1:21,600	1,800.00	27.27	2.93	74.38	0.1162
1:22,800	1,900.00	28.79	2.78	82.87	0.1295
1:24,000	2,000.00	30.30	2.64	91.83	0.1435
1:25,000	2,083.33	31.57	2.53	99.64	0.1557
1:31,680	2,640.00	40.00	2.00	160.00	0.2500
Method of calculation	$\dfrac{RFD}{12}$	$\dfrac{RFD}{792}$	$\dfrac{63,360}{RFD}$	$\dfrac{(RFD)^2}{6,272,640}$	$\dfrac{Acres/sq.\ in.}{640}$

[1]Conversions for scales not shown can be made from the relationships listed at the bottom of each column. Using the scale of 1:7,920 as an example (col. 1, line 1), the number of feet per inch is computed by dividing the representative fraction denominator (RFD) by 12 (no. of inches per foot). Thus, 7,920 ÷ 12 = 660 feet per inch (col. 2). By dividing the RFD by 792 (inches per chain), the number of chains per inch is derived (col. 3). Other calculations can be made similarly. Under column 4, the figure 63,360 represents the number of inches in one mile; in column 5, the figure 6,272,640 is the number of square inches in one acre; and in column 6, the number 640 is acres per square mile.

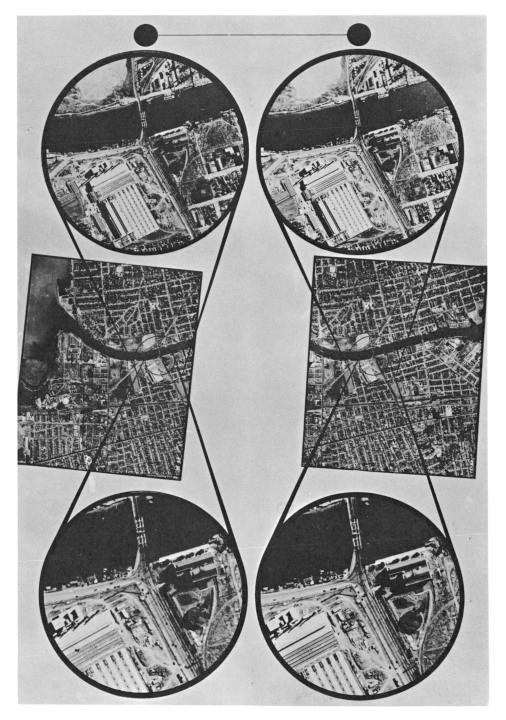

FIGURE 3-4. Stereograms of an urban-industrial area at three different scales. Courtesy of Abrams Aerial Survey Corp.

Image Displacement on Aerial Photos

On an accurate planimetric map, all features are depicted at their correct horizontal positions, and the observer thus has a truly vertical view of every detail shown. This standard cannot be met by aerial photographs, however, because of various sources of distortion or image displacement. Objects pictured on aerial photographs may fail to register in their correct plane positions because of (a) optical or photographic deficiencies, (b) tilting of the camera lens-axis at the instant of exposure, or (c) variations in local relief.

The meaning of optical distortion is well understood by anyone who has gazed through the sharp curvature of a "wrap-around" auto windshield, or stared at his image in a doubly convex carnival mirror. When optical distortion is due to an inferior camera lens, the recorded images are displaced radially toward or away from the principal point of the photograph. Image distortions may also be induced by faulty shutters, film shrinkage, or failure of the film-flattening mechanism in the camera focal plane. Fortunately for the photo interpreter, such difficulties rarely occur. Modern camera systems in the hands of experienced flight crews have all but eliminated this source of image displacement.

A tilted photograph presents a slightly oblique view rather than a truly vertical record. Almost all aerial photographs are tilted to some degree, for the perfect aerial camera stabilizer has yet to be developed. The focus of tilt displacement is referred to as the *isocenter,* a point occurring at the "hinge" formed by the tilted negative and an imaginary horizontal plane. Images are displaced radially toward the isocenter on the upper side of a tilted photograph and radially outward or away from the isocenter on the lower side. Along the axis of tilt, there is no displacement relative to an equivalent untilted photograph. For these reasons, scale checks should utilize measurements between points located at the same elevation and on opposite sides of the print center. In this way, errors due to tilt (which may be present but not apparent) tend to be somewhat compensating.

The exact angle and direction of tilt are rarely known to the interpreter, and precise location of the isocenter is therefore a tedious process. Furthermore, the presence of small amounts of tilt often goes undetected. As only the central portions of most contact prints are used for interpretation, photographic tilt amounting to less than 2 or 3 degrees can usually be ignored without serious consequences.[2] In such cases, it is assumed that the isocenter coincides with the easily located principal point.

The most significant source of image displacement on aerial photographs is relief, i.e., differences in the relative elevations of objects pictured. Relief displacement is by no means limited to mountains and deep gorges; all objects that extend above or below a specified ground datum have their photographic images displaced to a greater or lesser extent. Skyscrapers, houses, automobiles, trees, grass, and even people are affected by this characteristic *(Figure 3-5).* An aerial photograph completely devoid of relief displacement is difficult to visualize. Perhaps the closest approximation would be a vertical photograph of a calm water surface (e.g., Lake Tahoe) or an unmarred landscape such as the Utah salt flats.

Effects of Relief Displacement

The underlying cause of relief displacement can be traced to the perspective view "seen" by a camera lens pointed straight down toward the earth's surface. If a single exposure is precisely centered over a tall smokestack, the photographic image will appear merely as a

---

[2]When necessary, tilted negatives can be optically *rectified* to a vertical condition. The negative is placed in a special projector, and the opposite tilt angle is established between negative and photographic printing paper.

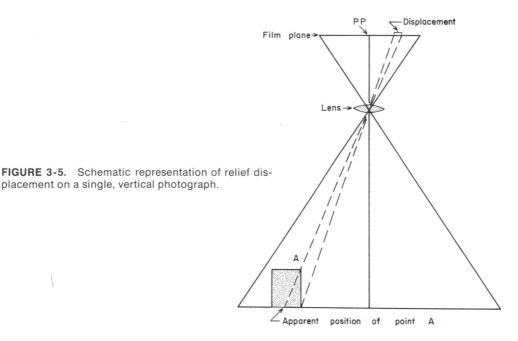

FIGURE 3-5. Schematic representation of relief displacement on a single, vertical photograph.

doughnut-shaped ring, perhaps not unlike that of an open-topped cistern only a few feet high. There is little image displacement here, for this is the one point where the camera lens affords a truly vertical view. By contrast, suppose another smokestack occurs near the *edge* of the print. In this instance, the camera eye looks more at the *side* of the smokestack than "down the barrel." The recorded image thus appears to lean radially *outward* from the center of the photograph. More specifically, displacement is radial from the *nadir,* a point that also coincides with the principal point on truly vertical photographs.[3] It can be stated that objects projecting *above* a specified datum are displaced radially *outward* from the nadir, while those *below* the datum are displaced radially *inward* toward the nadir. Irrespective of the direction of displacement, a line drawn from the nadir through a displaced image will pass through the true horizontal position of the object.

An outstanding example of relief displacement is illustrated in *Figure 3-6*. On the left photograph, the mountain peak is almost directly under the camera lens, and relief displacement is minimized. On the right photo, however, the face of the same cliff leans away from the nadir because of the perspective view of the camera lens. Trees along the valley road may be viewed three-dimensionally, but the abrupt rise of over 2,000 feet precludes stereoscopic fusion of the displaced peaks.

The numbered arrows in *Figure 3-6* substantiate the fact that objects at high elevations are displaced farther from their nadirs than features at or near ground datum. The distance between corresponding images at point 2 (high elevation) is much less than that between images at point 1 (low elevation). As outlined in the next chapter, this characteristic of relative image displacement on adjacent photographs can be used in the stereoscopic determination of actual differences in elevation.

The meteoritic crater pictured in *Figure 3-7* furnishes an example of relief displacement for images *below* ground datum. With an engineer's scale, it can be verified that

---

[3]The nadir is technically defined as the point at which the plane of the photograph is pierced by a vertical line extended from the ground through the center of the camera lens. The principal point is commonly accepted as the nadir position when photographic tilt does not exceed 2 or 3 degrees.

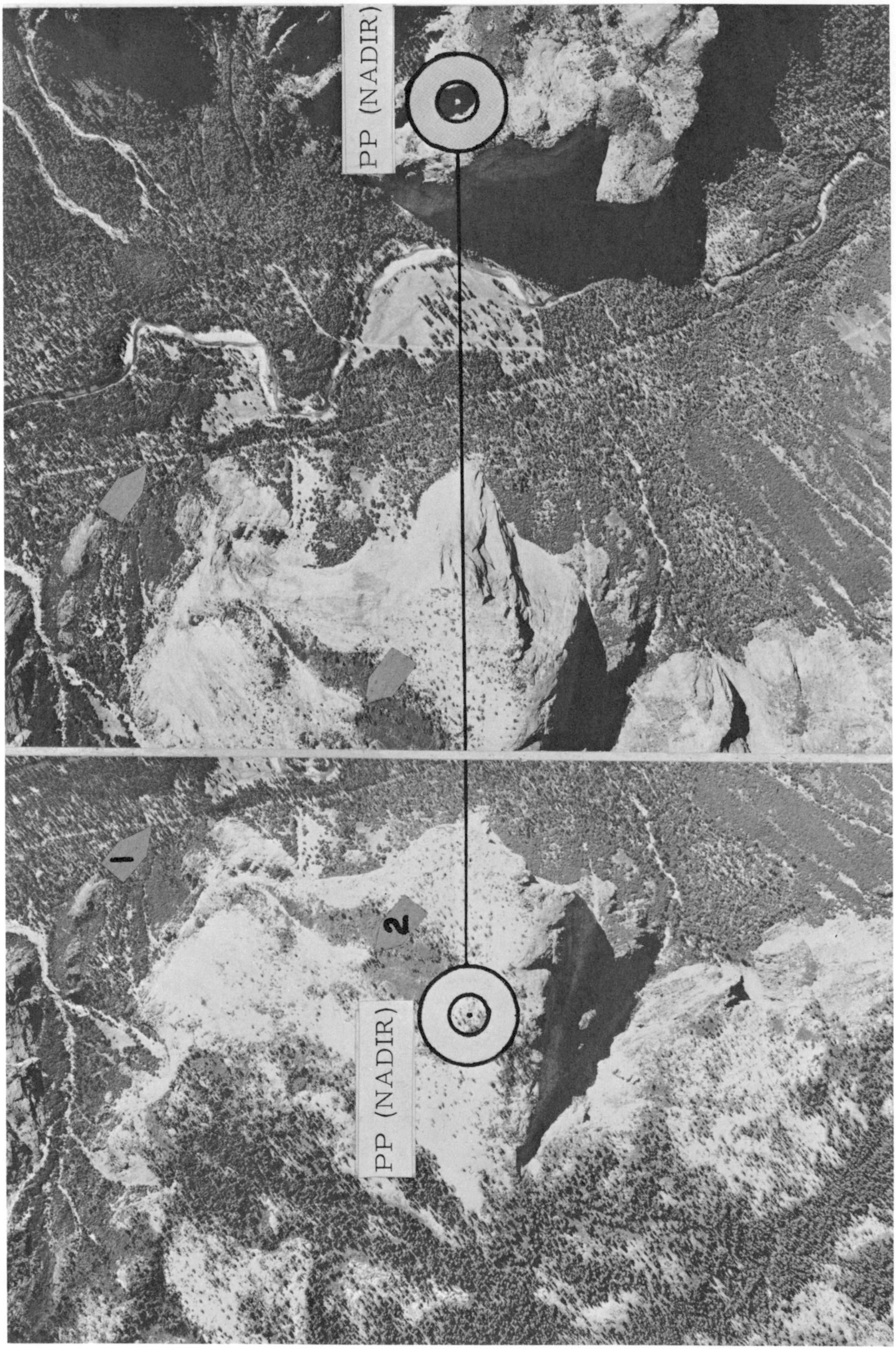

FIGURE 3-6. Stereogram of precipitous terrain in Yosemite National Park, California. The line connecting the two principal points (or nadirs) represents the path of flight. The excessive degree of image displacement makes stereoscopic viewing difficult except at lower elevations. Compare the difference in elevation between points 1 and 2.

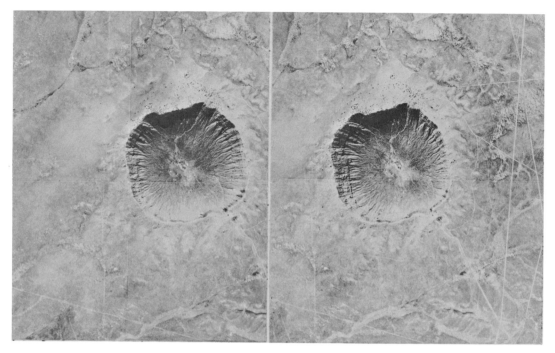

FIGURE 3-7. Stereogram of Meteor Crater, Coconino County, Arizona. Scale is about 3,350 feet per inch. The crater is nearly one mile across and approximately 600 feet deep. Courtesy of U.S. Department of Agriculture.

corresponding images at the bottom of the crater are farther apart than those at the rim surface (ground datum). Thus the two images of the 600-foot depression are displaced *toward* their respective nadirs (off the left and right print margins).

In summary, it may be concluded that the amount of relief displacement is directly correlated with the actual height (or depth) of an object and its distance from the nadir. Tall objects pictured near the edges of prints will exhibit maximum displacement. Displacement is affected also by the flight altitude, and hence by the focal length of the camera used. At a given photo scale, a 6-inch focal length will result in twice as much image displacement as a 12-inch focal length, because the former will be taken from one-half the altitude of the latter. While relief displacement constitutes a source of error in measuring horizontal distances on aerial photographs, it is this same characteristic that makes it possible to study overlapping prints stereoscopically. This point can be easily demonstrated by making two prints from the *same* negative; a three-dimensional view is unattainable due to a lack of relative image displacement.

Thus the goal of the aerial surveyor is to make certain there is sufficient image displacement to assure three-dimensional study and still avoid the excessive distortions that prevent stereoscopic fusion. As the amount of relief itself cannot be controlled, this objective must be accomplished by manipulations in flight altitudes and camera focal lengths. When it is desired to increase the exaggeration of the third dimension, as in relatively flat terrain, a focal length of 6 inches is commonly specified. Conversely, in extremely mountainous country, a 12-inch or longer lens might be used, because excessive displacement makes stereoscopic viewing uncomfortable.

Longer focal lengths are also required under level topographic conditions when tall objects (e.g., redwood trees) are photographed at very large scales. Exposures at a scale of 1:2,500 may necessitate use of focal lengths as long as 24 inches. The 8.25-inch camera focal length supposedly represents a compromise between 6 and 12 inches, but it is not as widely employed now as in previous years. The reason is that newer aerial cameras rarely use this focal length. As a rule, a modern 6-inch, distortion-free lens can be successfully used wherever 8.25-inch focal lengths have formerly been specified.

Measuring Heights of Displaced Objects

The exaggerated displacement of tall objects pictured near the edges of large-scale, vertical photographs sometimes permits accurate measurement of object heights on single prints. This specialized technique of height evaluation is feasible provided that:

1. The principal point can be accepted as the *nadir* position.

2. The flight altitude above the base of the object can be precisely determined.

3. Both the top and base of the object are clearly visible.

4. The degree of image displacement is great enough to be *accurately* measured with available equipment, e.g., an engineer's scale.

When all of these conditions can be met, object heights may be determined by this relationship:

$$\text{Height (in feet)} = \frac{D}{R} \text{ (A)}$$

where D is the length of the displaced image in *inches*
       R is the radial distance from the nadir to the top of the displaced image, in *inches*
       A is the altitude above the base of the object in *feet*

Practical application of this method can be illustrated by use of the left-hand view in *Figure 3-8*. This photograph was taken from a flight altitude of 3,000 feet with a camera focal length of 6 inches. Radial measurements from the assumed nadir position to tanks "A" and "B" may be substituted in the preceding formula:

$$\text{Height (Tank ``A")} = \frac{0.18}{2.34} \text{ (3,000)} = 231 \text{ feet}$$

$$\text{Height (Tank ``B")} = \frac{0.38}{5.00} \text{ (3,000)} = 228 \text{ feet}$$

Thus both tanks are about the same height, and the measurement of Tank "B" could be rechecked on the right-hand photograph:

$$\text{Height (Tank ``B")} = \frac{0.30}{3.84} \text{ (3,000)} = 234 \text{ feet}$$

In these examples, the three estimates of height show closer agreement than may be obtained by casual measurement. In the last computation, for instance, an error of only 0.02 inch in the length of the displaced image would have affected the final answer by ± 16 feet.

FIGURE 3-8. Stereogram of an industrial area in the upper Midwest, taken at a scale of about 500 feet per inch. On the left photo, the tanks marked "A" and "B" are actually the same height; tank "B" shows more image displacement because it is farther from the nadir. Tank "B" appears on both photographs, but the difference in displacement of the corresponding images makes stereoscopic fusion almost impossible. Courtesy of Abrams Aerial Survey Corp.

References

Landis, G. H., and Meyer, H. A.
  1954. The accuracy of scale determinations on aerial photographs. Jour. Forestry 52:863-864, illus.

Meyer, Merle P., and Trantow, L. H.
  1959. A comparison of 6-inch Planigon lens with conventional 8.25-inch lens aerial photography for forestry purposes. Jour. Forestry 57:634-636.

Moessner, Karl E.
  1960. Basic techniques in forest photo interpretation: A training handbook. U.S. Forest Serv., Intermountain Forest and Range Expt. Sta., 73 pp., illus.

Pope, Robert B.
  1957. The effect of photo scale on the accuracy of forestry measurements. Photogram. Engineering 23:869-873, illus.

Rogers, Earl J.
  1948. A short cut for scaling aerial photos. U.S. Forest Serv., Northeastern Forest Expt. Sta., Sta. Paper 20, 10 pp., illus.

Spurr, Stephen H.
  1960. *Photogrammetry and Photo-Interpretation,* 2nd ed. The Ronald Press Co., New York, N.Y., 472 pp., illus.

EXERCISE 4 — Sample Problems on Scale and Focal Length

1. If the lower stereogram in *Figure 3-4* is printed at a scale of 500 feet per inch, what are the scales of the upper and center stereograms shown in the same illustration? Express your answers as representative fractions.

    Center stereogram: RF = _____   Upper stereogram: RF = _____

2. Determine the RF of a photograph taken from 15,000 feet above MSL over a land surface having an elevation of 1,250 feet above MSL. Assume a camera focal length of 8.25 inches.

    RF = _____

3. Two points along a highway are known to be exactly one mile apart. If the corresponding photo distance is 0.330 foot, what is the RF of the photograph?

    RF = _____

4. Suppose you wish to obtain photographs at a scale of 4 inches per mile with a camera focal length of 6 inches. Average ground elevation of the area to be photographed is 1,500 feet above MSL. What flight altitude above MSL must be maintained to obtain the desired scale?

    _____feet

    What flight altitude would be required if the camera focal length were 12 inches?

    _____feet

5. On 1:2,400 photographs of a regulation baseball diamond, what photo measurement would be obtained for the distance from home plate to second base?

    _____inches

6. Assume that railroad passenger cars are 90 feet long and that freight cars are 40 feet long. What would be the lengths of these images on 1:20,000 aerial photographs?

    Passenger cars _____ inches;   Freight cars _____ inches

7. How many square miles are covered by 9 by 9-inch photographs at scales of:

    (a) 1:5,000?   (b) 1:10,000?   (c) 1:20,000?
    _____ sq. mi.   _____ sq. mi.   _____ sq. mi.

8. Suppose the smallest image that can be consistently distinguished on aerial photographs has a diameter of 1/200 inch. If your aerial camera has a focal length of 6 inches, what is the *maximum* flight altitude at which objects 2 feet in diameter could be recognized?

    _____ feet

9. A cultivated field measures 1½ by 3 inches on a photograph taken at a scale of 1:11,000. How many

    acres are in the field? _____ acres.   How many hectares? _____ hectares

EXERCISE 5—Laboratory Measurements of Photo Scale

1. The nominal scale of your own photographs as recorded in Exercise 3 is _____. For a more precise determination, compute the scale for each of your prints by ratios of several photo and ground distances. (Ground distances may be obtained from U.S.G.S. maps, from the lengths of known features such as section lines, or from actual field measurements.) Record below:

Description of line	Ground or map distance	Photo distance	RF
_____	_____	_____	_____
_____	_____	_____	_____
_____	_____	_____	_____
_____	_____	_____	_____
_____	_____	_____	_____
_____	_____	_____	_____

Average scale (RF) _____

2. Refer to Table 3-1 and convert the average scale to the following units:

   a. _____ feet per inch

   b. _____ chains per inch

   c. _____ inches per mile

   d. _____ acres per square inch

3. If the camera focal length is known, compute the flying height of the photographic aircraft above ground _____ feet

   Next determine the flying height above MSL _____ feet

4. Measure the dimensions of several accessible features on your photographs and convert them to ground distances. Then check these distances by ground measurement. Compare and explain possible reasons for differences.

Description of feature	Photo-derived dimensions	Ground check
_____	_____	_____
_____	_____	_____
_____	_____	_____
_____	_____	_____
_____	_____	_____

5. Become familiar with the mirror stereoscope. Compare its advantages and disadvantages with the lens stereoscope.

EXERCISE 6—Sample Problems on Relief Displacement

1. Determine the height of the smokestacks in the right-hand view of *Figure 3-8*. (Flight altitude is 3,000 feet above ground.)

_____ feet

2. Assume you have a 1:7,920 vertical photograph that includes the Eiffel Tower, a tall structure that was built for the Paris Exposition of 1889. If the camera has a 6-inch focal length, the displaced image is 0.542 inch long, and the distance from the nadir to the tip of the tower is 2.180 inches, what is the height of the tower?

_____ feet

3. On a photograph of California's "fog belt," the distance from the nadir to the top of a 340-foot redwood tree is measured as 3.00 inches. If the photograph was taken from an altitude of 3,600 feet, how much would you expect the image to be displaced on the photograph?

_____ inches

4. The top of the Empire State Building, a 102-storied structure built in 1930-31, appears 2.460 inches from the nadir of a photograph taken 6,150 feet above central Manhattan. If the displaced image is exactly one-half inch long, how tall is the building?

_____ feet

5. The Great Egyptian Pyramid of Khufu, having a base that was originally 768 feet square and and covering about 13 acres of land, is the largest known structure of its type. Assume the pyramid is photographed with a camera having a 12-inch focal length. If the length of the base measures 1.20 inches on the photograph, what is the scale of the print? If the length of the displaced pyramid image is 0.108 inch and the distance from the top of the pyramid to the nadir is 1.720 inches, what is the height of the pyramid?

_____ RF

_____ feet

CHAPTER **4**

Stereoscopic Parallax

Types of Parallax

If a nearby object is observed alternately with the left and right eye, its location will appear to shift from one position to another. This apparent displacement, caused by a change in the point of observation, is known as parallax. As detailed in the preceding chapter, parallax is a normal characteristic of overlapping aerial photographs, and it comprises the basis for three-dimensional viewing. The apparent elevation of an object is due to differences in its image displacement on adjacent prints.

Two measures of parallax must be obtained in determining object heights on stereoscopic pairs of photographs. *Absolute stereoscopic parallax* (X-parallax) is the sum of the distances of corresponding images from their respective nadirs. It is always measured *parallel* to the flight line.[1] *Differential parallax* is merely the difference in the absolute stereoscopic parallax at the top and base of the object being measured. The basic formula for determining object heights or differences in elevation from parallax measurements is:

$$\text{Height of object (ho)} = \frac{\text{H} \times \text{dP}}{\text{P} + \text{dP}}$$

where   H = height of aircraft above ground datum
        P = absolute stereoscopic parallax at base of object being measured
      dP = differential parallax

If object heights are to be determined in feet, the height of the photographing aircraft (H) must also be in feet. Once the exact photo scale has been ascertained, the flight altitude can be found by multiplying the RF denominator by the camera focal length. Absolute stereoscopic parallax (P) and differential parallax (dP) must be expressed *in the same units;* ordinarily, these units will be hundredths of millimeters or thousandths of inches.

For reasons of convenience and ease of measurement, the average photo base length of a stereo-pair is commonly substituted as the absolute stereoscopic parallax (P) in the solution of the parallax formula. This procedure produces reasonably accurate results if: (1) photographic tilt is less than 3 degrees; (2) both negatives of the stereo-pair were exposed from the same flight altitude; (3) both nadirs, or principal points, are at the same ground elevation; and (4) the base of the object to be measured is at essentially the same elevation as that of the principal points. In short, use of the average photo base as "P" presents no difficulties for near-vertical photography of relatively flat terrain.

---

[1] If the paired photographs are assumed to be vertical (i.e., tilted less than 3 degrees) and taken from the same flight altitude, Y-parallax or displacement at right angles to the flight line is considered nonexistent. Furthermore, principal points can be substituted for nadir locations in measuring absolute stereoscopic parallax.

Variations in the elevation of the two principal points of a stereo-pair will result in differing measurements of corresponding base lengths. In such instances, the use of the *average* photo base length supplies an estimate of the absolute stereoscopic parallax for an imaginary datum midway between the actual principal point elevations. A more serious situation is presented when the elevation at the base of the object being measured differs by more than 200 or 300 feet from that of the principal points. Here, a new value should be calculated for absolute stereoscopic parallax:

1. Set up the stereo-pair for normal viewing. Flight lines should be superimposed and images separated about 2.2 inches. Both prints should be firmly fastened down to avoid movement.

2. Measure the distance between the two principal points to the nearest 0.01 inch with an engineer's scale.

3. Measure the distance between corresponding images on the two photographs at or near the base of the desired object. Subtract this distance from that obtained in (2) to obtain the absolute stereoscopic parallax at the base of the object.

Direct Measurements of Parallax

Differential parallax (dP) is usually measured stereoscopically with a parallax wedge or parallax bar (stereometer) employing the "floating mark" principle. These instruments are discussed in the sections that follow. The concept of differential parallax can best be illustrated by direct scale measurement of heavily displaced images, and the stereo-pair of the Washington Monument *(Figure 4-1)* supplies an ideal example. The nominal scale of 1:4,800 is first corrected to an exact scale of 1:4,600 at the base of the monument. As a 12-inch camera focal length was used, the flying height above ground (H) is 4,600 feet.

Average photo base length (P) for the stereo-pair is 4.40 inches. Absolute stereoscopic parallax at the base and top of the monument is measured parallel to the line of flight with an engineer's scale; the difference (2.06 − 1.46 inches) is dP, the differential parallax of the displaced images. (As the monument has the shape of an obelisk, measurements were made at the midpoint of the base and vertically above this position at the pyramidal top.) Substituting the foregoing values in the parallax formula, we have:

$$\text{ho} = \frac{4,600' \times 0.60''}{4.40'' + 0.60''} = \frac{2,760}{5} = 552 \text{ feet}$$

This is an unusually precise estimate, for the actual height of the monument is 555 feet, 5 inches. Had the nominal scale of photography (1:4,800) been used instead of the corrected scale, the height would have been computed as 576 feet, an error of 21 feet. Errors of similar magnitude would result from inaccurate parallax measurements. Thus the necessity for precision can hardly be overemphasized. A diagrammatic explanation of differential parallax is shown in *Figure 4-2*.

Functions of Stereometers

The interpreter must recognize that the degree of stereoscopic parallax encountered on small-scale (high-altitude) photography is often much less than that illustrated by *Figures 4-1* and *4-2*. Therefore, differential parallax is usually measured under the stereoscope with a parallax wedge or stereometer, because a precise determination by direct measurement with an engineer's scale would be virtually impossible.

If a small dot is inked at precisely the same location on both prints of a stereo-pair, the two dots will merge into one when viewed through a stereoscope. Had one pair of dots been

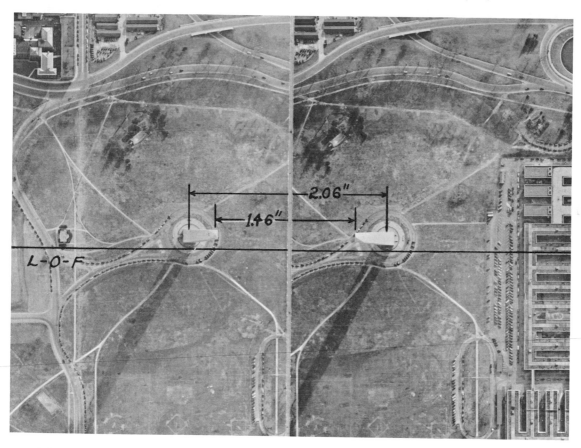

FIGURE 4-1. Stereo-pair of the Washington Monument, Washington, D.C. Note displacement of images parallel to line of flight (L-O-F) and measurements for determining differential parallax. Scale is about 385 feet per inch at base of monument.

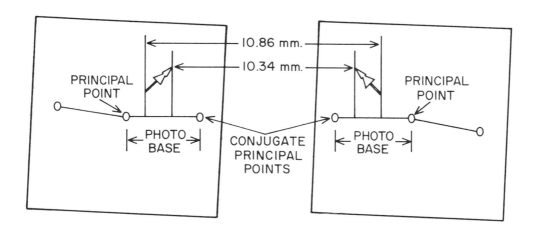

DIFFERENTIAL   PARALLAX (dP): 10.86 - 10.34 = 0.52 mm.

FIGURE 4-2. Direct measurement of differential parallax for a heavily displaced tree image. Note that base and height measurements are made exactly parallel to the photo base or line of flight.

placed on level ground and another pair on top of a tree or building, each pair will merge into a single mark; the first pair will appear to lie at ground level, while the second pair (being slightly closer together) will appear to "float" in space at the elevation of the object on which the dots were inked. If the distance between each pair of corresponding dots can be precisely measured, the algebraic difference will be a measure of differential parallax. The function of a stereometer is to measure such changes in parallax that are too small to be determined with an engineer's scale.

The Parallax Wedge

An inexpensive device often used for measuring differential parallax is the parallax wedge. The basic design, usually printed on transparent film or glass, consists of two rows of dots or graduated lines beginning about 2.5 inches apart and converging to about 1.8 inches apart. Graduations on the wedge are calibrated for making parallax readings to the nearest 0.002 inch *(Figure 4-3)*.

In use, the parallax wedge is placed over the stereoscopic image with the converging lines perpendicular to the line of flight and shifted until a single fused line of dots is seen sloping downward through the stereo-model. If corresponding images are separated by exactly 2 inches, a small portion of the wedge centered around the 2-inch separation of converging lines will fuse and appear as a single line. The line will appear to split above and below this section. Using the fused line of graduations, differential parallax is obtained by counting the number of dots or intervals between the point where a graduation appears to rest on the ground and the point where another graduation appears to "float" in the air at the same height as the top of the object.

In *Figure 4-3*, for example, the difference in parallax between the ground and the highest roof level of the building might be read as 10 intervals on the wedge or 0.020″ dP. Assuming a flight altitude (H) of 5,400 feet and a photo base length (P) of 1.850 inches, the building height may be determined by the parallax formula:

$$\text{ho} = \frac{5,400' \times 0.020''}{1.850'' + 0.020''} = \frac{108}{1.87} = 58 \text{ feet}$$

FIGURE 4-3. Parallax wedge correctly oriented over a stereogram of a large, flat-roofed building. Graduations on right-hand side indicate the separation of the converging lines to the nearest 0.002 inch.

The Parallax Bar or Stereometer

This instrument is more expensive than the parallax wedge and yields results of comparable accuracy. Many interpreters prefer the parallax bar because the floating dot is movable and easier to place on the ground and on the tops of objects. Stereometers of two different types are illustrated in *Figures 4-4* and *4-5.*

The typical parallax bar has two lenses attached to a metal frame that houses a vernier and a graduated metric scale. The left lens contains the fixed reference dot; the dot on the right lens can be moved laterally by means of the vernier. The bar is placed over the stereoscopic image parallel to the line of flight. The right-hand dot is moved until it fuses with the reference dot and appears to rest on the ground, and the vernier reading is recorded to the nearest 0.01 millimeter. Then the vernier is turned until the fused dot appears to "float" at the elevation of the object being measured. A second vernier reading is taken, and the difference between the two readings is the differential parallax (dP). This value can be substituted in the parallax formula without conversion if the absolute parallax (P) is also expressed in millimeters.

Most stereometers yield dP readings in millimeters, while P is more commonly measured in inches. Although conversion to identical units is not difficult, the solution of the parallax formula can be simplified by use of conversion factors as given in Table 4-1. Similar conversions for parallax wedge readings are given in Table 4-2. These two tables may be safely used only when dP is small with relation to P. With ordinary 9 by 9-inch aerial photos and an average overlap of 60 percent, the ratio of dP to P is 1:100 or smaller. If the ratio becomes as large as 1:50, however, values should be substituted directly in the parallax formula.

FIGURE 4-4. Lens stereoscope with attached stereometer. The knurled cylinder can be revolved to move the right-hand lens and create a floating dot. Courtesy of Carl Zeiss, Inc., New York.

FIGURE 4-5. Mirror stereoscope with inclined magnifying binoculars and an attached stereometer for measuring heights of objects. Courtesy of Carl Zeiss, Inc., New York.

TABLE 4-1. Parallax-bar conversion factors for devices reading to 0.01-mm. parallax (dP)[1]

Average photo base (P) Inches	Average flying height (H) above ground datum in feet																		Average photo base (P) Inches
	2,500	3,000	3,500	4,000	4,500	5,000	5,500	6,000	6,500	7,000	7,500	8,000	8,500	9,000	9,500	10,000	10,500	11,000	
Inches	— Object heights (ho) in feet per millimeter																	—	*Inches*
2.1	46	55	64	74	83	92	101	110	120	129	138	147	157	166	175	184	193	203	2.1
2.2	44	53	62	70	79	88	97	105	114	123	132	141	149	158	167	176	185	193	2.2
2.3	42	50	59	67	76	84	93	101	109	118	126	135	143	152	160	168	177	185	2.3
2.4	40	48	56	65	73	81	89	97	105	113	121	129	137	145	153	161	169	177	2.4
2.5	39	47	54	62	70	78	85	93	101	109	116	124	132	140	147	155	163	171	2.5
2.6	37	45	52	60	67	75	82	90	97	104	112	119	127	134	142	149	157	164	2.6
2.7	36	43	50	57	65	72	79	86	93	101	108	115	122	129	136	144	151	158	2.7
2.8	35	42	49	55	62	69	76	83	90	97	104	111	118	125	132	139	146	153	2.8
2.9	33	40	47	54	60	67	74	80	87	94	100	107	114	120	127	134	141	147	2.9
3.0	32	39	45	52	58	65	71	78	84	91	97	104	110	117	123	130	136	142	3.0
3.1	31	38	44	50	56	63	69	75	82	88	94	100	107	113	119	125	132	138	3.1
3.2	30	36	43	49	55	61	67	73	79	85	91	97	103	109	115	122	128	134	3.2
3.3	29	35	41	47	53	59	65	71	77	83	88	94	100	106	112	118	124	130	3.3
3.4	29	34	40	46	51	57	63	69	74	80	86	92	97	103	109	114	120	126	3.4
3.5	28	33	39	44	50	56	61	67	72	78	83	89	95	100	106	111	117	122	3.5
3.6	27	32	38	43	49	54	60	65	70	76	81	87	92	97	103	108	114	119	3.6
3.7	26	32	37	42	47	53	58	63	68	74	79	84	89	95	100	105	111	116	3.7
3.8	26	31	36	41	46	51	56	62	67	72	77	82	87	92	97	103	108	113	3.8
3.9	25	30	35	40	45	50	55	60	65	70	75	80	85	90	95	100	105	110	3.9
4.0	24	29	34	39	44	49	54	58	63	68	73	78	83	88	93	97	102	107	4.0
4.1	24	29	33	38	43	48	52	57	62	67	71	76	81	86	90	95	100	105	4.1
4.2	23	28	32	37	42	46	51	56	60	65	70	74	79	84	88	93	97	102	4.2
4.3	23	27	32	36	41	45	50	54	59	64	68	73	77	82	86	91	95	100	4.3
4.4	22	27	31	35	40	44	49	53	58	62	66	71	75	80	84	89	93	98	4.4
4.5	22	26	30	35	39	43	48	52	56	61	65	69	74	78	82	87	91	95	4.5

Average flying height (H) above ground datum in feet

— Object heights (ho) in feet per millimeter —

Average photo base (P) Inches	11,500	12,000	12,500	13,000	13,500	14,000	14,500	15,000	15,500	16,000	16,500	17,000	17,500	18,000	18,500	19,000	19,500	20,000	Average photo base (P) Inches
2.1	212	221	230	239	249	258	267	276	285	295	304	313	322	331	341	350	359	368	2.1
2.2	202	211	220	228	237	246	255	264	272	281	290	299	308	316	325	334	343	352	2.2
2.3	194	202	210	219	227	236	244	253	261	269	278	286	295	303	311	320	328	337	2.3
2.4	185	194	202	210	218	226	234	242	250	258	266	274	282	290	298	306	315	323	2.4
2.5	178	186	194	202	209	217	225	233	240	248	256	264	271	279	287	295	302	310	2.5
2.6	172	179	187	194	201	209	216	224	231	239	246	254	261	269	276	284	291	298	2.6
2.7	165	172	180	187	194	201	208	216	223	230	237	244	251	259	266	273	280	287	2.7
2.8	159	166	173	180	187	194	201	208	215	222	229	236	243	250	257	264	270	277	2.8
2.9	154	161	167	174	181	187	194	201	207	214	221	228	234	241	248	254	261	268	2.9
3.0	149	155	162	168	175	181	188	194	201	207	214	220	227	233	240	246	253	259	3.0
3.1	144	151	157	163	169	176	182	188	194	201	207	213	220	226	232	238	245	251	3.1
3.2	140	146	152	158	164	170	176	182	188	194	200	207	213	219	225	231	237	243	3.2
3.3	136	142	147	153	159	165	171	177	183	189	195	200	206	212	218	224	230	236	3.3
3.4	132	137	143	149	154	160	166	172	177	183	189	194	200	206	212	217	223	229	3.4
3.5	128	133	139	145	150	156	161	167	172	178	184	189	195	200	206	211	217	222	3.5
3.6	124	130	135	141	146	152	157	162	168	173	179	184	189	195	200	206	211	216	3.6
3.7	121	126	132	137	142	147	153	158	163	168	174	179	184	189	195	200	205	211	3.7
3.8	118	123	128	133	138	144	149	154	159	164	169	174	179	185	190	195	200	205	3.8
3.9	115	120	125	130	135	140	145	150	155	160	165	170	175	180	185	190	195	200	3.9
4.0	112	117	122	127	132	136	141	146	151	156	161	166	171	175	180	185	190	195	4.0
4.1	109	114	119	124	128	133	138	143	147	152	157	162	167	171	176	181	186	190	4.1
4.2	107	111	116	121	125	130	135	139	144	149	153	158	162	167	172	176	181	186	4.2
4.3	104	109	113	118	123	127	132	136	141	145	150	154	159	163	168	172	177	181	4.3
4.4	102	106	111	115	120	124	129	133	137	142	146	151	155	160	164	168	173	177	4.4
4.5	100	104	108	113	117	121	126	130	134	139	143	147	152	156	160	165	169	173	4.5

[1]To use table, measure parallax difference (dP) of object to nearest hundredth of a millimeter (as 0.41 mm., for example). If average photo base (P) is 3.1 inches and flying height (H) is 15,000 feet, the conversion factor of 188 is multiplied by 0.41 for an object height of 77 feet. Linear interpolations may be made in the table for determining conversion factors not shown.

TABLE 4-2. Parallax-wedge conversion factors for wedges reading to 0.002-inch parallax (dP)[1]

Average photo base (P)	Average flying height (H) above ground datum in feet										Average photo base (P)
Inches	2,000	4,000	6,000	8,000	10,000	12,000	14,000	16,000	18,000	20,000	Inches
	— — — — —	Object heights (ho) in feet per 0.002 inch								— —	
2.1	1.9	3.8	5.7	7.6	9.5	11.4	13.3	15.2	17.1	19.0	2.1
2.2	1.8	3.6	5.4	7.3	9.1	10.9	12.7	14.5	16.3	18.2	2.2
2.3	1.7	3.5	5.2	7.0	8.7	10.4	12.2	13.9	15.6	17.4	2.3
2.4	1.7	3.3	5.0	6.7	8.3	10.0	11.7	13.3	15.0	16.6	2.4
2.5	1.6	3.2	4.8	6.4	8.0	9.6	11.2	12.8	14.4	16.0	2.5
2.6	1.5	3.1	4.6	6.1	7.7	9.2	10.8	12.3	13.8	15.4	2.6
2.7	1.5	3.0	4.4	5.9	7.4	8.9	10.4	11.8	13.3	14.8	2.7
2.8	1.4	2.8	4.3	5.7	7.1	8.6	10.0	11.4	12.8	14.3	2.8
2.9	1.4	2.8	4.1	5.5	6.9	8.3	9.6	11.0	12.4	13.8	2.9
3.0	1.3	2.7	4.0	5.3	6.7	8.0	9.3	10.7	12.0	13.3	3.0
3.1	1.3	2.6	3.9	5.2	6.4	7.7	9.0	10.3	11.6	12.9	3.1
3.2	1.2	2.5	3.7	5.0	6.2	7.5	8.7	10.0	11.2	12.5	3.2
3.3	1.2	2.4	3.6	4.8	6.1	7.3	8.5	9.7	10.9	12.1	3.3
3.4	1.2	2.3	3.5	4.7	5.9	7.0	8.2	9.4	10.6	11.8	3.4
3.5	1.1	2.3	3.4	4.6	5.7	6.8	8.0	9.1	10.3	11.4	3.5
3.6	1.1	2.2	3.3	4.4	5.6	6.7	7.8	8.9	10.0	11.1	3.6
3.7	1.1	2.2	3.2	4.3	5.4	6.5	7.6	8.6	9.7	10.8	3.7
3.8	1.0	2.1	3.1	4.2	5.3	6.3	7.4	8.4	9.5	10.5	3.8
3.9	1.0	2.0	3.1	4.1	5.1	6.1	7.2	8.2	9.2	10.2	3.9
4.0	1.0	2.0	3.0	4.0	5.0	6.0	7.0	8.0	9.0	10.0	4.0
4.1	0.98	2.0	2.9	3.9	4.9	5.8	6.8	7.8	8.8	9.8	4.1
4.2	0.95	1.9	2.9	3.8	4.8	5.7	6.7	7.6	8.6	9.5	4.2
4.3	0.93	1.9	2.8	3.7	4.6	5.6	6.5	7.4	8.4	9.3	4.3
4.4	0.91	1.8	2.7	3.6	4.5	5.4	6.4	7.3	8.2	9.1	4.4
4.5	0.89	1.8	2.7	3.6	4.4	5.3	6.2	7.1	8.0	8.9	4.5

[1] To use table, measure parallax difference (dP) of object to nearest 0.002 inch (as 0.016 or 8 dot intervals on wedge). If average photo base (P) is 3.6 inches and flight altitude is 14,000 feet, the table value of 7.8 is multiplied by the 8 dot intervals for an object height of 62 feet. Linear interpolations may be made in the table for determining conversion factors not shown.

Precision of Height Determinations

Precision in measuring object heights depends on a number of factors, including the ability of the individual in his perception of stereoscopic parallax. Interpreters who can detect parallax differences of 0.002 inch (0.05 mm.) can often measure heights within approximately 10 feet on contact prints taken from altitudes of 10,000 to 15,000 feet. Greater precision may be possible in open, flat terrain where photo scale changes are minor and less skill is required in making ground-level parallax readings. Interpreters should be conscious of the following points as a means of improving the precision of height measurements:

1. In rough terrain, calculation of the exact scale and flying height for each overlap is desirable. For objects on high ridges or in deep ravines, it is better to compute new values for absolute stereoscopic parallax than to use the average photo base length.

2. Once a pair of photographs has been aligned for stereo-viewing, they should be fastened down to avoid movement. A slip of either print between readings at the base and top of an object will result in large errors.

3. To avoid single measurements of high variability, it is recommended that several parallax readings be made for each object and the results averaged.

References

Avery, T. Eugene.
  1966. Forester's guide to aerial photo interpretation. U.S. Department of Agriculture Handbook 308, Government Printing Office, Washington, D.C., 40 pp., illus.

_____ and Myhre, David.
  1959. Composite aerial volume table for southern Arkansas. U.S. Forest Serv., Southern Forest Expt. Sta., Occas. Paper 172, 9 pp., illus.

Hackman, Robert J.
  1960. The isopachometer — a new type parallax bar. Photogram. Engineering 26: 457-463, illus.

Johnson, Evert W.
  1958. Effect of photographic scale on precision of individual tree-height measurements. Photogram. Engineering 24:142-152, illus.

Moessner, Karl E.
  1961. Comparative usefulness of three parallax measuring instruments in the measurement and interpretation of forest stands. Photogram. Engineering 27: 705-709, illus.

_____ and Choate, Grover A.
  1966. Terrain slope estimation. Photogram. Engineering 32:67-75, illus.

Schut, G. H., and van Wijk, M. C.
  1965. The determination of tree heights from parallax measurements. Canadian Surveyor 19:415-427, illus.

EXERCISE 7—Heights by the Parallax Method

1. Refer to *Figure 3-6* in Chapter 3. Carefully measure the differential parallax between arrows 1 and 2 with an engineer's scale. Then determine the difference in elevation of the two points by the parallax formula. Photo base is 3.40 inches for the left print and 4.00 inches for the right print. Assume a scale of 1:20,000 and a camera focal length of 8.25 inches.

ho = _____

2. Refer to *Figure 3-7* in Chapter 3. Determine the depth of Meteor Crater by direct measurement of differential parallax. Assume flight line is parallel to bottom edge of prints. (H = 16,000 feet; P = 2.75 inches)

ho = _____

3. Refer to *Figure 4-6* illustrated here. Rank the designated features in height order, e.g., 1 = tallest, 2 = second tallest, and so on.

A_____ B_____ C_____ D_____ E_____

FIGURE 4-6. Stereogram of industrial plant near Detroit, Michigan. Photo scale is 500 feet per inch, aircraft flying height is 3,000 feet, and average photo base length is 3.37 inches. Courtesy of Abrams Aerial Survey Corp.

4. Complete the following form for use in measuring heights on your own photographs. Determine the *exact* scale of your prints before computing flying height. Then solve the parallax formula to determine (1) the change in elevation per millimeter of dP, and (2) the change in elevation per 0.002 inch of dP.

Stereo-overlap no.	Height (H) (feet)	Av. photo base length (P)		Change in height or elevation	
		(inches)	(millimeters)	Per 1.00 mm. dP	Per 0.002″ dP

5. Locate several objects such as trees, buildings, or smokestacks within the overlap zones of your photographs. Select features that are not likely to have changed since your exposures were made. Measure their heights with a stereometer (floating mark device) and record below. If feasible, check these heights by ground measurement for a comparison of results.

Stereo-overlap no.	Description of object	dP	Photo height	Ground check	Difference (+ or −)

CHAPTER 5

Stereograms, Shadow-Heights, and Areas

The Interpreter's Task

Because photo interpretation often involves a considerable amount of subjective judgment, it is commonly referred to as an art rather than an exact science. Actually, it is both. The interpreter must know how to use the scientific tools and methodology of the photogrammetric engineer; yet these objective findings must often be supplemented with deductive reasoning to supply a logical answer to the perennial question, "What's going on here?"

The skilled interpreter must have a large store of information at his fingertips to adequately perform his exacting task. He should have a sound general background in geography, geology, forestry, and other disciplines oriented toward the study of natural and cultural features. Complex features are rarely identified as a result of quick stereo-scanning. The interpreter who knows which features to expect in a given locality, as well as those not likely to occur, can make a more positive identification in a shorter period of time.

Under certain circumstances, the mental processes of deduction and association may permit "detection" of objects not actually visible on the photographs, e.g., a buried pipeline, or a camouflaged military airfield. The value of experience and imagination can hardly be overemphasized, for the interpreter who does not recognize an unusual object when standing alongside it cannot be expected to identify a similar feature on a small-scale print. Of course, there are situations, particularly in military intelligence work, where photographic limitations or a lack of associated information precludes "positive" identification of objects. In such cases, the terms "probable" or "possible" are customarily used to qualify the interpreter's findings.

While the cartographer or photogrammetric engineer is normally interested only in up-to-date mapping photography, the interpreter's job can often be made easier when comparative coverage is available. Comparative or "sequential" coverage refers to two or more sets of prints of the same area taken at different times. With favorable timing of photographic flights, changes in land use may be readily detected, and activities that might normally pass unnoticed are brought sharply into focus (Chapter 10). Specific applications of photo interpretation in agriculture, forestry, geology, engineering, urban analysis, and military intelligence are discussed in later chapters of this volume.

Photo Interpretation Keys

A photo interpretation key is a set of guidelines used to assist interpreters in rapidly identifying photographic features. Keys are valuable as training aids for neophyte interpreters and as reference or refresher material for more experienced personnel. Depending on the method of presenting diagnostic features, P.I. keys may be grouped into two general classes: *selective keys* and *elimination keys.*

Selective keys are usually made up of typical illustrations and descriptions of objects in a given category, e.g., industries. They are organized for comparative use; the interpreter merely selects the key example that most nearly coincides with the feature he must identify. By contrast, elimination keys require the user to follow a step-by-step procedure, working from the general to the specific. One of the more common forms of elimination keys is the dichotomous type. Here, the interpreter must continually select one of two contrasting alternatives until he progressively eliminates all but one item of the category—the one being sought.

When available, elimination keys are sometimes preferred to selective keys. On the other hand, elimination keys are more difficult to construct, and their use may result in erroneous identifications if the interpreter is forced to choose between two unfamiliar image characteristics. Studies by De Lancie, Steen, *et al.* (1957) have revealed no significant difference between types of keys as long as the material within each key is well organized.

The determination of the type of key and method of presentation to be used depends on (1) the number of objects or conditions to be recognized, and (2) the variability normally encountered within each classification. As a general rule, keys are much more easily constructed and applied in identifications of man-made features than for natural vegetation and landforms. For reliable interpretation of natural features, training and field experience is often essential to ensure consistent results. Examples of selective and elimination keys are included in Chapters 11 and 14.

Preparation of Stereograms

One of the best ways for an interpreter to build a file of reference material is by preparing sample stereograms for various classes of objects pictured on aerial photographs. Once a representative set of stereograms has been compiled, the interpreter can easily organize the material into a formalized selective or elimination key. Vertical, oblique, or terrestrial photographs can be used for stereograms; in some cases, two or more views are combined in the same illustration *(Figure 5-1)*. Ground stereograms made with a 35-mm. stereo-camera are often useful for supplementing vertical views.

Aerial stereograms are preferably prepared from single-weight, glossy prints. For maximum usefulness, all features in a given category (e.g., tree species, landforms, industries) should be pictured on prints of the same scale and film type. The following step-by-step procedure has been found useful in the preparation of stereograms from 9 by 9-inch contact prints:

1. Locate principal points and conjugate principal points; pin-point with fine needle holes.

2. Draw in flight lines for the overlapping pair; use a sharpened china-marking pencil or a soft lead pencil so that the lines may be easily removed later.

3. Delineate the desired view within a space exactly 2.2 inches wide as measured along the flight line. Enclose this view with parallel lines drawn exactly at right angles to the flight line *(Figure 5-2)*. Transfer to overlapping print by use of a lens stereoscope. Draw these lines with a hard pencil to indent the emulsion surface.

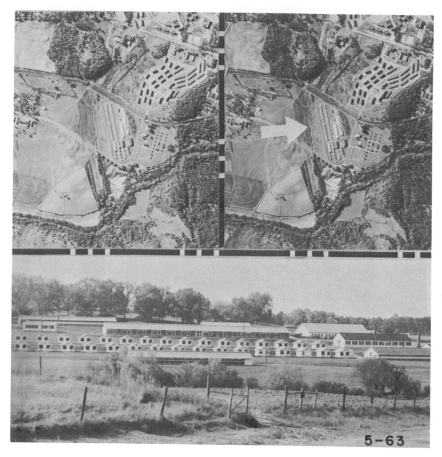

FIGURE 5-1. Combined vertical stereogram and low oblique aerial view of a chicken farm. The arrow indicates the orientation of the oblique view. Scale of vertical stereogram is about 1,700 feet per inch.

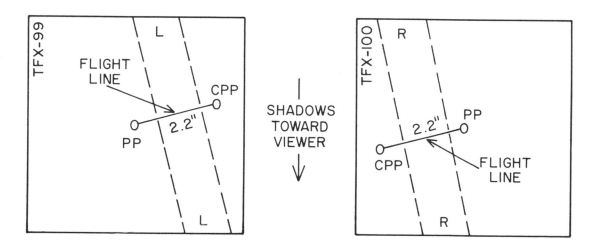

FIGURE 5-2. Method of delineating stereogram cutouts on 9 by 9-inch prints. The 2.2-inch viewing width may be varied slightly, provided it does not exceed the observer's interpupillary distance.

4. Orient prints with shadows falling toward observer; then designate the delineated portions to be cut as left (L) or right (R).

5. Recheck all items (steps 1 to 4). Obtain the following data *before* cutting out views:

Project symbol, roll and exposure numbers
Print scale in feet per inch
Date and time of photography
Average photo base length to nearest 0.1 inch
Camera focal length (if shown on prints)
Agency responsible for photography, such as U.S.D.A.

6. Cut out the two views and align flight line (be sure to check left and right notations). Tape together about ¹⁄₁₆ inch apart by using a strip of transparent tape on underside. Check view with a lens stereoscope.

7. Trim the stereo-pair in height to fit a standardized format such as that illustrated in *Figure 5-3*. Mount on card with rubber cement or gum arabic.

Systematic Filing of Stereograms

Organizations that accumulate large files of aerial photographs in the form of annotated stereograms sometimes experience difficulty in locating reference illustrations on short notice. In many cases, the mounting of these stereograms on standard edge-punched cards provides a solution to the problem of filing, indexing, and relocating selected aerial views. Stereogram cards may be numerically coded according to subject matter, geographic region, scale, season, date of photography, type of film, and other classifications. Once coded and notched, all cards in a particular category can be retrieved through a simple system of mechanical sorting with a wire needle. Fifty to one hundred cards can be handled per sort, and the system is well suited for stereogram files containing random mixtures of several hundred reference cards.

Stock cards may be purchased in several standard sizes, such as 2½ by 6½ inches, 3¼ by 7½ inches, 5 by 8 inches, and larger. A sample 5 by 8-inch stereogram card is illustrated in *Figure 5-3*. The marginal numbering scheme of 7-4-2-1 for each "field" of four holes is one of several standard digital arrangements; identifications of these fields and groupings of two fields into "sections" were accomplished by special printing.

Development of Codes

To make use of edge-punched cards, all marginal information to be entered must first be reduced to a logical system of numerical codes. For example, the general type of subject matter illustrated, i.e., card class, might be coded as follows:

1 – Forests and natural vegetation
2 – Agricultural crops and conservation practices
3 – Soils and erosional patterns
4 – Water, drainage systems, and shoreline features
5 – Range and wildlife management
6 – Landforms and physiographic features
7 – Structural geology
8 – Glaciation
9 – Mining and excavation
10 – Archeology

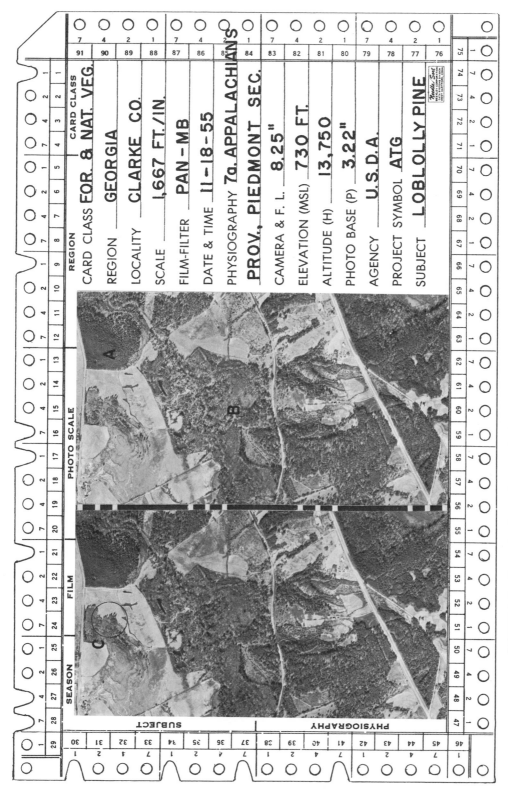

REGION

CARD CLASS

CARD CLASS FOR. & NAT. VEG.

REGION GEORGIA

LOCALITY CLARKE CO.

SCALE 1,667 FT./IN.

FILM-FILTER PAN-MB

DATE & TIME 11-18-55

PHYSIOGRAPHY 7q. APPALACHIANS PROV., PIEDMONT SEC.

CAMERA & F.L. 8.25"

ELEVATION (MSL) 730 FT.

ALTITUDE (H) 13,750

PHOTO BASE (P) 3.22"

AGENCY U.S.D.A.

PROJECT SYMBOL ATG

SUBJECT LOBLOLLY PINE

PHOTO SCALE

FILM

SEASON

SUBJECT

PHYSIOGRAPHY

FIGURE 5-3. Example of an edge-punched stereogram card. Original size was 5 by 8 inches. This particular imagery illustrates loblolly pines (A), bottomland hardwoods (B), and pine shadow patterns (C).

11 — Urban-residential patterns
12 — Industrial and transportation features
13 — Engineering structures
14 — Military and defense installations

Because just 14 categories are involved here, this classification requires only one of the 7-4-2-1 fields on a card. As seen from the following card-notching scheme, each field can accommodate numerical values from 0 to 14 (no punches to all four notches) for a total of 15 classifications.

Code	Notches Used	Code	Notches Used
1	1	8	7 and 1
2	2	9	7 and 2
3	2 and 1	10	7 and 2 and 1
4	4	11	7 and 4
5	4 and 1	12	7 and 4 and 1
6	4 and 2	13	7 and 4 and 2
7	7	14	7 and 4 and 2 and 1

Referring again to the notched card in *Figure 5-3*, it will be noted that the "card class" is coded as 1, indicating that the stereogram was prepared to illustrate some aspect of forests and natural vegetation. Further study of the marginal values on the card yields the following coded entries:

Coded Items	Interpretation of Codes
Region 10	Georgia
Photo Scale 17	Approximately 1,700 feet per inch
Film 1	Panchromatic
Season 11	November
Subject 81	Loblolly pine cover type
Physiography 07	Older Appalachians Province

The foregoing interpretations may be verified by reference to the sample codes listed subsequently. It will be noted that only two of the four card margins are utilized here, so the classifications coded could be increased considerably above that illustrated. As an alternative method of recording, the inner series of numbers (ranging from 1 to 91) could be used for *direct coding*, i.e., assigning a specific meaning to each individual number. This method is simple and provides for rapid card retrieval, but the amount of data that can be coded is limited in comparison with the use of the 7-4-2-1 fields.

Hand Notching and Sorting

Once the classification system and corresponding codes have been developed, card margins are usually notched with a special hand punch. To minimize errors, it is often advisable to first mark the holes to be notched with a pencil.

Sorting is accomplished with a special wire needle. A stack of 50 to 75 cards can be handled during each sort, provided they are perfectly aligned and carefully "fanned out" on the needle to avoid friction between cards. Selective sorting is merely a process of elimination — the cards *not wanted* are progressively removed from the deck. To make a selective sort of a numerical code, one should start at the left of the field (with the highest digit) and work toward the right-hand side or lower digits. For example, if the month of March is coded as 3 (2 and 1) in a 7-4-2-1 field, one would first sort on the digit 7; all cards that drop from the needle would be discarded. Then a sort is made on the digit 4, and again all cards that drop are discarded. The cards remaining at this point can have notches only in positions 2, 1, or both. Thus as the needle is passed through each of these holes, discards will be lifted out and the cards *remaining* (i.e., those notched in both the 2 and 1 positions) will represent the month of March. Similar procedures are followed for sorting in other fields *(Figure 5-4)*.

FIGURE 5-4. Use of a sorting needle for extracting cards from a mixed deck. By repeated sensing of holes in a given field, unwanted cards are progressively removed until only the desired stereograms remain in the deck.

Sample Stereogram Codes

The codes that follow are not intended to be all-inclusive, even for the description of forests and natural vegetation. Instead, they merely provide examples of the kinds of information that can be recorded on edge-punched cards. For the forest cover types, codes were derived from a numbering scheme published by the Society of American Foresters (1954). Physiographic classifications represent descriptive regions recognized by many professional geographers. For other categories, codes are self-explanatory.[1]

Region (state)
01 — Alabama
02 — Alaska
03 — Arizona
04 — Arkansas
05 — California
... etc.
50 — Wyoming

Photo Scale (in hundreds of feet/inch)
01 — 100
02 — 200
03 — 300
04 — 400
05 — 500
... etc.
20 — 2,000

[1]A more sophisticated image information processing system has been reported by Mumbower and Richards (1962).

Film
01 — Panchromatic
02 — Infrared
03 — Pan-infrared combination
04 — Conventional color
05 — Color infrared
06 — Radar imagery
07 — Thermal imagery

Season (month)
01 — January
02 — February
03 — March
04 — April
05 — May
. . . etc.
12 — December

Subject (forest cover type)
01 — Jack pine
02 — Black spruce — white spruce
03 — Jack pine — paper birch
04 — White spruce — balsam fir
05 — Balsam fir
. . . etc.
99 — Slash pine -- swamp tupelo

Physiography
01 — Laurentian Upland Province
02 — Arctic Archipelago Province
03 — Greenland Province
04 — Atlantic and Gulf Coastal Plain
05 — Continental Shelf
. . . etc.
31 — Lesser Antilles

Shadow Method of Height Determination

It has been previously shown that the heights of objects pictured on aerial photographs can be determined from image displacement on single prints or by measuring parallax differences on stereo-pairs. Under rather specialized conditions, heights may also be computed from measurements of shadow lengths. First, objects must be vertical, i.e., perpendicular to the earth's surface; second, shadows must be cast from the true tips rather than from the sides of objects; and third, shadows must fall on open, level ground where they are undistorted and easily measured *(Figure 5-5)*.

Because of the great distance between sun and earth, the rays of the sun are essentially parallel throughout the small area shown on vertical aerial photographs. Thus at any given moment, the length of an object's shadow will be directly proportional to its height. *Figure 5-6* illustrates the trigonometric relationship involved in determining object heights from shadow measurements. Angle "a" in this diagram is referred to as the angular elevation of the sun; the tangent of this angle multiplied by the shadow length provides a measure of object height. Therefore, the basic problem is the determination of the true value of angle "a." The sun's elevation cannot be measured directly, because it changes every hour of every day throughout the year. On the other hand, it may be easily computed if sharply defined objects of known height can be found on the photographs. For example, if a radio antenna known to be exactly 100 feet tall casts a shadow 75 feet long on level ground, the tangent of angle "a" can be found by transposing the equation in *Figure 5-6*:

$$\tan \text{``a''} = \frac{\text{Height of object in feet}}{\text{Shadow length in feet}} = \frac{100}{75} = 1.333$$

Other shadows can be measured on the same stereo-pair, and their lengths multiplied by 1.333 to determine the heights of corresponding objects. For accurate results, shadows should be carefully measured to the nearest 0.001 inch. This can be done with special micrometer devices or shadow "wedges" printed on transparent film or glass.

Other things being equal, precision of shadow-height measurements is highly dependent on the scale of photography. At a scale of 1:15,840 or 1,320 feet per inch, an error of 0.01 inch in shadow measurement is equivalent to 13.2 feet; at a scale of 1:5,000 or 417 feet per inch, a similar error would account for a difference of only 4.2 feet. An added complication is

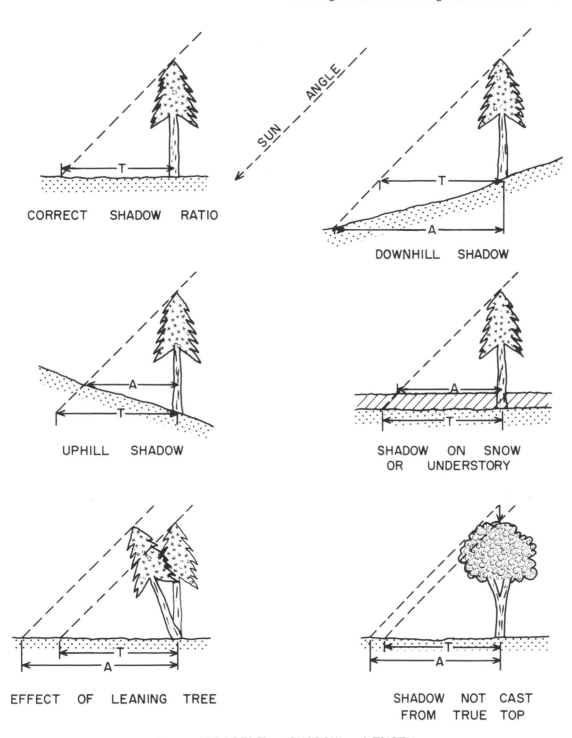

CORRECT SHADOW RATIO

DOWNHILL SHADOW

UPHILL SHADOW

SHADOW ON SNOW
OR UNDERSTORY

EFFECT OF LEANING TREE

SHADOW NOT CAST
FROM TRUE TOP

A = APPARENT SHADOW LENGTH
T = TRUE SHADOW LENGTH

FIGURE 5-5. Illustration of various factors affecting the length of shadows cast by trees or similar objects.

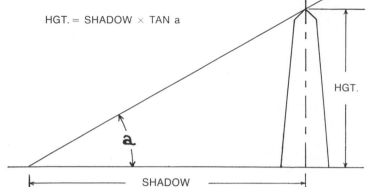

HGT. = SHADOW × TAN a

HGT.

a

SHADOW

FIGURE 5-6. Relationship of shadows and corresponding object heights.

that of determining the point from which the shadow is cast by a tall object. This problem is illustrated by a comparison of the various types of shadows shown in *Figure 5-7*.

Computing the Sun's Angular Elevation

The foregoing technique of determining the angular elevation of the sun works well where the heights of one or two objects are known or can easily be checked. When this method of computation is not feasible, however, the sun's elevation can be calculated by a more complex procedure requiring the use of special astronomical tables, i.e., a solar ephemeris.[2] Information needed is (1) month and day of photography, (2) time of photography (nearest hour), (3) latitude and longitude of photography, and (4) exact scale of photography. The angular elevation of the sun (angle "a" in *Figure 5-6*) is determined from this equation:

$$\text{Sin ``a''} = (\cos x)(\cos y)(\cos z) \pm (\sin x)(\sin y)$$

Where: **Angle x** is the sun's declination or latitude on the day of photography, corrected to Greenwich Civil Time, and read from a solar ephemeris

Angle y is the latitude of photography

Angle z is the hour angle, or the difference in longitude between the position of the sun and the locality of photography

The algebraic sign in the equation is *plus* from March 21 to September 23 and *minus* from September 24 to March 20 in the northern hemisphere; signs are reversed for the southern hemisphere. When the sin of angle "a" has been found, the angle itself is read from a table of trigonometric functions; then the tangent is determined for use in shadow-height conversions. To simplify solution of the equation, special computing forms have been developed by Johnson (1954).

For reliable height measurements, new values for angle "a" should be computed for each hour of the day, each day of photography, and for significant changes in the geographic location of photography. Although most interpreters prefer to use the parallax method of height determination, the shadow technique furnishes a valuable alternative when stereopairs of photographs are not available.

---

[2]Current solar ephemerides may be obtained from leading manufacturers of surveying equipment, military installations, or the U.S. Government Printing Office, Washington, D.C., 20250.

FIGURE 5-7. Stereogram of an oil refinery in midwestern United States. Scale is about 650 feet per inch. Compare shadows of cylindrical tanks versus those cast by tall smokestacks.

Object Counts

In certain photo interpretation activities, the ability to distinguish and count individual objects is of prime importance. Automobiles may be counted in traffic studies, trees in forest inventories, or ships and tanks in military operations. As a rule, man-made objects having some degree of uniformity (e.g., telephone poles) are more easily counted than natural features of the same size (e.g., dense stands of trees). The principal factors affecting counting accuracy are:

Size and shape of objects
Scale and resolution of photography
Spatial arrangements of objects
Tonal contrasts between objects and associated backgrounds
Type of film (e.g., infrared or camouflage-detection)
Use of stereo-pairs versus single prints for making counts

In *Figure 5-8*, individual railroad crossties and highway pavement cracks could be distinguished on the original prints of stereograms "B" and "C". Where large numbers of objects are closely spaced, counts are commonly made on sample plots of predetermined size. Tallies are expanded on the basis of the total area involved. For example, counts made on 10 one-acre plots randomly located in a woodland area might indicate an average of 50 trees per plot. If the woodland area is 160 acres, the estimated total number of standing trees is 50 × 160 or 800. Tree counts are discussed in greater detail in Chapter 11.

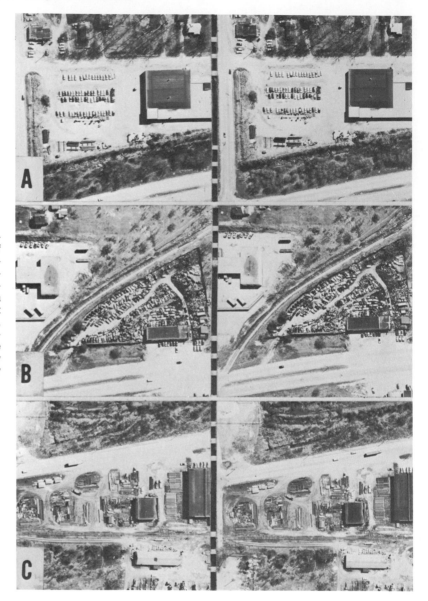

FIGURE 5-8. Three stereograms showing the effect of object size, shape, and arrangement on an interpreter's ability to count individual items. Automobiles in a parking lot are pictured at "A", wrecked cars at "B", and various stacks of structural materials at "C". Scale is 500 feet per inch. Courtesy of Abrams Aerial Survey Corp.

Compass Bearings and Distances

Vertical and near-vertical photographs present reliable records of angles; therefore, compass bearings or azimuths may be measured directly on prints with a simple protractor *(Figure 5-9).* Flight lines usually run north-south or east-west, but the edges of prints are rarely oriented exactly with the cardinal directions. For this reason, a line of true direction must be established before bearings can be accurately measured. Such reference lines can be plotted from existing maps or located directly on the ground by determining the bearing of any straight-line feature.

In *Figure 5-10,* the highway at the top of the print was established as a due north-south reference line. To determine the bearing of the buried pipeline (in direction of arrow), the included angle was measured with a protractor as 29°. Thus the pipeline bears 29°

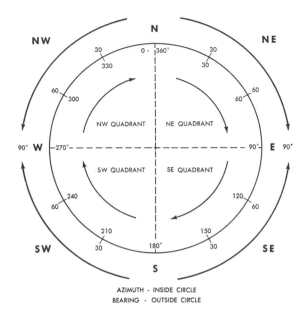

AZIMUTH - INSIDE CIRCLE
BEARING - OUTSIDE CIRCLE

FIGURE 5-9. Relationship of compass bearings and azimuths. Courtesy of U.S. Department of the Army.

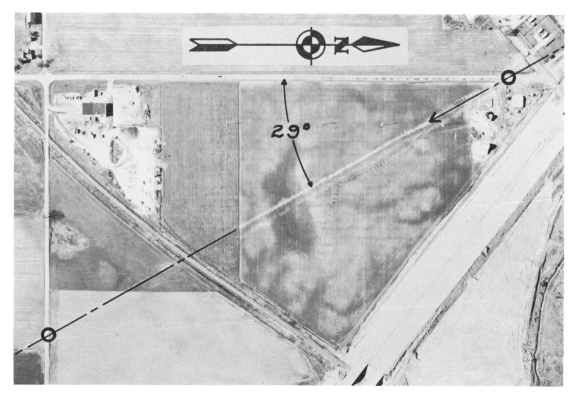

FIGURE 5-10. Measurement of the compass bearing and length of a buried pipeline. Scale is 500 feet per inch. Courtesy of Abrams Aerial Survey Corp.

east of due south. Expressed more conventionally, it has a bearing of S 29° E or an azimuth of $180° - 29° = 151°$.

As detailed in Chapter 3, photographic scales and measurements of distance may be subject to errors because of tilt or relief displacement. On essentially vertical photographs of flat terrain, however, distances may often be measured with fair precision. Even in steep topography, distances between points of the same elevation can be reliably determined on contact prints.

The photo measurement of the pipeline *(Figure 5-10)* between the two inked circles is 5.50 inches. If the nominal photo scale of 500 feet per inch is used, the ground distance is $5.50 \times 500 = 2,750$ feet. However, a ground check indicated a true photo scale of about 490 feet per inch. Thus the actual ground distance is approximately 5.50×490 or 2,695 feet. Accuracy, of course, is dependent on both precise photographic measurements and exact scale determinations. In this example, an error of 0.01 inch in the photo distance would result in a ground difference of about 5 feet. At a photo scale of 1:20,000, the same measurement error would be equal to almost 17 feet on the ground.

Area Measurements

Areas, like distances, are preferably measured on controlled base maps when precise results are essential. Reasonably precise area estimates can be made directly on contact prints in regions of level to gently rolling topography. The reliability of such estimates is dependent on the precision with which photo scales and area conversion factors are determined. Where topographic changes exceed a few hundred feet, large errors will be incurred unless new conversions are computed for each significant variation in land elevation. This point is illustrated in *Table 5-1* for 1:12,000 photographs. If the nominal scale is used, the area equivalent is 22.96 acres per square inch; on a plateau 500 feet above ground datum, the conversion is only 19.29 acres per square inch. Conversely, the value of 26.94 would be used for depressions 500 feet below the datum plane.

It will be assumed here that areas are to be measured directly on contact prints, for this is quite feasible for a large portion of the United States and Canada. Furthermore, the same techniques and general procedures are applicable to area determinations on base maps. The principal devices used for area measurement are (1) polar planimeters, (2) transects, and (3) dot grids.

Planimeters

Polar planimeters, sometimes called areameters, are available to most interpreters, although they are relatively expensive by comparison with other devices discussed here. In use, the pointer of the instrument is carefully run around the boundaries of the area in a *clockwise* direction. As a rule, the perimeter is traced two or three times for an average reading. From the vernier scale, the area in *square inches* or *square centimeters* is read and converted to desired units, usually acres or hectares, on the basis of photo or map scale.

A unique "photoelectric planimeter" has also been devised for measuring irregularly shaped areas. The areas to be measured are carefully cut from a base map, resulting in segments similar to the pieces of a jigsaw puzzle. Each map segment is placed between a light source and a set of photoelectric cells. The amount of light intercepted by the opaque segment is proportional to its size, and the area in square inches or acres is read directly from a specially graduated microammeter (Nash, 1948). Tests of this instrument indicate considerable savings in time as compared with tedious tracing required when using conventional polar planimeters.

TABLE 5-1. Effect of topographic changes on area equivalents for 1:12,000 aerial photographs[1]

Change in elevation	Actual flying height	Corrected photo scale	Equivalent area per square inch
feet	feet	R. F.	acres
- 1,000	7,000	1:14,000	31.25
- 900	6,900	1:13,800	30.36
- 800	6,800	1:13,600	29.49
- 700	6,700	1:13,400	28.63
- 600	6,600	1:13,200	27.78
- 500	6,500	1:13,000	26.94
- 400	6,400	1:12,800	26.12
- 300	6,300	1:12,600	25.31
- 200	6,200	1:12,400	24.51
- 100	6,100	1:12,200	23.73
0	6,000	1:12,000	22.96
+ 100	5,900	1:11,800	22.20
+ 200	5,800	1:11,600	21.45
+ 300	5,700	1:11,400	20.72
+ 400	5,600	1:11,200	20.00
+ 500	5,500	1:11,000	19.29
+ 600	5,400	1:10,800	18.60
+ 700	5,300	1:10,600	17.91
+ 800	5,200	1:10,400	17.24
+ 900	5,100	1:10,200	16.59
+ 1,000	5,000	1:10,000	15.94

[1]Assumes a camera focal length of six inches.

Transects

The transect method is basically a technique for proportioning a known area among various types of land classifications, such as forests, cultivated fields, and urban uses. An engineer's scale is aligned on the photos so as to cross topography and drainage at right angles. The length of each type along the scale is recorded to the nearest tenth of an inch. Proportions are developed by relating the total measure of a given classification to the total linear distance. For example, if 10 equally spaced, parallel lines 15 inches long are tallied on a given photograph, the total transect length is 150 inches. If woodlands are intercepted for a total measure of 30 inches, this particular type classification would be assigned an acreage equivalent to 30 ÷ 150 or 20 percent of the total area. The transect method is simple and requires a minimum of equipment. For deriving area proportions on photo index sheets, special transparent overlays can be improvised for locating transect lines.

Dot Grids

The preferred method of measuring areas on contact prints is by use of dot grids. These are transparent overlays with dots systematically arranged on a grid pattern *(Figure 5-11)*. Grids are aligned with photo fiducial marks or tract boundaries to avoid positioning bias and dots are tallied for each area classification. The value assigned to each dot is dependent on the scale of photography. First, the number of acres per square inch is computed. This figure is then divided by the number of dots per square inch on the grid to obtain the acreage represented by each dot. At a scale of 1:7,920, for example, the area conversion factor is 10 acres per square inch. If a grid with 25 dots per square inch is used, the value assigned to each dot is 10 ÷ 25 or 0.4 acre. When the total tract area is already known, areas of type classifications or subdivisions may be calculated by proportions of dots falling in each category. This technique is analogous to the transect method.

The recommended dot grid intensity, i.e., number of dots per square inch, depends on the map or photo scale, the size of area involved, and the desired precision. For tracts of

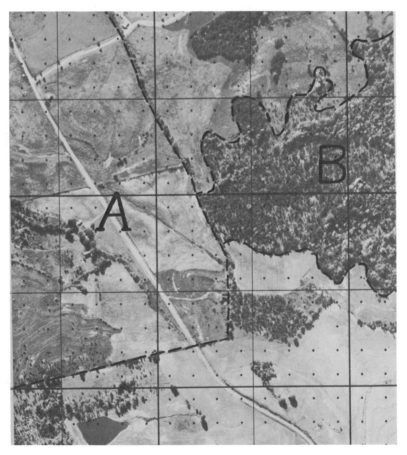

FIGURE 5-11. Dot grid with 16 dots per square inch oriented over a photograph taken at a scale of 660 feet per inch.

one square mile or less in size, it is desirable to use a dot intensity that will result in a conversion factor of ¼ acre to 1 acre per dot. Grids having 64 dots per square inch are commonly used with 1:20,000 scale photographs, for example. As one square inch equals 63.77 acres at photo scale, each dot represents 0.996 acre.

For readers interested in a statistical approach, dot-sampling intensity can also be computed for various levels of precision by use of a formula based on the binomial distribution. However, in applying this technique, dots should be selected by random location rather than by using grids with systematic dot spacings. Area measurements in terms of acres have been stressed here, but conversions to other common units may be made by reference to *Table 5-2.*

TABLE 5-2.   Conversions for several units of area measurement.

Square feet	Square chains	Acres	Square miles	Square meters	Hectares	Square Kilometers
4,356	1	0.1	0.000156	404.687	0.040469	0.000405
43,560	10	1	0.0015625	4,046.87	0.404687	0.004047
27,878,400	6,400	640	1	2,589,998	258.9998	2.589998
107,638.7	24.7104	2.47104	0.003861	10,000	1	0.01
10,763,867	2,471.04	247.104	0.386101	1,000,000	100	1

References

Anonymous.
1957. The needle sort instruction manual. Business Forms, Inc., West Hartford, Conn., 14 pp., illus.

Chester, G. S.
1965. A method of preparing an edge-punched card literature reference file. Forestry Chron. 41:207-214, illus.

Colwell, Robert N.
1963. To measure is to know — or is it? Photogram. Engineering 29:71-83, illus.

De Lancie, R., Steen, W. W., Pippin, R. E., and Shapiro, A.
1957. Quantitative evaluation of photo interpretation keys. Photogram. Engineering 23:858-864, illus.

Heath, Gordon R.
1955. An associative method of regional photo interpretation. Photogram. Engineering 21:589-598, illus.

Johnson, Evert W.
1954. "Shadow-height" computations made easier. Jour. Forestry 52:438-442, illus.

Kramer, P. R., and Sturgeon, E. E.
1942. Transect method of estimating forest area from aerial photo index sheets. Jour. Forestry 40:693-696, illus.

Mumbower, Leonard E., and Richards, Thomas W.
1962. Image information processing for photo interpretation operations. Photogram. Engineering 28:569-578, illus.

Nash, A. J.
1948. A photoelectric planimeter. Surveying and Mapping 8:64-69, illus.

Society of American Foresters.
1954. Forest cover types of North America, exclusive of Mexico. SAF Committee on Forest Types, Washington, D.C., 67 pp., illus.

Tryon, Theodore C., Hale, Gerald A., and Young, Harold E.
1955. Dot gridding air photos and maps. Photogram. Engineering 21:737-738.

Wilson, R. C.
1949. The relief displacement factor in forest area estimates by dot templets on aerial photographs. Photogram. Engineering 15:225-236, illus.

Young, Harold E.
1955. The need for quantitative evaluation of the photo interpretation system. Photogram. Engineering 21:712-714.

EXERCISE 8—Shadow-Height Measurements

1. Obtain several overlapping photographs of an accessible local area. By ground measurement of two or more tall objects whose shadows fall on level ground, compute an average value for the tangent of the angular elevation of the sun.

Stereo-overlap no.	Photo scale (ft./in.)	Description of object	Actual height (feet)	Shadow length		Tangent of angle "a"
				Photo (inches)	Photo (feet)	
				Average value:		

2. Using the average tangent value obtained above and the average photo scale in feet per inch, compute a conversion factor indicating the height of objects on the ground (in feet) per 0.001 inch of shadow length.

_____ feet per 0.001 inch

3. With a micrometer wedge or other measuring device reading to 0.001 inch, determine the heights of several features (trees, buildings, etc.) from their shadow lengths. Wherever possible, use the same features previously measured by the parallax method. Compare results of both methods with ground measurements, if feasible.

Stereo-overlap no.	Description of object	Shadow length (inches)	Shadow height (feet)	Parallax height (feet)	Actual height (feet)

4. Compute the angular elevation of the sun by the equation method outlined in the preceding pages. Compare the value derived for the tangent of angle "a" with that obtained from field measurements. Discuss advantages and disadvantages of the two methods of calculation for use in shadow-height determinations.

EXERCISE 9 — Bearings, Counts, and Areas

1. Refer to *Figure 5-12*. Assuming that the top of this photograph is due south, in which direction is the aircraft flying? If the photograph was taken at about 35° North latitude in the United States, estimate the time of photography to the nearest hour.

Aircraft direction of flight _____ degrees (azimuth)

Time of photography _____ (a.m.) (p.m.)

FIGURE 5-12. Photograph of a commercial airliner approaching an airport near Charlotte, North Carolina.

2. Count the total number of aircraft in *Figure 5-13*. _____
Then measure the length and width of the three identical buildings in the left-center portion of

the photograph. _____ feet wide by _____ feet long. How many square feet

of floor space is in each building? _____ sq. ft.

3. Make a quick ocular estimate of the number of automobiles parked in the lot shown in *Figure 5-14*.

Then count the cars for a comparison. Estimate: _____ cars. Count: _____ cars.

4. Refer to *Figure 5-11*. Determine the acreage of areas "A" and "B" by using the overprinted dot

grid. Area "A": _____ acres. Area "B": _____ acres. Check your answers by

using the transect method. Area "A": _____ acres. Area "B": _____ acres.

5. Using your own photographs, select several areas of irregular shape and determine their acreages
by using both a planimeter and an appropriate dot grid. Record results to two decimal places in
the table below and compare differences obtained.

Description of area	Area by dot grid (___dots/sq. inch)	Area by planimeter (Avg. 3 readings)	Difference in readings
	- Acres -		

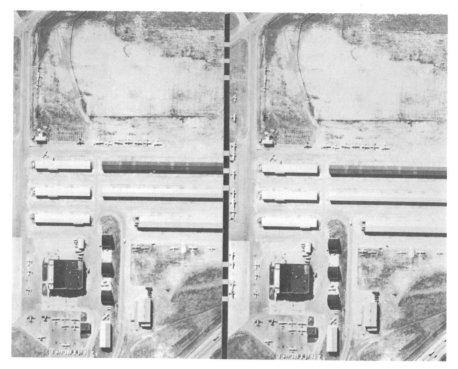

FIGURE 5-13. Small planes parked on an airport ramp near Milwaukee, Wisconsin. Scale is 400 feet per inch.

FIGURE 5-14. Automobiles in a large parking lot. Scale is 660 feet per inch.

CHAPTER 6

Films and Filters for Aerial Photography

Light Sensitivity and Spectral Reflectance

Seven image qualities contributing to the recognition of features on aerial photographs have been previously enumerated. These are shape, size, photographic tone, pattern, shadow, topographic location, and texture. It now appears appropriate to add stereoscopic parallax, i.e., the value of the third dimension, to this list. Finally, there are certain image characteristics that are directly dependent on the selection of a photographic film, filter, and season of exposure. Of special interest here are the factors of resolution and light sensitivity of the film.

Resolution, or resolving power, refers to the sharpness of detail afforded by the combination of film qualities and the camera lens system. In photographic terms, it is commonly expressed as the maximum number of lines per millimeter that can be resolved or seen as individual lines. Any magnification beyond that required to make the line-count for the resolution of the final print will only decrease the image quality and interpretation possibilities of the photographs.

The light sensitivity of a film implies more than an indication of its "speed," or A.S.A. exposure index. Of additional importance is the range of light wavelengths to which the film responds. Light waves are measured in millimicrons,[1] and the portion of the spectrum visible to the human eye includes wavelengths of about 400 to 700 millimicrons *(Figure 6-1)*. However, film emulsions may be sensitized to a wider or narrower span of wavelengths to produce varying tonal contrasts on the finished print.

It should now be apparent that the image quality or photographic tone is dependent on both the spectral reflectance of an object and the degree of film sensitivity to different wavelengths of reflected light. Thus if it is desired to differentiate between various types of healthy vegetation, a knowledge of foliage reflectance characteristics under varying light conditions is essential *(Figure 6-2)*. Photo interpreters are ordinarily limited to two basic types of black-and-white film (panchromatic and infrared) and two variants of color emulsions (conventional color and infrared color film). Nevertheless, when these films are correctly exposed through proper filters, a wide range of light sensitivity can be made available for producing desired tonal contrasts.

---

[1] A millimicron is equivalent to one-millionth of a millimeter. Expressed in another way, there are about 25,400,000 millimicrons per inch.

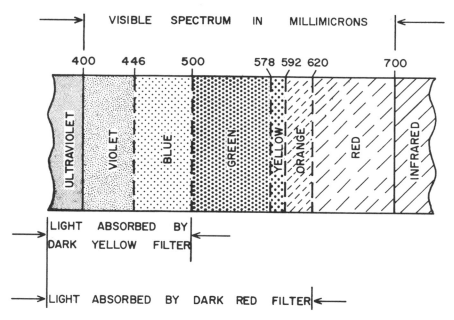

FIGURE 6-1. Schematic diagram of the visible spectrum. Color divisions are for illustrative purposes only; hues actually blend continuously from one wavelength to another.

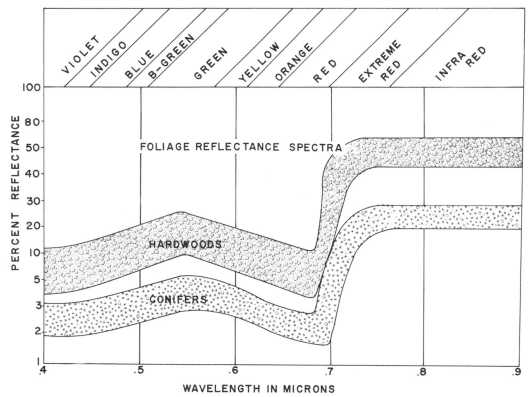

FIGURE 6-2. Hypothetical spectral reflectance curves for deciduous versus coniferous tree foliage. To assure tonal separation of these foliage types on aerial photographs, the film selected should have a high degree of sensitivity in the range of 0.7 to 0.9 micron.

Haze Filters for Black-and-White Films

Aerial films are usually exposed through haze-cutting filters placed in front of the camera lens. Such filters are essential, because small dust and moisture particles in the air scatter light rays, preventing distant images from registering on the film. Scattering of light rays also destroys fine detail on the photographs. The effect of haze increases with the height of the air column that must be penetrated; therefore, it is significantly greater in high-altitude photography. Due to their short wavelengths, blue light rays are scattered to a much greater extent than green and red rays. A "minus blue" filter reduces the effect of haze by absorbing the short rays and transmitting only the longer wavelengths to the film. Because haze-cutting filters remove part of the available light, longer film exposures are required. The ratio of the increased exposure to the normal exposure is known as the "filter factor." A list of filters often used for black-and-white photography is given in *Table 6-1*.

TABLE 6-1.   Kodak Wratten filters commonly used for panchromatic and infrared films[1]

Wratten no.	Special designation	Filter color	Light absorbed	Filter factor[2]		Uses or effects
				Pan	IR	
3	Aero No. 1	Light yellow	Ultraviolet, violet, some blue	1.5	—	Panchromatic
12	Minus blue	Medium yellow	Ultraviolet, violet, most blue	2.0	1.5	Panchromatic and modified infrared
15	G	Dark yellow	Ultraviolet, violet, all blue	2.0	1.5	Panchromatic and modified infrared
25	A	Red	Ultraviolet, violet, blue, green	4	2	Infrared with high contrast
89B	—	Dark red	Ultraviolet and most of visible spectrum	—	3	Infrared with extreme contrast

[1]Adopted from "Kodak Materials for Aerial Photography," Eastman Kodak Co.
[2]Filter factors are suggestive only; actual factor depends on prevailing light and atmospheric conditions.

Haze Filters for Color Films

Filters used with color films are different from those employed with black-and-white emulsions, because all colors of light must be taken into consideration. Scattering of the short, invisible wavelengths of ultraviolet light increases the haze effect on color film; thus a desirable filter should absorb all ultraviolet and as much blue light as required for a correctly "balanced" color transparency. Such filters are usually colorless (ultraviolet) or pale yellow (minus blue). As a rule, haze filters for color films have filter factors of one, i.e., their density does not require exposure increases.

Panchromatic Film

The principal film used for aerial mapping and interpretation in the United States is panchromatic, a black-and-white negative material having approximately the same range of sensitivity as that of the human eye. Standard speed (Super XX) panchromatic film provides reasonably good tonal contrast, a wide exposure latitude, satisfactory resolving power, and low graininess. "Pan" film, as it is called, has slightly higher than normal sensitivity to red light, thus permitting greater speed through haze filters. The normal A.S.A. exposure index is 100.

Images on panchromatic photographs are rendered in varying shades of gray, with each tone comparable to the density of an object's color as seen by the human eye. Panchromatic film is superior for distinguishing objects of truly different colors, but its lack of high sensitivity to green light makes separation of vegetative types (e.g., tree species) difficult. A light or medium yellow haze filter is generally used for exposures on panchromatic film.

A high-speed version of panchromatic black-and-white film is Tri-X, an emulsion designed for exposure under minimum light intensities. The A.S.A. rating of Tri-X is 200, or twice the speed of Super XX. It is exposed through the same types of haze filters as standard panchromatic, and except for increased graininess, produces similar tonal rendition.

Infrared Film

Infrared black-and-white film is primarily sensitive to blue-violet and infrared light radiations. It is sometimes exposed through red or dark red filters; thus exposures can be made by red and infrared wavelengths only. Realistically, this type of photography may best be described as "near-infrared," for most exposures utilize only a small band of infrared radiation ranging from about 700 to 900 millimicrons. The gray tones on infrared film result from the degree of infrared reflectiveness of an object rather than from its true color. For example, broad-leaved vegetation is highly reflective and therefore photographs in light tones; coniferous or needle-leaf vegetation tends to absorb infrared radiation and consequently registers in much darker tones. This characteristic makes infrared film particularly useful for delineating timber types and for detecting camouflage when noninfrared reflective green paint or cut vegetation has been used.

Bodies of water absorb infrared light to a high degree and usually register quite dark on the film (unless heavily silt-laden). This rendition is useful in determining the extent of river tributaries, tidal and shorelines, swamps, and canals. On the other hand, the dark tone often inhibits detection of such underwater hazards as reefs, shoals, and channel obstructions. In some cases, the unusual tone rendition of infrared photography blends light objects such as dirt roads with light-toned vegetation. Furthermore, the dark (black) shadows on infrared prints are a source of annoyance in the interpretation of ground detail.

Photography taken with infrared film normally penetrates haze better than panchromatic, but it will not penetrate extremely dense haze or moist clouds. The recommended A.S.A. exposure rating is 125. When infrared film is exposed through yellow haze filters, the resulting compromise in tonal contrast is sometimes referred to as "modified" infrared. Exposure with red filters greatly increases contrast, especially among types of vegetation, but often at some sacrifice of image sharpness. *Figure 6-3* illustrates comparative panchromatic and infrared photography of an area in Georgia. Close inspection of this illustration confirms the fact that neither film has a clear-cut superiority over the other. When a choice of the two emulsions is available, the selection will depend mainly on the objectives of interpretation.

As shown by arrows, the panchromatic print is better for identifying woods roads (A), recently plowed fields (B), small trees (C), and field contours (D). Also, images such as tree crowns appear sharper on the panchromatic photograph, and shadows are less offensive. By contrast, the infrared print is more useful for identifying coniferous (dark crowns)

FIGURE 6-3. Summer panchromatic (left) and infrared photography of an area in northern Georgia. Exposures were made simultaneously with a dual aerial camera system. Panchromatic exposures were made with a minus blue filter, the infrared with a red filter. Courtesy of U.S. Forest Service.

versus broad-leaved (light crowns) trees (E), small bodies of water and minor stream courses (F), and differences between fallow and cultivated fields (G). Based on these examples, the topographic mapper or civil engineer might select panchromatic film, while the forester or game manager would probably choose infrared. The military interpreter would likely request both types of coverage, if feasible.

Conventional Color Film

Kodak Ektachrome Aero Film and similar Anscochrome emulsions are reversal color films of the subtractive type. They are sensitized to all visible colors and provide positive transparencies with natural color rendition when properly exposed and processed. Until recently, most aerial color films had A.S.A. exposure ratings of about 40. Today, however, film speeds are three to four times as fast, and the newer emulsions have improved definition and less granularity than before.

Color film has a limited exposure latitude as compared with black-and-white emulsions, and it is preferably exposed under conditions of bright sunlight. Without the correct exposure and proper filter, pictures are likely to be of poor quality. A typical daylight exposure for Kodak Ektachrome Aero Film would be 1/250 second at f/11 (Tarkington and Sorem, 1963). This particular emulsion has proved especially valuable for identifying soil types, rock outcrops, and industrial stockpiles. Color film also has good qualities of water-penetrability, and it is therefore valuable for subsurface exploration, hydrographic control, and the delineation of shoreline features. A portable light table has been devised by Wear (1960) to alleviate the problem of studying color transparencies with a stereoscope in the field.

Since the largest single cost item in obtaining new aerial photography is that of aircraft operation, color photography is not excessively expensive as compared with black-and-white photography. Although film and processing costs are greater, these factors are not normally significant in terms of the *total* cost of a special photographic survey.

Infrared Color or Camouflage-Detection Film

Kodak Ektachrome infrared aero film is a false-color, reversal film. It was originally designed to emphasize the difference in infrared reflection between live, healthy vegetation and visually similar objects painted with infrared-absorbing green paints to simulate the color of foliage. The emulsion is sensitive to green, red, and infrared radiation. A yellow filter, such as the Wratten no. 12 or 15, is used to absorb blue wavelengths of radiation. Although the film's speed is not designated according to the usual A.S.A. system, a typical exposure in bright sunlight might be obtained with a camera lens setting of 1/250 second at f/8 or 1/500 second at f/5.6.

When the film is processed as recommended, the resulting transparencies display colors that are false for most natural features. The utility of this film in camouflage detection is obvious. Natural deciduous foliage appears magenta or red, while painted pseudo-foliage shows up as purple or blue. Camouflaged targets are most easily detected by comparing pictures on this film with conventional color transparencies.

Although infrared color film was originally developed for locating targets of military importance, it has proved quite useful in specialized interpretation projects such as the early detection of plant diseases and insect outbreaks in forest stands. Basic to such applications is the identification of tree species or cover types, a task that requires information on the infrared reflectivity of various types of foliage. There is a near similarity in visual color between deciduous and evergreen trees. Because healthy deciduous trees have a much higher infrared reflectivity than healthy evergreens, there are distinct differences between the colors of these trees as seen by this film.

In spring and summer, healthy deciduous trees photograph magenta or red, and healthy evergreens photograph bluish-purple. Deciduous leaves or evergreen needles that are dead or dying usually photograph as a bright green because such leaves or needles have lost their infrared reflectivity. Healthy deciduous trees whose leaves have simply turned red or yellow in the autumn still retain some of their infrared reflectivity, so that red leaves photograph yellow and yellow leaves photograph white.

Infrared color film is additionally valuable for conducting studies of water pollution. The black-and-white photograph shown in *Figure 6-4* was originally exposed on infrared color or camouflage-detection film. From this and other illustrations appearing in this chapter, it can be concluded that no single film emulsion serves all purposes. Instead, the varied tones and patterns produced by different ranges of film sensitivity complement each other, and the maximum amount of information can be extracted only when several types of imagery covering a given subject are interpreted in concert.

Kodak Aero-Neg Color System

The Kodak Aero-Neg system is based on the use of a special Ektachrome color film that is first processed to a negative. From this single negative, special techniques provide for the production of color prints, black-and-white prints, color diapositives, black-and-white diapositives, or color transparencies. These can be reproduced as enlargements, reductions, or as contact-scale photographs.

FIGURE 6-4. The mouth of the Maumee River at Lake Erie showing water and cultural features associated with water pollution: (1) sewage disposal plant, (2) sewage effluent discharged into river, and (3) breakwater that impedes circulation of effluent into Lake Erie. The original photograph was taken on infrared color film. Scale is about 3 inches per mile. Courtesy of U.S. Department of the Interior, Geological Survey.

With this system, the interpreter has an opportunity of selecting a variety of end results from one aerial exposure. The versatility of the Aero-Neg color system should make it especially popular with geographers, foresters, and natural resource managers who desire color photographs for office interpretation as well as conventional black-and-white contact prints for field use.

Seasons for Black-and-White Photography

The optimum season for scheduling photographic flights depends on the nature of features to be identified or mapped, the film to be used, and the number of days suitable for aerial photography within a given period of time. Unfortunately, extended periods of clear, sunny weather may not occur during the season when photography is desired. As evidence of this fact, *Table 6-2* was compiled from Weather Bureau records to illustrate the average number of "photographic days" per month in each state.

An initial consideration in choosing a suitable time of year for aerial photography is the objective of the project, i.e., the specific information to be derived from the photographs. On the basis of generally divergent objectives, users of aerial photographs may be arbitrarily divided into two principal groups: (1) persons engaged in topographic mapping, urban planning, and evaluation of terrain features, and (2) those primarily concerned with assessment of vegetation and management of wildland areas. The first group might logically include cartographers, civil engineers, geologists, and geographers, while foresters, plant ecologists, range and wildlife managers would fall into the second category.

For topographic mapping, photography is usually taken either in spring or fall when deciduous vegetation is bare and the ground is essentially free of snow cover. Only during these periods can terrain features be adequately distinguished and contours precisely delineated. As differences in vegetation are rarely of significance, mapping photography is usually taken on panchromatic film with a yellow filter. Similar coverage would be specified by geologists interested in stratigraphic mapping and by engineers concerned with proposed highway routes and location of borrow pits. Although summer photography may suffice in an emergency, dense canopies of foliage greatly inhibit the efficient evaluation of ground detail. Of course, infrared exposures might be used for such projects as mapping water courses and drainage features.

Interpreters interested in vegetation analyses prefer photography that will enable them to readily differentiate between various plant associations. As a minimum, it is essential that softwoods, hardwoods, and mixtures of the two groups be separable. Either panchromatic or infrared photographs taken in winter will show sharp tonal contrasts between deciduous and evergreen species, but trees lacking foliage cannot be adequately assessed for ecological or timber inventory purposes *(Figure 6-5)*. If photography is planned during the dormant season, however, panchromatic film should be specified. There is no advantage in using infrared film under such conditions, because shadows are more offensive, resolution may be poorer, and costs are slightly higher.

When deciduous plants constitute an important component of the vegetative complex, photography is usually planned during the growing season. Panchromatic photography exposed when foliage is fully developed and pigmented usually depicts all healthy vegetation in a uniformly grayish tone *(Figure 6-3)*. The lack of contrast between various species-groups makes reliable cover type identifications difficult in some regions and virtually impossible in others. Although this may not be a serious handicap in western regions where conifers predominate, it severely reduces the interpretation value of photo-

TABLE 6-2. Average number of days suitable for aerial photography, by state and month of year[1]

NAME OF STATE[2]	Jan.	Feb.	Mar.	Apr.	May	June	July	Aug.	Sept.	Oct.	Nov.	Dec.	Total per year
Alabama	6.4	6.4	6.9	6.5	6.2	4.1	2.4	2.9	5.9	11.4	9.7	6.3	75.1
Arizona	15.3	13.2	15.7	18.3	22.0	23.7	15.8	15.8	20.2	21.5	18.3	16.2	216.0
Arkansas	7.0	6.9	6.6	6.5	5.6	5.8	5.7	7.2	9.1	11.8	9.0	7.8	89.0
California	7.4	6.7	8.4	9.3	9.7	11.5	12.7	12.8	13.3	13.1	10.8	8.6	124.3
Colorado	7.5	5.8	5.7	4.6	4.6	7.0	5.5	5.4	10.3	11.3	9.4	8.4	85.5
Connecticut	6.1	7.1	7.6	6.4	6.8	5.2	5.4	6.4	6.7	9.1	6.1	6.6	79.5
Delaware	5.5	5.7	5.6	5.2	5.5	4.0	4.5	4.7	6.6	9.2	6.4	5.5	68.4
Florida	5.9	6.7	7.4	6.7	5.0	2.7	1.4	1.5	2.8	6.0	7.7	6.3	60.1
Georgia	6.8	7.1	7.9	7.3	6.6	4.1	2.4	3.0	5.6	10.8	10.6	7.3	79.5
Idaho	2.7	3.7	4.3	4.6	5.5	8.8	13.3	18.4	12.5	9.8	5.7	3.5	92.8
Illinois	4.9	4.7	4.8	5.1	5.1	4.5	6.3	6.5	7.9	9.0	6.4	5.1	70.3
Indiana	4.2	3.8	4.2	4.5	4.4	3.7	4.9	5.4	7.1	9.2	6.2	4.4	62.0
Iowa	5.8	5.4	4.8	5.3	5.0	4.8	7.2	6.6	7.8	8.9	5.9	5.4	72.9
Kansas	8.5	7.3	6.7	5.8	5.6	6.2	8.7	8.2	9.6	10.7	9.6	8.4	95.3
Kentucky	4.8	4.8	5.2	5.4	6.1	5.8	7.2	6.3	8.4	10.7	7.2	4.9	76.8
Louisiana	6.9	6.3	6.6	6.9	6.2	5.7	3.9	4.7	7.3	11.3	9.6	6.8	82.2
Maine	5.6	6.3	5.8	4.8	3.8	3.4	3.4	4.6	5.8	6.8	4.0	5.3	59.6
Maryland	5.2	5.5	5.4	5.0	5.0	3.8	4.1	4.3	6.3	8.9	6.0	5.4	64.9
Massachusetts	3.6	4.2	4.5	4.0	3.5	2.5	2.2	3.6	4.2	5.1	3.5	3.4	44.3
Michigan	2.2	3.1	4.1	5.0	4.8	4.6	5.4	4.6	4.6	4.3	1.9	1.9	46.5
Minnesota	5.4	5.8	5.2	5.8	5.6	4.9	7.1	6.8	6.2	6.3	4.2	5.1	68.4
Mississippi	6.3	5.8	6.8	6.3	5.7	5.5	3.2	3.8	6.6	11.8	9.4	6.2	77.4
Missouri	7.4	7.1	6.8	6.8	6.8	6.8	9.2	8.9	9.9	11.6	9.2	7.3	97.8
Montana	3.5	3.7	3.5	4.1	3.8	4.2	9.9	9.0	7.3	6.9	4.3	4.0	64.2
Nebraska	6.9	5.7	5.3	4.9	4.7	5.5	8.4	7.4	8.9	10.2	7.1	6.9	81.9
Nevada	6.7	6.2	7.5	8.4	8.7	13.8	18.6	18.8	16.9	14.2	10.1	7.4	137.3
New Hampshire	3.3	3.8	4.1	3.7	3.2	2.2	2.0	3.0	3.8	4.4	2.8	2.9	39.2
New Jersey	6.1	6.2	6.1	5.6	6.5	4.5	5.3	5.6	7.1	9.9	7.3	5.9	76.1
New Mexico	10.5	8.4	8.7	8.3	8.1	10.5	5.4	5.3	10.2	14.0	12.7	12.3	114.4
New York	2.3	2.9	4.1	4.9	5.5	4.8	4.8	4.7	5.5	5.1	2.5	2.0	49.1
North Carolina	6.8	6.8	7.3	7.1	6.7	4.2	3.6	3.9	6.1	11.1	10.1	7.4	81.1
North Dakota	5.0	4.9	4.4	5.3	5.1	4.3	7.5	7.2	6.7	6.6	4.3	5.3	66.6
Ohio	3.5	3.1	4.1	4.8	5.8	5.1	6.2	6.2	7.3	7.1	4.3	2.9	60.4
Oklahoma	8.0	6.7	6.5	5.8	5.4	6.7	7.6	8.7	9.5	10.8	10.3	8.3	94.3
Oregon	2.0	2.6	3.0	4.7	5.0	6.8	13.4	13.2	9.5	6.2	2.9	2.1	71.4
Pennsylvania	3.0	3.2	3.9	4.2	4.9	3.7	3.9	4.2	5.8	6.4	3.4	2.5	49.1
Rhode Island	4.9	5.3	6.6	5.8	5.9	4.0	5.1	6.1	6.6	7.8	5.3	4.4	67.8
South Carolina	6.4	7.0	7.1	7.0	6.0	3.3	2.3	2.9	5.0	10.1	10.3	7.2	74.6
South Dakota	5.9	5.4	4.9	4.8	4.5	5.0	8.2	8.3	8.6	8.9	6.4	6.7	77.6
Tennessee	5.3	5.5	6.2	5.4	5.7	4.5	4.2	5.1	7.1	11.2	8.8	5.9	74.9
Texas	7.8	6.3	7.2	7.1	6.4	7.4	5.7	6.7	7.6	11.1	8.9	7.9	90.1
Utah	7.1	5.8	7.0	7.1	7.8	12.6	11.0	11.3	14.2	13.7	10.4	7.6	115.6
Vermont	2.9	2.9	3.3	3.1	2.7	1.7	1.6	2.0	3.2	3.2	1.5	1.8	29.9
Virginia	5.4	5.6	5.6	6.1	5.9	4.1	4.3	4.4	6.0	9.2	7.1	5.6	69.3
Washington	1.3	2.1	2.6	3.7	3.8	5.1	11.6	11.1	7.5	4.9	1.6	1.2	56.5
West Virginia	2.3	2.2	3.6	3.8	4.2	3.0	3.2	3.0	4.0	4.7	3.2	2.0	39.2
Wisconsin	4.9	5.3	4.6	5.1	5.4	4.6	7.0	6.5	6.4	7.2	4.4	4.7	66.1
Wyoming	4.7	4.5	4.3	3.8	3.2	4.8	6.9	6.7	8.2	7.9	5.7	5.5	66.2

[1]Compiled from U.S. Weather Bureau Records. Figures shown represent the number of days per month with 10 percent cloud cover or less. Averages should be used with discretion, as wide variations may occur from one part of a state to another.

[2]Data unavailable for Alaska and Hawaii.

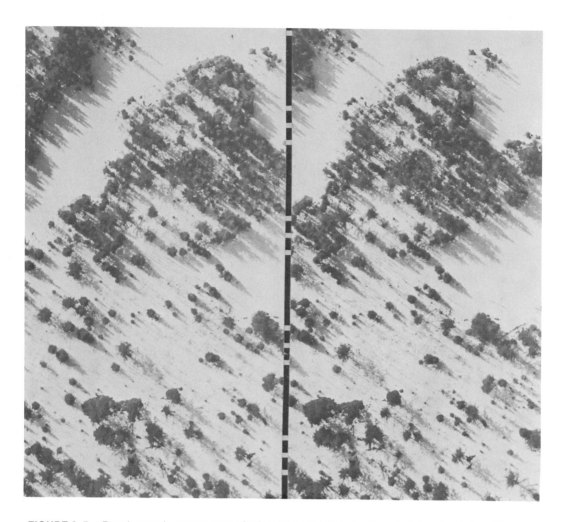

FIGURE 6-5. Panchromatic stereogram of a forest area in Ontario, Canada, taken in winter with snow on the ground. Coniferous trees are readily distinguished, but assessment of deciduous species is difficult. Scale is about 150 feet per inch.

graphs in eastern or southern mixed forests. As a partial solution to the problem, photographic flights can be limited to spring or fall seasons when there are striking tonal contrasts in foliage coloration among various trees and shrubs *(Figure 6-6)*.

In the Lake States, it has been found that panchromatic film provides best results in late fall—just before deciduous tree species such as aspen or tamarack shed their leaves. For a brief period of perhaps two weeks duration, foliage color differences will result in good photographic contrasts between most of the important timber species. This time schedule should produce equally satisfactory prints in the northeast, inasmuch as species associations are similar to those in the Lake States.

Correctly exposed infrared photography of mixed hardwood and coniferous forests displays excellent tonal contrasts between the two groups, but here again the season of photography must be carefully chosen. The early period of leaf development appears to be the best time for infrared photography. In southern and southeastern United States,

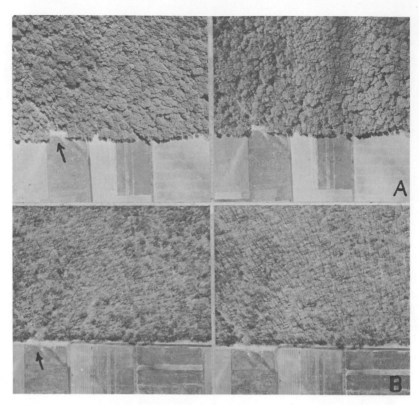

FIGURE 6-6. Paired stereograms of an area in Ingham County, Michigan, taken in May on panchromatic film. Rapid development of tree foliage is illustrated by the fact that photographs at "A" were made just 5 days after those at "B". Scale is 500 feet per inch. Courtesy of Abrams Aerial Survey Corp.

superior infrared exposures are obtained in late spring and early summer—after all trees have produced some foliage, but prior to maximum pigmentation. If large expenditures are anticipated for infrared photography, the interpreter should request print samples from several aerial survey companies. It is a matter of record that infrared photography has lost favor in some regions because of insufficient knowledge of its exposure characteristics under varying seasonal conditions. On the other hand, the fact that national forests in Arkansas, Michigan, and Minnesota have been photographed with infrared film indicates its utility under diverse vegetative conditions.

References

Anonymous.
1967. Kodak Aero-Neg color system. Eastman Kodak Co., Rochester, N.Y. Data Book M-40, 48 pp., illus.

———. 1964. Kodak data for aerial photography. Eastman Kodak Co., Rochester, N.Y. Pub. M-125, 20 pp., illus.

Anson, Abraham.
1966. Color photo comparison. Photogram. Engineering 32:286-297, illus.

Becking, Rudolf W.
1959. Forestry applications of aerial color photography. Photogram. Engineering 25:559-565.

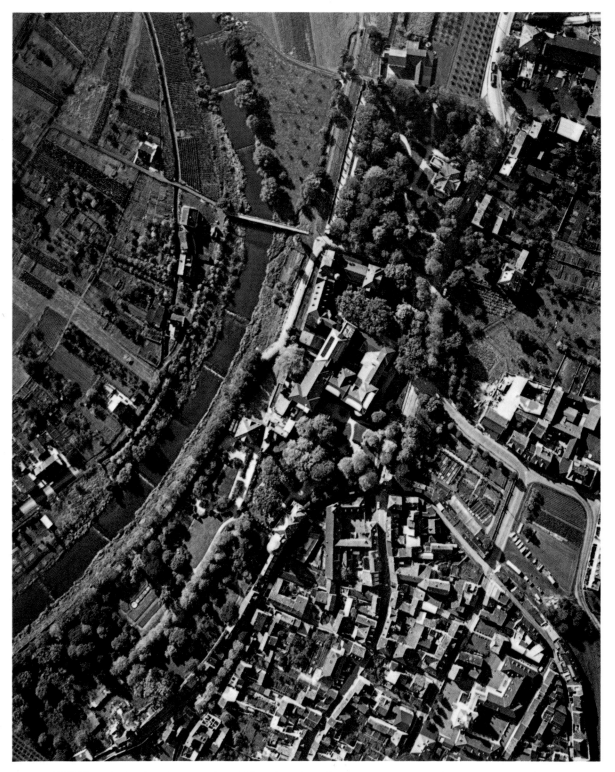

PLATE 1. Agfacolor photography of Ahrweiler, West Germany. Scale is about 210 feet per inch. Compare with panchromatic and infrared views of the same area in Figure 6-7. Courtesy of Carl Zeiss, Inc., New York.

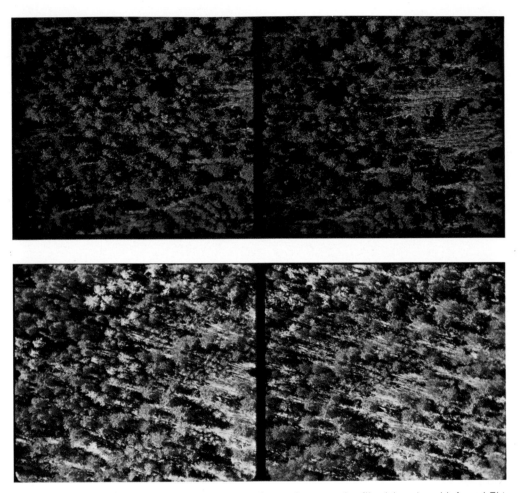

PLATE 2. Comparative 70-mm. stereograms on Anscochrome color film (above) and infrared Ektachrome film (below). Ponderosa pine trees killed by bark beetles are rendered in reddish-brown tones on conventional color film and in yellowish-green tones on infrared color film. Scale is 132 feet per inch. Courtesy of U.S. Forest Service Remote Sensing Project, Berkeley, California.

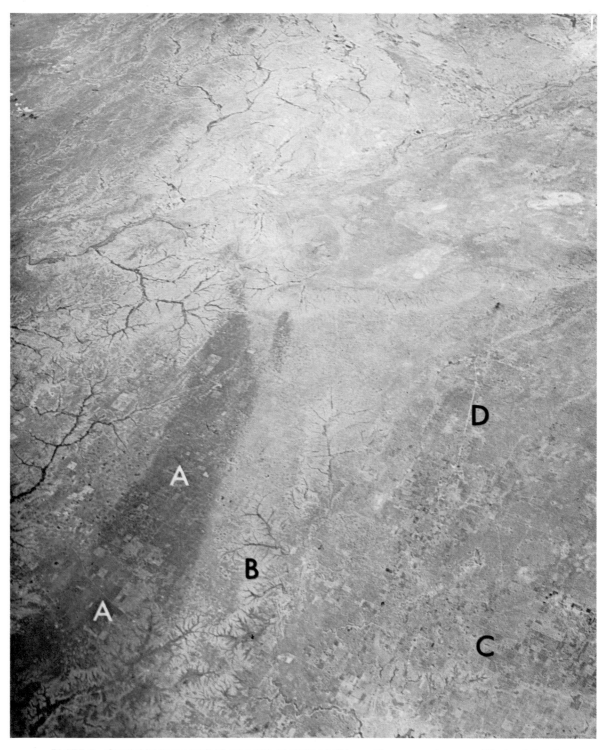

PLATE 3. Gemini IV spacecraft photograph of Midland-Odessa, Texas, area from an altitude of about 110 miles. The dark band indicates moist soil resulting from a recent rain shower (A). Note also the dendritic drainage patterns (B), cultivated fields (C), and prominent highway (D). Courtesy of National Aeronautics and Space Administration.

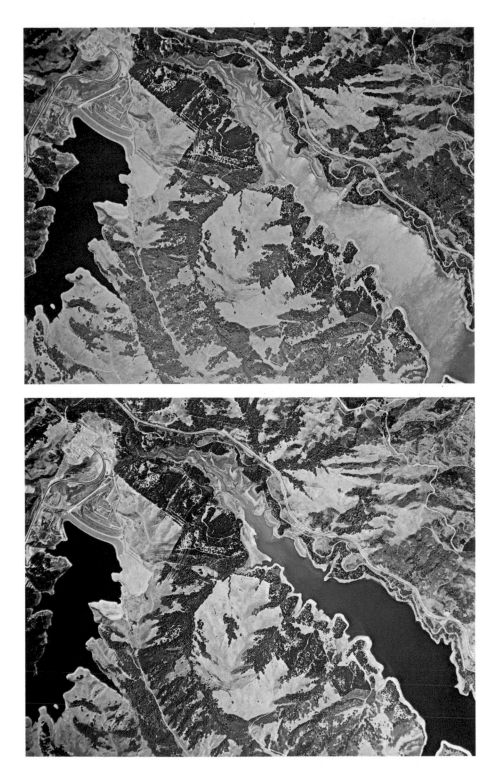

PLATE 4. Aerial Ektachrome photography (upper view) and Ektachrome aero infrared coverage (lower view) of two reservoirs in Contra Costa County, California. Annotated black-and-white views of the same area are shown in Chapter 13, Figure 13-9. Scale is about 2,800 feet per inch. Courtesy of U.S. Forest Service Remote Sensing Project, Berkeley, California.

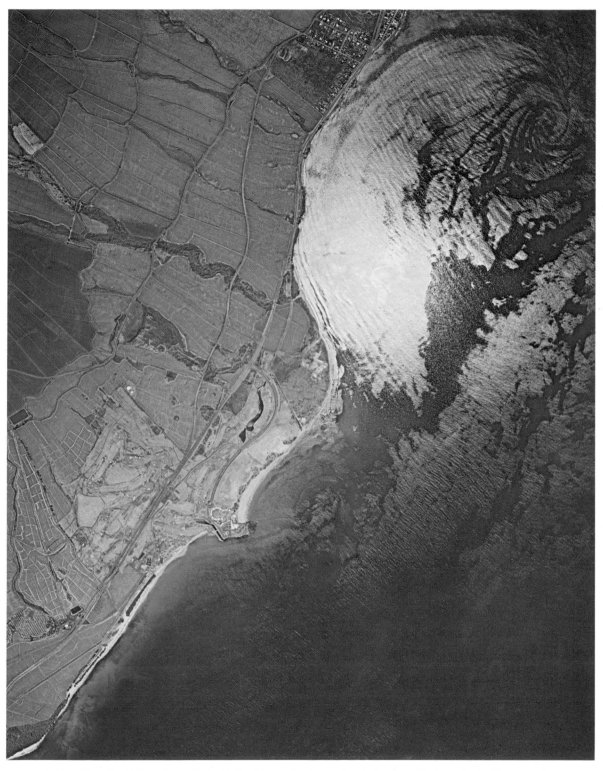

PLATE 5. Coastal section of Maui Island, Hawaii, at a scale of about 830 feet per inch. The smooth, green carpet-like vegetation represents irrigated fields of sugar cane. Courtesy of U.S. Department of Commerce, Coast and Geodetic Survey.

PLATE 6. Rocky coastal area near Cross Sound, Alaska, at a scale of about 420 feet per inch. Spruce trees have become established on some of the rock islets and large amounts of kelp can be seen in the water surrounding the islets. Courtesy of U.S. Department of Commerce, Coast and Geodetic Survey.

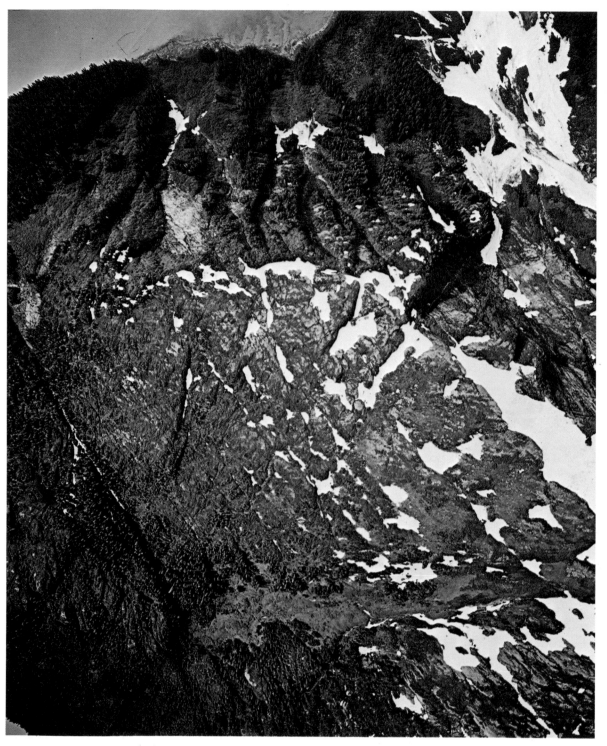

PLATE 7. Coastline area near Juneau, Alaska, at a scale of about 830 feet per inch. Large amounts of snow are visible, even though the exposure was made during August. Large trees are principally spruce (dark tones). The light-toned lesser vegetation includes such species as willows and alders. Courtesy of U.S. Department of Commerce, Coast and Geodetic Survey.

PLATE 8. Petroleum industry along the west shore of the Delaware River at a scale of about 500 feet per inch. Tree crowns are beginning to change colors in this autumn photograph. Courtesy of U.S. Department of Commerce, Coast and Geodetic Survey.

Colwell, Robert N.
1960. Some uses of infrared aerial photography in the management of wildland areas. Photogram. Engineering 26: 774-785, illus.

Cooper, Charles F., and Smith, Freeman M.
1966. Color aerial photography: toy or tool? Jour. Forestry 64:373-378.

Land, Edwin H.
1959. Experiments in color vision. Scientific American reprint, W. H. Freeman and Co., San Francisco, Calif., 14 pp., illus

Myhre, David W., and Meyer, Merle P.
1961. Variations in aerial photo image recovery resulting from differences in film and printing technique. Photogram. Engineering 27:595-599, illus.

Steen, W. W., and Little, J. C.
1959. A new portable reflectance spectrophotometer for the selection of film and filters for aerial photography. Photogram. Engineering 25:615-618, illus.

Swanson, Lawrence W.
1964. Aerial photography and photogrammetry in the Coast and Geodetic Survey. Photogram. Engineering 30:699-726, illus.

Tarkington, Raife G., and Sorem, Allan L.
1963. Color and false-color films for aerial photography. Photogram. Engineering 29:88-95, illus.

Walker, John E.
1961. Progress in spectral reflectance film-filter research applicable to engineering and geologic studies. Photogram. Engineering 27:445-450, illus.

Wear, John F.
1960. Interpretation methods and field use of aerial color photos. Photogram. Engineering 26:805-808, illus.

Welch, R.
1966. A comparison of aerial films in the study of the Breidamerkur glacier area, Iceland. The Photogram. Record 28:289-306, illus.

Winterberg, Richard P., and Wulfeck, Joseph W.
1961. Additive color photography and projection for military photo interpretation. Photogram. Engineering 27:450-460, illus.

EXERCISE 10 — Comparison of Panchromatic and Infrared Photography

1. List at least four reasons why objects may register in different tones on black-and-white photographs.

a. _____

b. _____

c. _____

d. _____

2. What is the primary purpose of using photographic filters? Which filter is most commonly used with both panchromatic and infrared film?

3. Assume that a red filter used with panchromatic film has a filter factor of 4. If an exposure meter indicates a lens setting of 1/100 second at f/8, what should be the f/stop when the filter is used with a shutter speed of 1/100 second? _____

4. List relative advantages and disadvantages of taking aerial photographs for vegetation studies during the different seasons of the year.

Season	Foliage stage	Advantages	Disadvantages
Winter	Dormant season		
Spring	Light green, immature		
Summer	Dark green Pigmentation		
Fall	Maximum coloration		

5. Study the paired panchromatic and infrared views in *Figure 6-7*. Make a list of features that can be recognized, and compare the tonal differences of these features on the two photographs. Tabulate as follows:

Feature identified	Panchromatic tone	Infrared tone	Preferred film and comments

FIGURE 6-7. Panchromatic (left) and infrared photography of Ahrweiler, West Germany. Scale is about 210 feet per inch. Courtesy of Carl Zeiss, Inc., New York.

CHAPTER 7

Sources of Aerial Photographs and Maps

Prints from U.S. Government Agencies

Most of the United States has been photographed in recent years for various federal agencies. The key to this photography is available free in map form as the "Status of Aerial Photography in the U.S." Copies may be obtained by writing to:

Map Information Office
U.S. Department of the Interior
Geological Survey
Washington, D.C. 20240

This map shows all areas of the United States, by counties, that have been photographed by or for: Agricultural Stabilization and Conservation Service, Soil Conservation Service, Forest Service, Geological Survey, Corps of Engineers, Air Force, Coast and Geodetic Survey, and commercial firms. Names and addresses of agencies holding the negatives for the photographs are printed on the back of the map, and inquiries should be sent directly to the appropriate organization. There is no central laboratory that can furnish prints of all government photography.

Negatives for the largest proportion of recent aerial photography are held by three agencies in the U.S. Department of Agriculture: Agricultural Stabilization and Conservation Service (ASCS), Forest Service (FS), and Soil Conservation Service (SCS). Standard ASCS coverage is panchromatic minus-blue photography taken at a scale of 1:20,000 (1,667 feet per inch). Forest Service and SCS photography may be on either panchromatic or infrared film, and scales of 1:15,840 (1,320 feet per inch) and 1:12,000 (1,000 feet per inch) are often available. Most USDA photography has been obtained with aerial cameras having 8.25-inch or 12-inch focal lengths. Negatives of various scales are held by the Geological Survey in the U.S. Department of Interior. Prints are available for purchase at cost from U.S. Geological Survey, Federal Center, Denver, Colorado, 80225.

Photographic prints may be obtained with glossy or semi-matte finishes. Glossy prints provide fine image resolution and contrast, but exhibit an offensive glare under ordinary illumination. Also they are difficult to write upon and may develop emulsion cracks under excessive handling. Semi-matte prints are usually preferred, because they are less reflective and more receptive to pencil and ink markings. Either single- or double-weight prints can be obtained from most agencies. Single-weight papers are suitable for office use, take up less filing space, and are easy to handle under the lens stereoscope. Double-weight prints are preferred for field use, however, as they are less subject to dimensional changes and withstand handling better than single-weight prints. Most USDA photography is furnished on double-weight, semi-matte paper, unless otherwise specified. Contact prints may be obtained on special low-shrink, waterproof papers at a slight increase in price.

Some USDA laboratories offer three degrees of print contrast: "soft" for mapping, "normal" for general use, and "contrast" for timber survey work. The contrast of aerial prints should be specified if a choice is available. The photograph should present maximum tonal differences between timber types without loss of image detail in light and dark areas. Although contrast is limited primarily by the quality of the original exposure, new electronic printing devices get excellent contrast from all but the poorest negatives.

Ordering ASCS Photography

Photo index sheets or index mosaics, showing the relative positions of all individual photographs within a given county *(Figure 7-1)*, can be examined at local offices of the Agricultural Stabilization and Conservation Service or the Soil Conservation Service. The number of index sheets per county varies from one to six or more.

To decide which prints to order, the boundaries of the desired area can be outlined on the photo index. All photographs that overlap this area, partially or completely, should be included to insure stereo-coverage. An estimate of the number of prints required to cover various-sized areas can be made from *Table 7-1*. Prints should be listed by county symbol, roll number, and exposure number. Other items to specify in ordering are: date of photography, scale, print weight, and type of finish desired.

Photographs of the following states should be ordered from:

Western Laboratory
Aerial Photography Division
ASCS—USDA
2505 Parley's Way
Salt Lake City, Utah 84109

Arizona	Idaho	Nebraska	Oregon
Arkansas	Kansas	Nevada	South Dakota
California	Louisiana	New Mexico	Texas
Colorado	Minnesota	North Dakota	Utah
Hawaii	Montana	Oklahoma	Washington
			Wyoming

Photography of Alaska and Vermont is not available through the ASCS. Photographs of the remaining states should be ordered from:

Eastern Laboratory
Aerial Photography Division
ASCS—USDA
45 South French Broad Avenue
Asheville, North Carolina 28802

Alabama	Iowa	Missouri	Rhode Island
Connecticut	Kentucky	New Hampshire	South Carolina
Delaware	Maine	New Jersey	Tennessee
Florida	Maryland	New York	Virginia
Georgia	Massachusetts	North Carolina	West Virginia
Illinois	Michigan	Ohio	Wisconsin
Indiana	Mississippi	Pennsylvania	

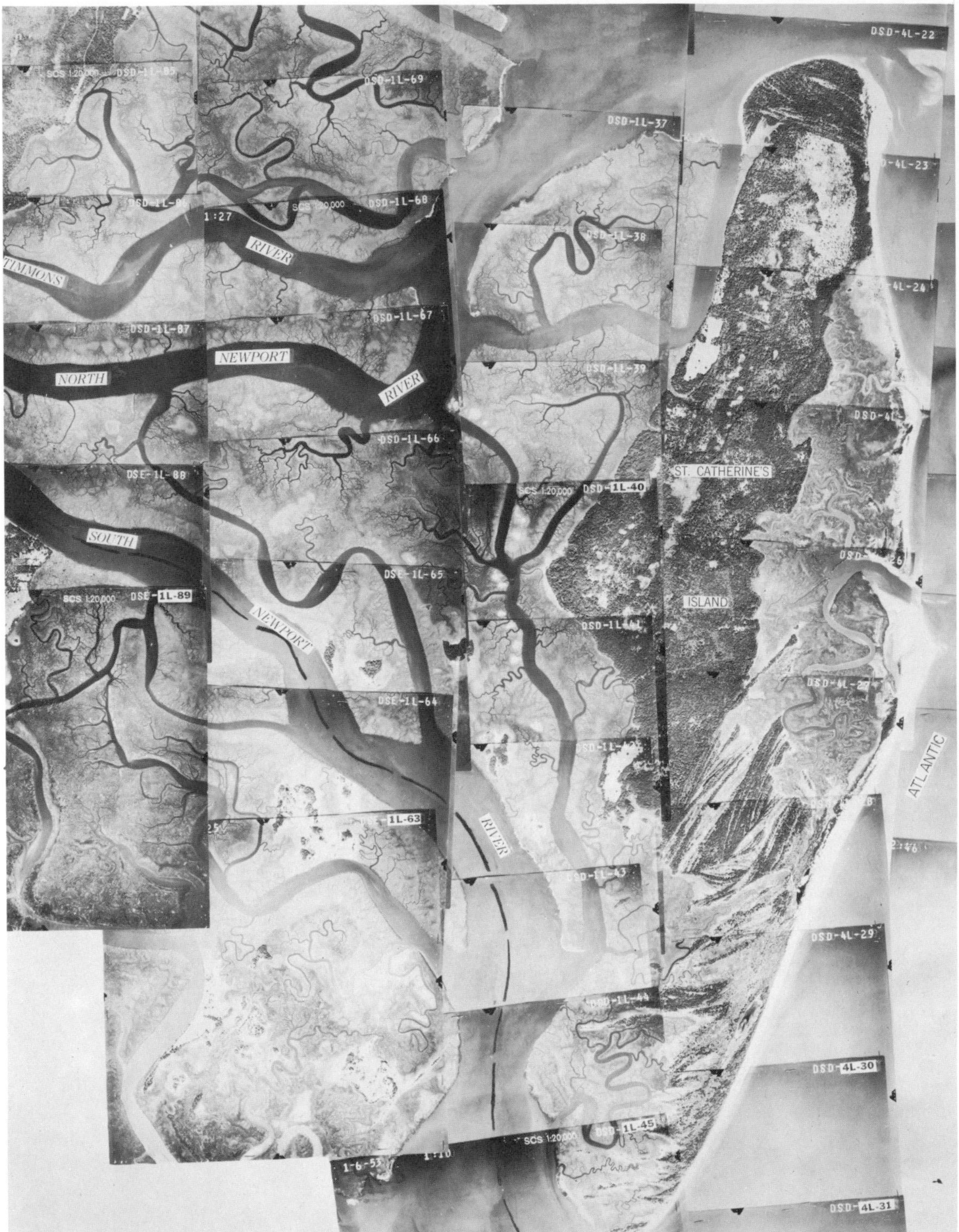

FIGURE 7-1. Portion of an aerial photo index sheet covering tidal marshes and St. Catherine's Island off the Georgia coast. Courtesy of U.S. Department of Agriculture.

TABLE 7-1. Approximate number of 9- by 9-inch prints required for stereoscopic coverage, by size of area and photo scale[1]

Size of Area	Aerial Photo Scale				
	1:20,000 or 1,667 ft./in.	1:15,840 or 1,320 ft./in.	1:12,000 or 1,000 ft./in.	1:9,600 or 800 ft./in.	1:7,920 or 660 ft./in.
Square miles	- - - - - - - - - - - - - - - - Number of Prints - - - - - - - - - - - - - - -				
25	12	19	32	50	74
50	23	37	64	99	148
100	46	74	128	198	296
200	92	148	256	396	592
400	184	296	512	792	1,184
800	368	592	1,024	1,584	2,368
1,500	685	1,091	1,900	2,965	4,364
2,500	1,142	1,819	3,166	4,941	7,276
5,000	2,284	3,638	6,332	9,882	14,552

[1]Assumes an average forward overlap of 60 percent and an average sidelap of 30 percent, or an effective area of about 22 square inches per print.

Photographic order blanks, including current prices, can be obtained by writing to the appropriate laboratory. Print orders must be accompanied by payment in advance, and six to eight weeks should be allowed for delivery. Although four scales of print enlargements are available for purchase, standard 9 by 9-inch contact prints are recommended for stereoscopic study.

Ordering SCS Photography

Some areas of the United States, notably counties bordering the Atlantic Ocean, are not covered by ASCS photography. In some instances, photo coverage of these areas may be purchased from:

Soil Conservation Service
Cartographic Division
U.S. Department of Agriculture
Hyattsville, Maryland 20251

Ordering Forest Service Photography

Aerial photographs of the National Forests are available at scales of 1:15,840 (1,320 feet per inch) or 1:12,000 (1,000 feet per inch). Coverage includes the Chugach and part of the Tongass National Forests in Alaska but does not include Hawaii. Some photographs are on infrared film. Prices quoted for ASCS coverage will generally apply to the Forest Service.

Forest Service photography of Alaska and eastern United States may be ordered from:

Chief, Forest Service
U.S. Department of Agriculture
Washington, D.C. 20250

Photographic coverage of western United States (Forest Service, Regions 1-6) is obtained through the appropriate Regional Forester as follows:

Region	Address
1	Federal Building, Missoula, Montana 59801
2	Federal Center, Building 85, Denver, Colorado 80225
3	Federal Building, 517 Gold Avenue, S.W., Albuquerque, New Mexico 87101
4	Forest Service Building, Ogden, Utah 84403
5	630 Sansome Street, San Francisco, California 94111
6	P. O. Box 3623, Portland, Oregon 97208

Prints from the Canadian Government

The National Air Photo Library of Canada contains approximately 3 million oblique, vertical, and trimetrogon photographs that provide aerial coverage of most of the country. Established in 1925, this library serves as a central repository for all survey photography done by and for the federal government, including a copy of each photograph and information on the flight lines, the flying agency, the film, and camera operations.

Contact prints can be supplied on the following papers: double-weight matte; double-weight glossy; double-weight glossy, dried matte; single-weight glossy; single-weight glossy, dried matte; resisto (light-weight, semi-gloss, water-resistant). Enlargements, mosaics, diapositive mapping plates, and glass-mounted lantern slides of photographs are also available for purchase.

To obtain additional information on Canadian photographic coverage, interested parties should write:

National Air Photo Library
Room 180, Surveys and Mapping Building
615 Booth Street
Ottawa 4, Canada

To speed up the selection of photographs, requests should include (1) a map or tracing outlining the area for which prints are desired, (2) the purpose for which the photographs are to be used, and (3) whether stereoscopic coverage is desired. Clients will be advised as to cost. Remittances should be made payable to the Receiver General of Canada.

Prints from Private Companies

A wide selection of photographic negatives are held by private aerial survey companies in the United States and Canada. As a rule, prints can be ordered directly from these companies after obtaining permission of the original purchaser. A large share of the available coverage has been obtained on panchromatic film with aerial cameras having 6-inch, distortion-free lenses. As a result, prints are ideally suited for stereoscopic study because of fine image resolution and a high degree of three-dimensional exaggeration. Scales are often 1:15,840 or larger for recent photography. In addition to contact prints and photo index sheets, most aerial mapping organizations will also sell reproductions of special atlas sheets or controlled mosaics. These items are often useful for pictorial displays and administrative planning.

Prints purchased from private companies may cost more than those from federal agencies, but they are often of higher quality and at larger scales—factors that may offset any price differential. Quotations and photo indexes can be obtained by direct inquiry to the appropriate company. Names and addresses of leading photogrammetric concerns are available in current issues of *Photogrammetric Engineering,* the journal of the American Society of Photogrammetry.

Contract Aerial Photography

Although many persons rely largely on existing aerial photographs for interpretation and mapping, such coverage may be unsuitable because of age, season, film-filter combination, or scale. As a result, there is considerable interest in the purchase of new photography taken specifically to meet the requirements of a given project. Although photo interpreters rarely take their own photographs, they may have the responsibility of drawing up preliminary specifications or flight plans, estimating costs, and inspecting the finished product.

Other things being equal, the two factors normally having the greatest influence on photographic costs are scale and size of area involved. Prices per square mile increase as scales become larger and as the area covered becomes smaller. When the scale is doubled (as from 1:15,480 to 1:7,920), four times as many prints are required, with a proportionate increase in cost. For coverage at 1:15,840 (4 inches per mile), a good camera crew can photograph 750 to 900 square miles in 5 to 8 hours of flying time. Hence, photo coverage of small tracts will be influenced more by the cost of moving the plane and crew than by the actual flying time that may be involved.

Both experienced personnel and modern equipment are essential for obtaining high-quality exposures that are necessary for precise photogrammetric work *(Figures 7-2, 7-3, and 7-4)*. Aerial photographs that fail to supply the quantity and quality of information desired cannot be considered inexpensive by any standard. It is therefore wise to negotiate only with reputable aerial survey firms that maintain high standards in their work.

Costs of contract aerial photography will obviously change with time, locality, weather conditions, film and filter specified, and fluctuations in the business activities of aerial mapping companies. As any quotation must reflect a set of fixed conditions, it is not surprising that there have been few published accounts of photographic prices. A cost-estimating and scheduling determination procedure for aerial surveying, ground control, and map compilation work has been reported by Aguilar (1967).

Technical Specifications for Aerial Photography

When the decision to purchase new photography has been made, technical specifications are usually summarized in a formal contract. Such agreements assume a variety of forms, but most of the following items are covered to some degree. Readers interested in additional contract details should refer to the *Manual of Photographic Interpretation (op. cit.)* or to sample specifications prepared by various federal agencies.

Business arrangements. These include such items as the cost of the aerial survey, posting of a performance bond, assumption of risks and damages, provision for periodic inspection of work, reflights, cancellation privileges, schedules for delivery and payments, and ownership and storage of negatives.

Area to be photographed. Includes location, size, and boundaries. These are ordinarily indicated on flight maps supplied by purchaser.

Type of photographic film and filter. Such items as A.S.A. exposure rating and dimensional stability of film base may be specified.

FIGURE 7-2. Any seven types of aerial cameras can be carried in this USAF Boeing photo-reconnaissance version of the B-47 jet bomber. Also shown here are cartridge flares and flash bombs. Official U.S. Air Force photograph.

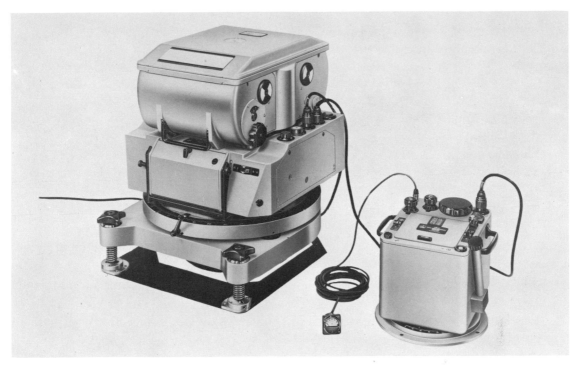

FIGURE 7-3. Zeiss RMK-A-15/23 aerial camera. Focal length is 6 inches and negative size is 9 by 9 inches. Courtesy of Carl Zeiss, Inc., New York.

FIGURE 7-4. Simplified cross-section of an aerial camera.

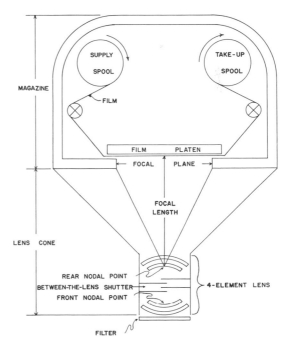

Negative scale. Maximum scale deviation normally allowed is ± 5 percent.

The aerial camera. A National Bureau of Standards calibration report may be required. Other camera specifications include size of negative format, method of flattening film during exposure, type of shutter, focal length, distortion characteristics of lens, and resolving power.

Position of flight lines. Lines are to be parallel, oriented in correct compass direction, and within a stated distance from positions drawn on flight maps.

Overlap. Usually set at 55 to 65 percent (averaging 60 percent) along line of flight, and 15 to 45 percent (averaging 30 percent) between adjacent lines. At the ends of each flight line, two photo centers should fall outside tract boundary.

Print alignment. Crab or drift is not to affect more than 10 percent of the print width for any three consecutive photographs.

Tilt. Should not exceed 2 or 3 degrees for a single exposure, nor average more than 1 degree for the entire project.

Time of photography. Both season of year and time of day (or minimum sun angle) are usually specified.

Base maps. If base maps or radial line plots are required, responsibility for ground control (field surveying) should be established.

Film processing. Included here are procedures for developing and drying negatives, indexing and editing film rolls, and type of photographic paper (weight, finish, contrast) to be used.

Quality of negatives and prints. Should be free from stains, scratches, and blemishes that detract from intended use.

Materials to be delivered. Two sets of contact prints and one set of index sheets are usually supplied. A copy of the original flight log may also be specified. Additional items such as enlargements, mosaics, maps, or plan-and-profile sheets should be listed in detail.

Inspection of Contract Aerial Photography

Following completion of a photographic survey, it is customary for a representative of the purchaser to make a technical inspection of all prints, index sheets, and negatives. If the project was awarded to a reputable aerial survey firm at the beginning, the inspection and official acceptance of materials becomes a mere formality. In other instances, careful scrutinization may be required to determine whether the photography meets the standards set forth in the contract specifications.

Infrequent purchasers of aerial photography may have difficulty in evaluating the finished product, for acceptance or rejection of photographic flights often requires checks of such items as film titling, overlap, scale, and print quality. As a means of translating technical specifications into guides for the neophyte inspector, an itemized inspection checklist as designed by Avery and Meyer (1962) may prove useful.

All prints should be dated in the upper left corner; project, roll, and exposure numbers should be shown in the upper right corner of each photograph. Nominal photo scale, as 1:15,840, and local standard time are ordinarily placed at the top center of the first and last exposures in each flight line. The center of the photographic flight strip should be within a specified distance of the position plotted on original flight maps. Maximum deviation is usually set at 25 percent of the mean sidelap distance. The inspector should also check to make sure that the compass bearing of each flight line is within 5 degrees of the specified direction and that adjacent lines are within 5 degrees of parallel.

Photographic Tilt and Scale Checks

Tilt is most commonly encountered on prints near the ends of flight lines where exposures are made as the aircraft banks into a turn for the next strip. It is difficult to detect a small degree of tilt, but excessive amounts are quite evident on photographs of flat terrain having rectangular land subdivision. In such instances, the oblique camera view results in an apparent convergence of grid patterns and parallel lines.

Because of the time required, photo-scale checks are seldom made for individual prints. Instead, 10 or more overlapping prints are selected from each flight line for a check of the average scale across an expanded geographic transect. After the prints have been taped down in mosaic fashion, the distance between two points is carefully measured. By computing a simple ratio between the photo measurement and the corresponding distance on the flight map, average print scale can be quickly read from *Table 7-2*. Allowing for variations in local relief, this average should be within ± 5 percent of the specified scale.

Assessing Print Quality

Print quality is usually the most difficult item for a new inspector to evaluate because of the lack of standards or criteria of comparison. Heavy reliance must be placed on subjective judgment in deciding whether a given photographic defect constitutes a reasonable basis for rejection. Some of the print "defects" shown in *Figure 7-5*, for example, may be of minor importance for certain photo interpretation projects. Although original exposures may be of high quality, carelessness in printing may produce photographs with poor contrast, stains, or blurred detail. For this reason, film negatives should be available for inspection over a light table. Special techniques in printing will often produce high-quality photographs even when negatives have poor density characteristics.

Topographic Maps for Flight Planning

An aerial flight plan is simply a reliable map depicting the area to be photographed, scale of photography desired, and proposed location and altitude of flight lines. Even though the final version may be prepared by an aerial survey firm, it is usually to the purchaser's advantage to draw up a preliminary plan prior to issuing bid invitations.

Topographic quadrangle sheets, ranging in scale from 1:24,000 to 1:250,000, are among the best maps readily available for preparing flight plans *(Table 7-3)*. In the United States, these maps can be purchased at nominal cost from two principal distribution centers. Maps for areas west of the Mississippi River, including all of Louisiana and Minnesota, can be purchased from:

U.S. Geological Survey
Distribution Section
Federal Center
Denver, Colorado 80225

TABLE 7-2. Conversion ratios for determining the average scale of aerial photographs[1]

Flight map scales (R.F.)					Aerial Photo Scale (R.F.)
1:250,000	1:125,000	1:62,500	1:31,680	1:24,000	
Scale conversion ratios					
35.7	17.8	8.9	4.52	3.43	1:7,000
33.3	16.7	8.3	4.22	3.20	1:7,500
31.2	15.6	7.8	3.96	3.00	1:8,000
29.4	14.7	7.4	3.73	2.82	1:8,500
27.8	13.9	6.9	3.52	2.67	1:9,000
26.3	13.2	6.6	3.33	2.53	1:9,500
25.0	12.5	6.2	3.17	2.40	1:10,000
23.8	11.9	6.0	3.02	2.28	1:10,500
22.7	11.4	5.7	2.88	2.18	1:11,000
21.7	10.9	5.4	2.75	2.09	1:11,500
20.8	10.4	5.2	2.64	2.00	1:12,000
20.0	10.0	5.0	2.53	1.92	1:12,500
19.2	9.6	4.8	2.44	1.85	1:13,000
18.5	9.2	4.6	2.35	1.78	1:13,500
17.8	8.9	4.5	2.26	1.71	1:14,000
17.2	8.6	4.3	2.18	1.66	1:14,500
16.7	8.3	4.2	2.11	1.60	1:15,000
16.1	8.1	4.0	2.04	1.55	1:15,500
15.6	7.8	3.9	1.98	1.50	1:16,000
15.2	7.6	3.8	1.92	1.45	1:16,500
14.7	7.4	3.7	1.86	1.41	1:17,000
14.3	7.1	3.6	1.81	1.37	1:17,500
13.9	6.9	3.5	1.76	1.33	1:18,000
13.5	6.7	3.4	1.71	1.30	1:18,500
13.1	6.6	3.3	1.67	1.26	1:19,000
12.8	6.4	3.2	1.62	1.23	1:19,500
12.5	6.2	3.1	1.58	1.20	1:20,000
12.2	6.1	3.0	1.54	1.17	1:20,500

[1]To use the table, several contact prints should be lapped in mosaic fashion. Measure distance between two points easily recognized on photos and flight-map. With a photo distance of 18.8 inches and a map distance of 2.0 inches, ratio is 9.4. Assuming a flight-map scale of 1:125,000, this ratio is interpolated above as representing a photo scale of approximately 1:13,250.

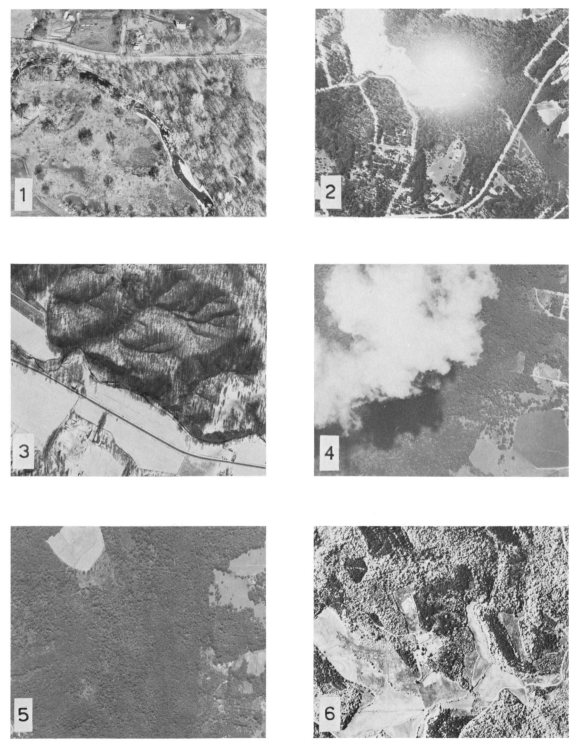

FIGURE 7-5. Illustration of several factors affecting image quality on aerial photographs. (1) Tilted photograph (note oblique view), (2) hotspot or sunspot, (3) snow cover and long shadows, (4) clouds and cloud shadows, (5) insufficient print contrast, and (6) excessive print contrast.

TABLE 7-3.   Scales of national topographic maps available from the U.S. Geological Survey

Map series and scale	Quadrangle size (latitude − longitude)	Quadrangle area (square miles)
Puerto Rico 1:20,000	7½ by 7½ minutes	71
United States 1:24,000	7½ by 7½ minutes	49 to 70
United States 1:62,500	15 by 15 minutes	197 to 282
Alaska 1:63,360	15 by 20-36 minutes	207 to 281
United States 1:250,000	1 by 2 degrees[1]	4,580 to 8,669
United States 1:1,000,000	4 by 6 degrees[1]	73,734 to 102,759

[1] Maps of Alaska and Hawaii vary from these standards.

For areas east of the Mississippi River, including Puerto Rico and the Virgin Islands, maps may be purchased from:

U.S. Geological Survey
Distribution Section
Washington, D.C. 20240

Maps of Hawaii may be ordered at either address.

In Canada, series maps of the national topographic system range in scale from 1:25,000 to 1:1,000,000. These may be purchased from:

Map Distribution Office
Surveys and Mapping Branch
Department of Mines and Technical Surveys
615 Booth Street
Ottawa 4, Canada

The National Atlas Project

Following recommendations from the National Academy of Sciences and the National Research Council, the U.S. Geological Survey is preparing a National Atlas of the United States. The objective is to create a reference tool of high quality for use by members of Congress, government agencies, business and industrial organizations, libraries, educational institutions, and scholars.

The National Atlas will be a volume of approximately 475 pages. Most of the United States maps will be devoted to coverage of physical characteristics (relief, geology, climate, water resources, soils and vegetation), history (discovery, exploration, territorial growth, settlement, battlefields, and scientific expeditions), economic status (agriculture, industry, resources, transportation, and finance), social conditions (population distribution and structure, educational achievement, centers of art, culture, and scientific research), administrative subdivisions (counties, judicial and election districts, time zones, etc.), and status of coverage by aerial photos and map or chart series.

In the back of the atlas will be a few world maps to show the place of the United States in world affairs, and a detailed index which will include geographical coordinates, an alpha-numeric code, generic identifications and, where appropriate, the population or elevation of places named.

Text in the atlas will be limited, with a few exceptions, to map captions and explanations, but references will be provided to more detailed maps and documentation of each subject. Many of the maps will be sold separately and may be purchased from the U.S. Geological Survey, Washington, D.C. 20242, as they are published. Revision is planned on a continuing basis.

A Sample Flight Plan

This example illustrates the various calculations involved in preparing an aerial flight plan for an area of 80 square miles. Basic information required is as follows:

Scale of base map: 1:62,500 or 1 inch = 5,208 feet
Size of area: 8 miles E-W by 10 miles N-S, or 42,240 feet by 52,800 feet
Average ground elevation above mean sea level: 1,200 feet
Average forward overlap: 60 percent
Sidelap: 15 to 45 percent, averaging approximately 30 percent
Negative format: 9 × 9 inches or 11,880 feet by 11,880 feet on the ground
Camera focal length: 6 inches or 0.5 foot

Items to be computed in preparing the flight plan are:

a. Flying height above ground and height above mean sea level
b. Direction and number of flight lines
c. Ground distance between flight lines
d. Actual percent of sidelap
e. Map distance between flight lines
f. Ground distance between exposures on each line
g. Map distance between exposures on each line
h. Number of exposures on each line and total number of exposures

Flight Map Computations

a. Flying height above ground datum: height = focal length × scale denominator, or
$$H = 0.5' \times 15,840 = 7,920 \text{ feet above ground}$$

Flying height above mean sea level: 7,920 + 1,200 = 9,120 feet

b. Direction of flight lines: North-South, following long dimension of tract.

Number of flight lines: Assuming an average sidelap of 30 percent, the lateral gain from one line to another is 70 percent of the print width, or 0.70 × 11,880 = 8,316 feet between lines. The number of *intervals* between lines is found by dividing the tract width (42,240 feet) by 8,316. The result is 5.08 or 5 *intervals* and 6 *flight lines*.

c. Ground distance between flight lines:
Tract width (42,240) ÷ 5 intervals = 8,448 feet between lines

d. Actual percent of sidelap:
$$\frac{\text{Sidelap}}{\text{percent}} = \frac{\text{Print width (ft.)} - \text{Spacing (ft.)}}{\text{Print width (ft.)}} \times 100$$

$$\frac{\text{Sidelap}}{\text{percent}} = \frac{11,880 - 8,448}{11,880} \times 100 = 28.9 \text{ percent}$$

e. Map distance between flight lines (map scale: 1″ = 5,208 feet):
$$\frac{1''}{5,208'} = \frac{X''}{8,448'}; X = 1.62'' \text{ between lines on map}$$

f. Ground distance between exposures on each line: Assuming an average forward overlap of 60 percent, the spacing between successive exposures is 40 percent of the print width, or $0.40 \times 11{,}880 = 4{,}752$ feet.

g. Map distance between exposures on each line:

$$\frac{1''}{5{,}208'} = \frac{X''}{4{,}752''}; \; X = 0.91'' \text{ between exposures on map}$$

h. Number of exposures on each line: Number of *intervals* between exposures is found by dividing tract length (52,800 feet) by $4{,}752 = 11.11$ *intervals*. This would require 12 exposures *inside* the area, assuming that the first exposure is centered over one tract boundary. In addition, two extra exposures are commonly made at the ends of each line; thus a total of $12 + 2 + 2 = 16$ *exposures* would be taken on each flight line.

Total number of exposures required to cover entire tract: 6 lines $\times$ 16 exposures per line = 96 exposures.

References

Aguilar, Antonio M.
  1967. Cost analysis for aerial surveying. Photogram. Engineering 33:81-89, illus.

Avery, T. Eugene.
  1962. Airphoto coverage currently used by private forest industries. Photogram. Engineering 28:509-511.

_____.
  1960. A checklist for airphoto inspections. Photogram. Engineering 26:81-84, illus.

_____ and Meyer, Merle P.
  1962. Contracting for forest aerial photography in the United States. U.S. Forest Serv., Lake States Forest Expt. Sta., Station Paper 96, 37 pp., illus.

Meyer, Merle P.
  1957. A preliminary study of the influence of photo paper characteristics upon stereo image perception. Photogram. Engineering 23:149-155, illus.

Stone, Kirk H.
  1960. World air photo coverage. Photogram. Engineering 27:214-227, illus.

U.S. Department of Agriculture.
  1965. Specifications for aerial photography. U.S. Forest Serv., Div of Engineering, Washington, D.C., 28 pp., illus. (mimeo.)

Wright, Marshall S., Jr.
  1960. What does photogrammetric mapping really cost? Photogram. Engineering 26:452-454.

EXERCISE 11 — Preparation of a Flight Map for Aerial Photography

1. Assume you must plan a photographic mission for an area covered by a topographic map such as that printed inside the back cover of this book. Your instructor will supply basic data on photo scale desired, overlap, camera focal length, and so on. Compute the following values by the methods outlined in the preceding example:

    a. Flying height above ground datum _____ feet

       Flying height above MSL _____ feet

    b. Direction of flight lines _____

       Number of flight lines _____

    c. Ground distance between flight lines _____ feet

    d. Actual percent of sidelap _____ percent

    e. Map distance between flight lines_____ inches

    f. Ground distance between exposures on each line _____ feet

    g. Map distance between exposures on each line _____ inches

    h. Number of exposures on each line _____

       Total number of exposures _____

2. Use the foregoing data to convert your topographic map into a finished flight plan. Show location, direction, and altitude of all flight lines, positions of all print centers, actual percent of sidelap, and so on. Add an appropriate title at the bottom of the map sheet.

CHAPTER 8

Mapping From Aerial Photographs

Planimetric Base Maps

In areas of flat terrain where photographic scales can be precisely determined, direct print tracings may serve many useful purposes; nevertheless, such tracings cannot be technically referred to as true maps. Although the vertical aerial photograph presents a correct record of *angles,* constant changes in horizontal scale preclude accurate measurements of distance on simple overlays. The obvious alternative is to transfer photographic detail to reliable base maps of uniform scale. *Planimetric maps* are those that show the correct horizontal or plan position of natural and cultural features; maps that also show elevational differences (e.g., contour lines) are termed *topographic maps.*

Construction of an original base map can be an expensive and time-consuming procedure. Therefore, existing maps should be used for the transfer of photographic detail wherever feasible. Geological Survey topographic quadrangle sheets at a scale of 1:24,000 provide excellent, low-cost base maps. Topographic maps may also be obtained from the Maps and Surveys Branch of the Tennessee Valley Authority, Chattanooga, Tennessee; and from the Mississippi River Commission, Corps of Engineers, Vicksburg, Mississippi, or Chicago, Illinois.

County maps, usually available from state highway departments, may also serve as base maps when a high level of accuracy is not required. They often show township, range, and section lines, in addition to geographic coordinates (longitude and latitude) to the nearest 5 minutes. County maps are usually printed at a scale of about one-half inch per mile. Although compass bearings of section lines are not generally shown, such maps are much more reliable than oversimplified plats showing idealized townships and sections oriented exactly with the cardinal directions.

Regardless of the base map selected, some enlargement or reduction is ordinarily required before transferring print detail, because differences between photographic and map scales must be reconciled. This may be accomplished optically by using special instruments described later, or by reconstructing the map at the approximate scale of the contact prints. A pantograph may be used to facilitate the drafting process.

General Land Office Plats

General Land Office (GLO) plats provide another satisfactory means of compiling planimetric base maps. Most of the United States west of the Mississippi River and north of the Ohio River, plus Alabama, Mississippi, and portions of Florida, was originally subdivided under the U.S. Public Land Survey *(Figure 8-1)*. Township, range, and section lines are often visible on aerial photographs. If enough such lines and corners can be identified, GLO plats can be constructed as base maps by using field notes available at state capitals or county surveyors' offices. The accuracy of this method depends upon the number of grid lines and corners that can be pin-pointed on the aerial photographs. The basic procedure is as follows:

A GLO plat showing sections, quarter-sections, and forties is drawn to the average photo scale from survey field notes. As many of the same lines and corners as possible are pin-pointed on the aerial photographs, preferably arranged in a systematic framework throughout the project area. Ownership maps, county highway maps, and topographic quadrangle sheets may be helpful in identifying such corners, but additional points must usually be found by taking the photographs into the field.

When photo interpretation has been completed, the annotated detail is transferred to the plat, one square of the grid being completed at a time. If the plat and photos are of the same scale, transfer can be speeded up by direct tracing over a light table; where scales differ, a proportionate grid system can be used. Photo detail is "forced" into corresponding squares on the base map. Transfer of detail should not be extended outside of the framework of control, because large errors may be incurred.

Map Projections

A map projection is merely an orderly system of representing the earth's surface on a plane. Actually the approximately spherical form of the globe cannot be flattened into a

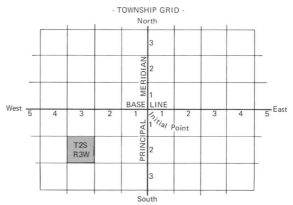

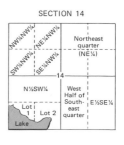

FIGURE 8-1. Subdivisions of the U.S. Public Land Survey.

map without incurring distortion of shapes or areal relationships. For small areas mapped at moderate scales (e.g., a small county), the curvature of the earth is so slight that distortion is negligible and often ignored. As larger areas (e.g., several counties or an entire state) are encompassed, however, distortion increases and it becomes impossible to represent a portion of the earth's surface precisely on a flat map sheet.

Historically, a large number of map projections have been devised, but only a relatively small number have enjoyed wide usage. There is no one projection that is best for all shapes and sizes of areas; all are designed for special purposes, and the value of a given projection depends on its specific use. Ideally a map projection provides a true representation of both shapes and areas, but in practice, these two characteristics cannot be obtained on the same map. Projections that retain the true shapes of geographical units are referred to as *conformal;* those that provide correct area relationships are termed *equal-area* or *equivalent.* Other features of an ideal map projection include properties of true distance, true direction, and ease of plotting. As no projection meets all of these requirements, the properties of three projections commonly used in the middle latitudes will be cited: (1) Mercator, (2) Lambert conformal conic, and (3) polyconic. Descriptions are taken primarily from a U.S. Army field manual.

Mercator Projection

This is a mathematically derived projection in which parallels and meridians are projected onto a cylinder tangent to the earth at the equator *(Figure 8-2).* When the cylinder is laid out flat, the meridians appear as vertical straight lines. Meridians are evenly spaced and true to scale at the equator or at the selected "standard parallel"[1] of latitude. Lines

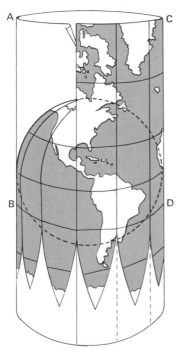

FIGURE 8-2. Derivation of the Mercator projection.

FIGURE 8-3. State map drawn on a Mercator projection.

[1] Any parallel along which linear measurements are the same as for a globe of equal scale. A meridian that has this property is called a central meridian.

of latitude are also straight and parallel, but they do not fall at their normally projected positions; instead, they are mathematically spaced to produce the property of conformality or true shape *(Figure 8-3)*. For any *small area* (e.g., a one-degree square), the relation of scale along meridians and parallels is the same as on the globe. Scale changes are slight in the mid-latitudes, amounting to only about 3 percent at 30° north or south of the equator. However, since the meridians do not converge, areas in the higher latitudes are greatly enlarged (not distorted) when the equator is used as the standard parallel. Although relatively true shapes are maintained, the map scale is doubly exaggerated at 60° and increased by six times at 80°. Thus on a Mercator map of the world, Greenland appears larger than South America, although it is actually only about one-ninth as large. Polar regions are at infinity and hence cannot be shown on a Mercator projection.

The Mercator projection, devised around 1569 by a Dutch cartographer, is the oldest and probably the best known projection in the world because of its continuous use for nautical charts. An outstanding feature of the Mercator is that all straight lines are "loxodromes" or "rhumb lines," i.e., lines of true bearing or azimuth. As parallels and meridians form a rectangular grid, it is easily plotted. The Mercator is widely used for navigational purposes in the mid-latitudes and it is the standard projection for Navy hydrographic and air-navigation charts.

Lambert Conformal Conic Projection

This projection, developed by a German mathematician, is derived by projecting lines from the center of the globe onto a simple cone. The cone intersects the earth along two standard parallels of latitude, both of which are on the same side of the equator *(Figure 8-4)*. All meridians are converging straight lines that meet at a common point beyond the limits

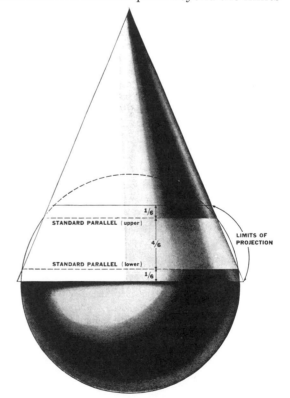

FIGURE 8-4. Derivation of the Lambert conformal conic projection.

STANDARD PARALLEL (upper)

STANDARD PARALLEL (lower)

1/6

4/6

1/6

LIMITS OF PROJECTION

of the map. Parallels are concentric circles whose center is at the intersection point of the meridians. Parallels and meridians cross at right angles, an essential of conformality.

To minimize and distribute scale errors, the two standard parallels are chosen to enclose two-thirds of the north-south map area. Between these parallels, the scale will be too small, and beyond them, too large. If the north-south extent of maps is limited, however, maximum scale errors will rarely exceed one percent. Area exaggeration between and near the standard parallels is relatively slight; thus the projection provides good directional and shape relationships for areas having their long axes running in an east-west belt. The Lambert conformal conic is the most commonly used projection for sectional aeronautical charts of the United States.

Polyconic Projection

Because of its suitability for large-scale maps of relatively small areas, the polyconic projection is ordinarily of greatest interest to photo interpreters. It is derived by projecting lines from the center of the earth onto a series of cones, each of which is tangent to a parallel of latitude. The central meridian of the area to be mapped is a straight line along which the linear scale is correct. Parallels are represented by arcs of circles that are not concentric, but the centers of which all lie in the extension of the central meridian. Distances between parallels along the central meridian are proportional to true distances on the earth's surface. Spacings between meridians are similarly proportioned. The projection is neither conformal nor equivalent, but for small areas, both qualities are closely approximated.

For large areas, north-south distortion increases rapidly with increasing distance from the central meridian. Because of this, it is customary to limit the width of the projection and to use the central meridian of the area to be mapped as the central meridian of the projection. In short, the projection is best suited to areas whose long axes lie in a north-south direction. The polyconic projection is used for almost all topographic maps compiled by U.S. government agencies. Special tables have been computed that permit its use anywhere in the world.

Radial Line Triangulation

If acceptable planimetric maps cannot be compiled from the foregoing methods, the usual alternative is to construct a new map based on a "radial line plot." A radial line plot is a photogrammetric triangulation procedure, usually controlled by ground surveys, by which the photo images are oriented and placed in proper relationship to one another. To a large degree, the field descriptions of available ground control points dictates the nature of the base map constructed. If control points are based on the U.S. Public Land Survey, a GLO plat would be constructed; if they are tied to a state coordinate system, the corresponding rectangular grid would be used; and if locations are described in terms of latitude and longitude, a suitable map projection would constitute the basic plotting framework.

On a vertical or near-vertical photograph, the principal point, isocenter, and nadir are assumed to occupy the same location. Thus a line drawn radially from the principal point to a given object will *pass through* the true location of the object. Expressed in another way, any displacement of photo images will occur along lines radiating from the center of the photograph. This concept is the basis for constructing maps controlled by radial line plots.

The principle of radial line triangulation can be illustrated with any two overlapping prints. If a straight line is drawn from the principal point of each photo through images of the *same* object, the two lines will intersect at the correct position of the object when the prints are lapped in mosaic fashion with flight lines superimposed. By repeating this procedure for several selected "wing points"[2] on each photograph, the entire group of prints can be correctly oriented and tied to a base map. It is presumed here that some of the wing points will also serve as ground control points. Ground control points are most effective when located around the perimeter of the project area, e.g., near the exterior boundaries. Even for small areas, a good radial line plot requires a minimum of one or two ground control points near each corner of the area being mapped, and most of these points should be common to at least three photographs.

Construction of a radial line plot for a small area (e.g., 10 to 20 square miles) is normally accomplished by using transparent paper templets. Larger radial line plots are preferably constructed by commercial mapping companies that are fully equipped for handling such work. In these instances, slotted templets may be used *(Figures 8-5, 8-6)* or triangulation may be performed directly with first-order stereoplotting instruments.

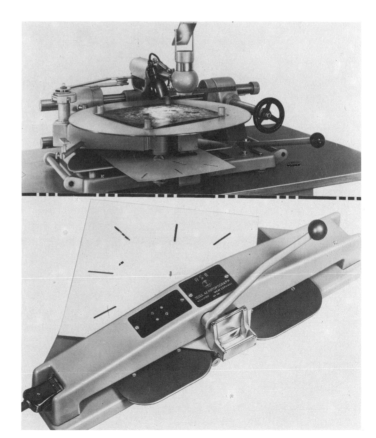

FIGURE 8-5. Two types of radial sectors used for cutting slotted templets. Courtesy of Carl Zeiss, Inc., New York.

---

[2]A wing point is any selected photo feature in the sidelap and overlap zone which can be easily pin-pointed on all prints upon which it appears. *Figure 2-12* illustrates an ideal distribution of wing points for six overlapping photographs.

FIGURE 8-6. Assembly of slotted templets for a large radial line plot. Each templet represents a 9 by 9-inch aerial photograph. Courtesy of Aero Service Division of Litton Industries.

Constructing a Radial Line Plot

As the use of transparent paper templets is the least expensive method of making a radial line plot for a small number of photographs, this procedure is outlined here. The same basic steps can be followed when slotted templets are available. At least six overlapping prints (three prints each in two adjacent flight lines) are needed. Principal points, conjugate principal points, and flight lines should be located and inked as described in earlier chapters.

1. Draw a suitable base map of the project area at the prescribed scale. All ground control points should be precisely plotted on the base map and marked with 0.2-inch diameter circles. Exact locations of control points may be obtained from ground surveys, GLO plats, or by using a network of known triangulation stations.

2. With a sharp china-marking pencil, outline the boundary of the project area on all photographs. Draw the line just *outside* the boundaries to avoid obscuring needed detail.

3. Pin-point ground control points on all photographs and mark with 0.2-inch circles in colored ink (to contrast with PP's and CPP's). At least two, and preferably three, control points should be common to one pair of overlapping prints when the transparent templet method is used.

4. Locate wing points (well-defined features easily pin-pointed on overlapping prints) near the middle of the sidelap zone and perpendicular to PP's and CPP's. If a control

point has already been picked within one inch of a planned wing point, the wing point may be omitted. Except for the first and last photo in each flight line, all prints will have six wing points. These will be common to 2, 3, 4, 5, or 6 overlapping photographs. Mark with a 0.2-inch diameter inked circles—the same color and size as those used to designate PP's and CPP's.

5. Prepare 9 by 9-inch squares of tracing paper for each photograph. Tape down each print over a light table with the transparent templet on top. Then, using a 4H pencil,

    a. Pin-point all PP's, CPP's, control points, wing points, and trace exact position of flight lines.

    b. Use a straightedge to align each wing and control point with the PP. Draw radial lines extending about 1.5 inches on either side of wing and control points.

    c. Label each templet by writing the appropriate exposure number aside PP's and CPP's. Wing and control points should carry the same designation on all templets upon which they appear.

6. Tape down the base map over a large light table. Assembly of the radial line plot may begin with any transparent templet which includes three control points. (If the slotted method is used, a templet having one or two control points can be positioned first.) Shift templet over top of base map until radial lines drawn through control points precisely intersect the same locations on the map. Fasten down with drafting tape.

7. The second templet positioned will be one in the same flight line that overlaps the first. With the common flight line superimposed, the templet is shifted back and forth *along the flight line* until radial lines representing control points pass through base map positions (just as with the first templet). Intersections of radial lines from wing points will be obtained simultaneously. The second templet is then taped down.

8. Remaining templets in the first flight line are added in order of overlap position. When one flight line has been completed, assembly of the adjacent line should begin with the templet having the greatest amount of ground control, and so on. Radial lines from wing points, as well as those from control points, should precisely intersect at the same point. A wing point that appears on six photographs will thus be represented by a six-way "cross" of radial lines. In all instances, flight lines must be superimposed, and the templets may be shifted *only along the flight line* to obtain intersections with radial lines from adjacent templets. The result will be an assembly similar to that shown in *Figure 8-7*.

9. When all templets have been correctly positioned and taped down, use a needle to punch through all PP's, CPP's, and wing point intersections. In this way, all points are located on the base map. Remove templets, mark all transferred points on the map with 0.2-inch diameter penciled circles, and label with appropriate designations as in step 5-c.

10. The radial line plot is now complete. Photographic detail may be transferred to the base map with instruments described in the next section.

Transferring Detail from Single Prints

Following completion of photo interpretation and preparation of a radial line plot, the next phase of map compilation is the transfer of photographic features to the base map. Although direct tracings may suffice under special circumstances, it is usually more efficient to use one of several photogrammetric devices designed for this purpose. The two types of instruments most commonly employed for transferring planimetric detail from single

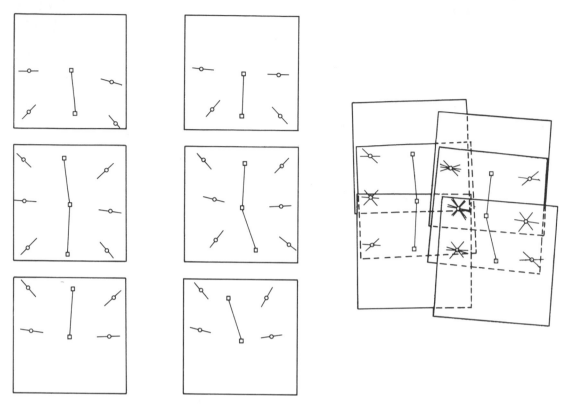

FIGURE 8-7. Diagram of paper templets (left) and assembly into a radial line plot (right). Compare with Figure 2-12.

prints are camera lucidas and reflecting projectors. As these instruments do not provide for stereoscopic viewing, the desired features should be annotated on alternate prints prior to the transfer process.[3]

One of the more common types of camera lucidas is the vertical sketchmaster pictured in *Figure 8-8*. This device employs a full-silvered and a semi-transparent or semi-silvered mirror to superimpose photo and map images. The annotated contact print is placed face up on the platform, directly under a large, full-silvered mirror. Photo images are reflected from the large mirror to a semi-silvered mirror in the eyepiece housing. When the interpreter looks into the eyepiece, the semi-transparent mirror provides a monocular view of the reflected photo image and the base map simultaneously.

To transfer photographic detail to the radial line plot, the instrument is raised or lowered by adjusting the legs until both map and photograph appear at the same scale. Any combination of three common control or wing points is carefully matched; features that fall within the triangle thus formed are traced onto the base map. The instrument is then shifted and the legs readjusted until three more circles can be superimposed. Planimetric detail is thus transferred, one triangle at a time, until the base map is completed. Photo image displacement due to tilt or topography may result in slightly offset features (e.g., a highway) along common sides of triangles. Such discrepancies must be resolved by "hedging" locations until smooth, continuous lines are obtained.

---

[3]If 9 by 9-inch photographs with 60 percent endlap and 30 percent sidelap are assumed, alternate prints will have effective (non-overlapping) areas of about 6.3 by 7.2 inches. Only one-half as many prints must be handled during the transfer process if annotations are confined to alternate photographs.

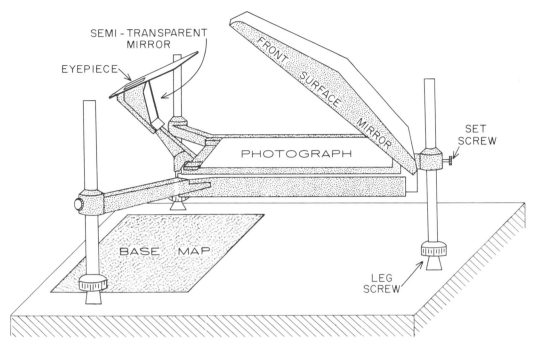

FIGURE 8-8. Schematic diagram of a vertical sketchmaster. A semi-silvered eyepiece mirror enables the operator to view photograph and map simultaneously.

Most sketchmasters provide for a relatively narrow range of scale changes; the type shown in *Figure 8-8* has a scale range of about 0.7X to 1.5X, while the model pictured in *Figure 8-9* accommodates changes of 0.4X to 2.8X. Base maps should therefore be drawn at the approximate photo scale when the sketchmaster is used for the transfer of detail.

FIGURE 8-9. LUZ Aero-sketchmaster with aerial photograph held in position by magnets. This self-illuminated camera lucida operates on the same basic principle as the device pictured in Figure 8-8. Courtesy of Carl Zeiss, Inc., New York.

Reflecting projectors are quite similar in operation to ordinary photographic enlargers. A contact print is placed opposite a light source and a full-silvered mirror set at 45° from the vertical. The photo image is thereby reflected through a lens and onto a tracing surface, usually a table top. Reflecting projectors offer a greater range of scale adjustments and more table-top "elbow room" than vertical sketchmasters; however, they are somewhat less portable and must ordinarily be used in a semi-darkened room *(Figure 8-10)*. Devices used for stereoscopic transfer of detail from aerial photographs to base maps are pictured on succeeding pages.

Ground Control for Topographic Maps

At the turn of the century, the compilation of topographic maps was largely dependent on field surveys. Such maps now are produced by photogrammetric methods, and field work is limited to obtaining a network of horizontal and vertical ground control required for accurate stereoplotting. Ground control points are carefully located positions that show longitude and latitude or elevation above mean sea level. Horizontal control is needed to maintain correct scale, position, and orientation of the map. For this purpose, the grid coordinates of many points within the area to be mapped must be determined by field surveys. Similarly, vertical control is needed for the correct location of contours. Therefore, elevations of many points must also be determined in the field.

Control points become the framework on which map detail is assembled. This framework determines the accuracy with which the positions and elevations of map features may be shown and makes it possible to join maps of abutting quadrangles without a break in the continuity of map detail. The control points are usually marked on the ground by metal tables set in rock or masonry, and are shown on maps by appropriate symbols. Some marks serve for both horizontal and vertical control.

FIGURE 8-10. Desk-model reflecting projector. A contact print can be placed behind the spring-held panel and detail traced onto a base map positioned below. Courtesy of Reed Research, Inc.

Compilation of Topographic Maps

Typical steps in the production of topographic quadrangles are as follows:

1. Vertical photography of the area to be mapped is obtained, usually on panchromatic film. Scale of photography is geared to the desired contour interval and the stereoplotting instrument to be used for map compilation.

2. Film is developed and a set of contact prints made for selection of ground control. Horizontal and vertical controls are established by field surveys, and control points are marked on contact prints *(Figure 8-11)*.

3. Glass diapositives (usually 9 by 9 inches) are made from each film negative for use in stereoplotting instruments *(Figure 8-12)*. The positive-image plates are oriented in the plotter so that they occupy the same relative positions in space as the original film negatives. Tie-ins to the base map or "manuscript" are established by use of ground control points. The resulting stereoscopic set-up is referred to as a stereo-model.

4. Contours, drainage, and culture are automatically traced onto the map manuscript by manipulation of a floating dot within the stereo-model. When all detail has been transferred from a given stereo-model, one diapositive is replaced, and an adjacent model is correctly oriented and tied in to the manuscript by a process known as "bridging."

5. The completed map manuscript is checked for errors and omissions. Detail is then traced onto a polyester film base by a technique known as "scribing" *(Figure 8-13)*. Separate scribe-sheets and negatives are made for each item to be lithographed or printed in a different tone on the finished map. Maps issued by such agencies as the Geological Survey and Tennessee Valley Authority are usually printed in five colors.

Business activities of many private aerial survey companies are oriented toward the production of topographic maps for use in city planning, real estate zoning and development, and highway engineering. Maps compiled for these purposes may require contour intervals of 1 to 5 feet, rather than the 10 to 20-foot intervals usually shown on government topographic quadrangles. In addition, cross-section or profile maps may be compiled to supplement information provided by vertical map presentations.

National Map Accuracy Standards

National standards for the horizontal and vertical accuracy of topographic maps were adopted by U.S. Government mapping agencies in 1941, and maps that meet these standards carry a statement to that effect in the lower margin. The main provisions of these standards state that the horizontal positions of at least 90 percent of the well-defined features must be correctly plotted within one-fiftieth inch on the published map, and that the elevations of 90 percent of the points tested vertically shall agree with the elevations interpolated from the contour lines within one-half the contour interval. This tolerance allowed for horizontal positions is equivalent to 40 feet on the ground for 1:24,000-scale maps and about 100 feet on the ground for 1:62,500-scale maps.

To keep maps up to date, they must be revised periodically. The useful life of a topographic map is influenced by the standards to which it was made, and the changes that have taken place since its original publication. Because these changes vary greatly from one area to another, it is not possible to establish a definite time interval for revision.

Maps are appraised for accuracy and content and are scheduled for revision according to their classification and the needs of map users. Revision methods vary but usually are a combination of photogrammetric and field procedures designed to bring the map content up to date and to maintain or improve its original accuracy.

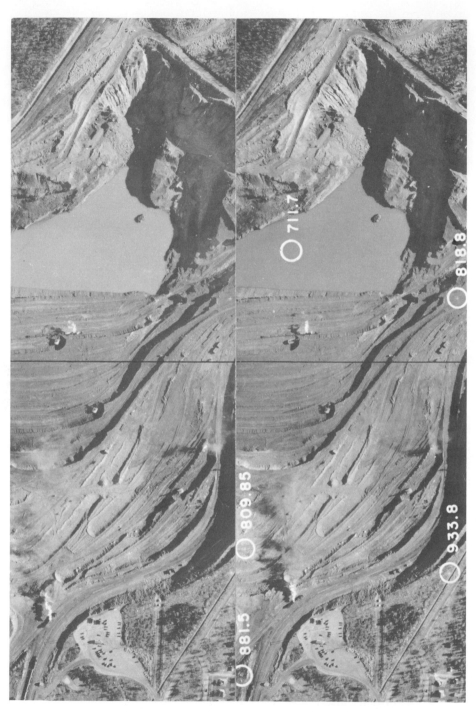

FIGURE 8-11. Stereogram of open-pit iron mine near Hibbing, Minnesota, taken from a flight altitude of about 3,300 feet. Scale is about 400 feet per inch, and average photo base length is 3.40 inches. Numbered points represent vertical ground control, i.e., elevations above mean sea level. Courtesy of Abrams Aerial Survey Corp.

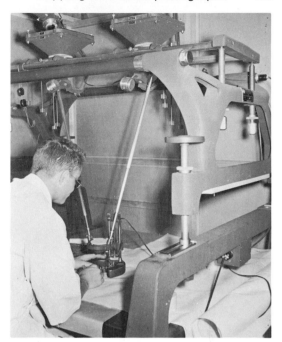

FIGURE 8-12. The Kelsh Plotter, a first-order instrument that employs the anaglyph principle to create a stereo-model of terrain features. Courtesy of Abrams Aerial Survey Corp.

FIGURE 8-13. The technique of "scribing" has largely replaced conventional inked draftings in preparing finished maps. The polyester film base ("scribecoat") is dimensionally stable and provides lines of high uniformity and sharpness. Maps are reproduced photographically from the scribed manuscript. Courtesy of Abrams Aerial Survey Corp.

Topographic Maps from Paper Prints

Photo interpreters directly concerned with topographic mapping are ordinarily interested in plotting devices designed for use with paper prints rather than glass diapositives. Representative of this group of instruments is the Zeiss Stereotope, a compact stereoplotter built around a magnifying mirror stereoscope, stereometer (parallax bar), and tracing pantograph *(Figure 8-14)*. The Stereotope is constructed primarily for making topographic maps at scales ranging between 1:25,000 and 1:100,000. With cameras commonly in use and currently obtainable flying heights, the recommended ratio of map scale to photo scale lies roughly between 0.7X and 1.6X.

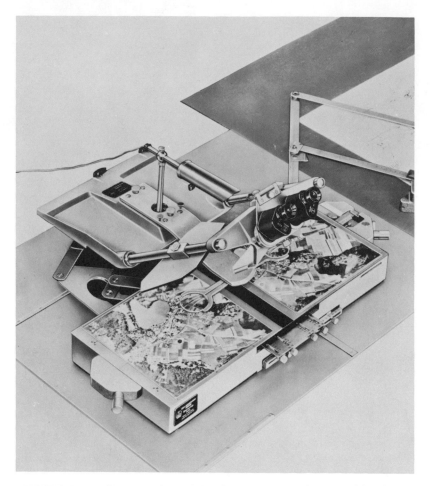

FIGURE 8-14. Close-up view of the Stereotope showing movable photo carriages and floating-mark lenses. Courtesy of Carl Zeiss, Inc., New York.

In use, the floating mark lenses remain stationary and centered in the field of view, while corrections for X- and Y-parallax are made by moving the right-hand photo carriage. Although both photographs remain flat on the special carriages, allowance for tilt can be made by a mechanical computing device that corrects the parallax readings obtained for a given stereo-pair. The instrument is rugged, compact, and portable. If high-quality, vertical photographs are available on low-shrink papers, accuracy of results will be comparable to that shown in *Figure 8-15*.

The relative accuracy of various stereoscopic plotting instruments is usually expressed in terms of the precision with which contours can be reliably determined. The contour factor (usually termed "C-factor") of a given plotter, multiplied by the desired contour interval, determines the maximum flight altitude that can be used for compiling topographic maps of the accepted accuracy standard.

C-factors are not precise ratings, and at times they can be quite misleading. For example, the C-factor of the Stereotope is usually considered to be around 250 to 350. A 10-foot contour interval would theoretically limit the flight altitude to about 2,500 feet. However,

FIGURE 8-15. Vertical photograph of a German city showing perspective contours plotted with the Stereotope. Scale is approximately 1:10,000; flight altitude: 7,500 feet; contour interval: 10 feet. Courtesy of Carl Zeiss, Inc., New York.

10-foot contours are shown in *Figure 8-15* for a flight altitude of 7,500 feet. In this case, the C-factor was actually closer to 750. The Kelsh plotter *(Figure 8-12)* has a C-factor of 1,200 to 1,500.

Form Lines

Although precise topographic work should not be attempted without instruments specifically designed for drawing contours, approximate "form lines" can be sketched with a simple stereoscope and stereometer. Form lines are defined as relative contours that are drawn from visual observation to show the general configuration of terrain; thus they do not necessarily represent true elevations nor have a uniform contour interval.

If large-scale photographs of steep terrain are available, interpreters can often differentiate form lines having intervals of 20 to 50 feet. Skilled interpreters may delineate these relative contours with only a stereoscope, but it is advantageous to measure several extremes of elevation with a stereometer or parallax bar. Exercise 12 has been prepared as a guide for interpreters interested in this technique.

Aerial Photo Mosaics

An aerial photo mosaic is an assembly of two or more aerial photographs that have been cut and matched together systematically to form a composite view of the area covered by the photographs. The mosaic gives the appearance of a single photograph, producing a complete record of the area. Mosaics are particularly useful for military terrain analyses and for studying certain natural resources. Source areas for construction materials such as building stone, sand, gravel, and timber can often be determined through the study of mosaics.

Although several categories of mosaics are recognized, most of them can be conveniently grouped into two general classes: *controlled* and *uncontrolled*. A controlled mosaic is an assembly of ratioed or rectified prints that are laid to ground control which is supplemented by radial line triangulation. With the accuracy required of ratioed or rectified prints, all mismatches of detail are eliminated, and reliable measurements may be made directly on the mosaic. With an uncontrolled mosaic, photographic detail is matched without the aid of ground control. Only the central area of each photograph is used. Detail is matched with adjacent center areas, and the assembly is pasted to a stable base to form the mosaic. The scale of uncontrolled mosaics is not uniform, so precise measurements of distances and areas cannot be made upon them.

Preparation of controlled mosaics is an expensive process involving highly trained technicians. In addition to requiring prints that match in terms of scale, tone, and freedom from tilt, edges of photographs must be bevel-cut and sanded before an adhesive is applied to the backing. Therefore, the succeeding discussion is based on a simplified do-it-yourself method of assembling uncontrolled mosaics as described by Meyer (1962).

Preparing an Uncontrolled Mosaic

In the step-by-step procedure that follows, the use of single-weight, contact prints is presumed. Print edges are square-cut (not beveled) for a butt-joint assembly. Supplies needed are a metal straightedge, china-marking pencil, sharp knife, rubber cement, drafting tape, photographs, and a hardboard base for mounting.

1. Photographs are first arranged in flight line sequence as in assembling an ordinary index mosaic. (Refer back to *Figure 7-1*.)

2. Starting with the middle flight line, photographic detail is matched in the *center* of each overlap area. As each overlapping print is matched, it should be taped down to avoid movement. Photos from adjacent strips are fitted together in a similar manner, giving priority to endlap detail, but also matching sidelap detail as closely as possible. Close matches are important only in the centers of overlap areas.

3. After all photographs have been precisely lapped and taped down, "match lines" are drawn to delineate the usable or effective area of each print. Such lines are best drawn with a china-marking pencil and a straightedge. Exact positions of match lines depend on photographic detail; lakes, roads, or square parcels of land should not be bisected, if this can be avoided by shifting match lines slightly.

4. When all endlap and sidelap match lines have been drawn in their final positions, the mosaic is taped to a piece of plywood and made ready for cutting. Once cutting has begun, the mosaic must not be moved. Therefore, it is important that it be firmly attached to the cutting surface and that individual photos are fastened securely to one another. Cutting cleanly through several thicknesses of photos requires a sharp knife and considerable pressure. A knife with a stout handle and replaceable razor-type blades is recommended.

5. After cutting, the effective areas of each print are retained, and each flight line is loosely taped together to keep the component sections in order. Final assembly, beginning with the middle flight line, is accomplished by cementing the print sections to a sturdy hard-board backing. Although variations in print scale usually preclude perfect matches of detail, the more important cultural features can usually be closely matched if these photo sections are cemented first.

References

Giroux, Mary J.
  1966. Maps: basic tools for national growth. Dept. of Mines and Technical Surveys, Ottawa, Canada, 30 pp., illus.

Heyden, Rev. Francis J.
  1963. Maps as the heritage of mankind. Photogram. Engineering 29: 573-579, illus.

Johnson, Evert W.
  1954. Ground control for planimetric base maps. Jour. Forestry 52:89-95, illus.

Meyer, Dan.
  1962. Mosaics you can make. Photogram. Engineering 28:167-171, illus.

  1961. A reflecting projector you can build. Photogram. Engineering 27:76-78, illus.

Raisz, Erwin.
  1962. *Principles of Cartography.* McGraw-Hill Book Co., New York, N.Y. 315 pp., illus.

Robinson, Arthur H.
  1953. *Elements of Cartography.* John Wiley and Sons, Inc., New York, N.Y. 254 pp., illus.

Scher, Marvin B.
  1955. Stereotemplet triangulation. Photogram. Engineering 21:655-664, illus.

U.S. Department of the Army.
  1964. Elements of surveying, TM 5-232. Government Printing Office, Washington, D.C., 247 pp., illus.

U.S. Department of the Interior.
  1952. Restoration of lost or obliterated corners and subdivision of sections. Government Printing Office, Washington, D.C. 40 pp., illus.

U.S. Tennessee Valley Authority.
  1965. How topographic maps are made. Maps and Surveys Branch, Chattanooga, Tenn., 28 pp., illus.

EXERCISE 12—Form Line Sketching with a Simple Stereometer

1. Obtain a stereo-pair of 9 by 9-inch contact prints illustrating pronounced topographic relief, such as that shown in *Figure 8-11*. Outline a rectangular area of about 3.5 by 6.0 inches in the central part of the overlap zone (mark only on one print).

2. Using an engineer's scale, lay off a ½ by ½-inch system of grid points within the selected rectangle. Mark each point with a very fine penciled cross.

3. Determine the average photo base (P) and flying height (H) of the stereo-pair for use in obtaining parallax conversions.

4. With a simple stereometer, find the lowest elevational plane within the delineated rectangle. If a lake or river is visible, the lowest water surface may be selected as the reference plane.

5. Assuming the selected reference plane to be the equivalent of mean sea level (i.e., zero elevation), measure the elevation of each grid point within the rectangle. Record these values (in feet) on an overlay traced from the marked photograph.

6. Study the gridded area under the stereoscope and sketch in form lines or approximate contours by interpolation between points of known elevation. Supplement the grid points with added measurements, if necessary. Draw trial lines with a china-marking pencil so that changes and corrections can be easily made. If a third-order stereoplotting instrument such as the Stereotope is available, contours may be traced directly at a specified contour interval, such as 20 or 30 feet. In such instances, grid points described here may be omitted.

7. When discrepancies and irregularities have been resolved, draft a finished overlay of the contoured area. Label each form line with its approximate relative elevation. Add pertinent topographic symbols, scale, and legend.

8. On a sheet of cross-section paper (10 by 10 squares per inch), draw a profile representing a transect across the area of greatest elevational change. Indicate the location of the profile line on both photograph and finished overlay.

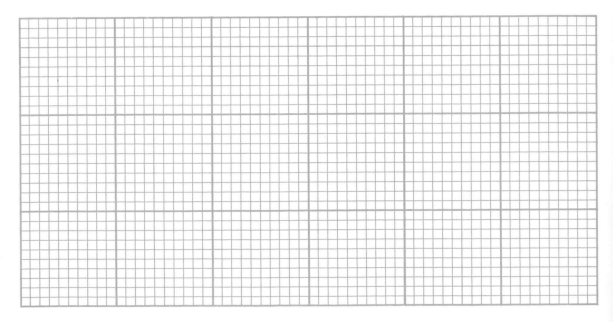

CHAPTER 9

Remote Sensing Techniques

Introduction

This chapter outlines three different methods used to obtain large-scale, low-altitude aerial photographs, and also provides an introduction to "remote sensing" of various terrain features. Large-scale photography described herein is arbitrarily limited to scales of 500 feet per inch and larger. Included are discussions of continuous strip photography, 70-mm. photography, and low-altitude helicopter photography.

Remote sensing may be defined as the detection, recognition, or evaluation of objects by means of distant sensing or recording devices. An astronomical telescope, an aerial camera in a supersonic jet aircraft, or a sonar installation in a submarine are all forms of remote sensors. The nocturnal bat employs a remote-sensing technique to guide its flight in darkness; a similar principle is embodied in radar equipment.

Remote sensors also include various earth-orbiting satellites that are becoming more and more useful as platforms for obtaining various kinds of photographic and nonphotographic aerial imagery. In later sections on remote sensing, emphasis is placed on interpretation of imagery derived from infrared sensors or "thermal mappers," from airborne radar equipment, and from orbital space flights.

Continuous Strip Photography

Continuous strip photographs are taken with a highly specialized camera system that permits large-scale stereoscopic coverage at very low altitudes from fast-moving aircraft. To eliminate blurred images on the negative, the film is continuously moved past a narrow slit-type aperture. The film velocity is based upon the ground speed of the plane and its height above the ground. The film and image velocities are synchronized so that little or no image blur occurs, and so that each point along the ground is photographed as the line-of-sight passes over it.

The camera includes two matched lenses, with the right lens ahead of the slit and the left lens to the rear. Each lens, while photographing ground objects continuously, exposes only *half* of the film width; the right lens "sees" an object before the plane passes over it, and the left lens after the passing of the plane (Wohl and Sickle, 1959).

The narrow slit-aperture and longitudinal displacement of the two lenses *(Figure 9-1)* represent two lines-of-sight, one forward and the other rearward, intersecting at a parallax angle. Once the lens angles have been precisely set, a constant degree of parallax is established in the direction of the flight path *(Figure 9-2)*. The resulting continuous photo-

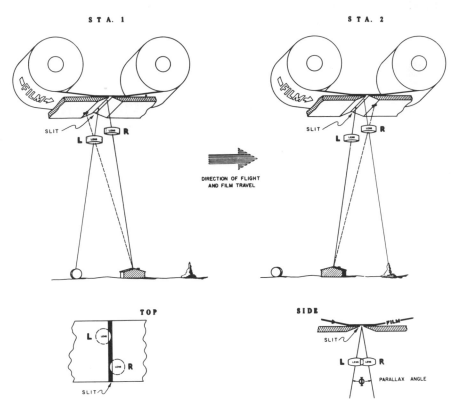

FIGURE 9-1. Plan and side views of a continuous strip camera. The stereo base is achieved in the direction of flight by offsetting the lenses, one forward and one rearward. Increasing the parallax angle increases the stereo air base and vertical exaggeration of the third dimension. Courtesy of Chicago Aerial Survey.

graph can be studied stereoscopically with a special viewer equipped with a stereo-comparator for measuring object heights or differences in elevation.

Continuous strip photography is adaptable to a wide variety of photogrammetric problems. It has been successfully used for analyzing automobile traffic distribution; discovery of taxable real estate; and for surveys of highways, railroads, and power transmission lines. At a scale of 100 feet per inch, a strip of terrain nearly 90 miles long can be shown on one unbroken picture. Contact prints can be made at scales as large as 6 feet per inch for studying such items as crack patterns in airport runways. Continuous strip photography probably has additional potential in geologic interpretation and vegetative analyses.

Large-Scale 70-mm. Photography

In recent years, a number of specialized photo interpretation studies have concentrated on the use of large-scale 70-mm. color or black-and-white photography (Aldrich, 1966). Low-altitude exposures are commonly made along widely spaced sample strips to provide supplementary details on areas having complete photographic coverage at smaller scales. Special aerial cameras utilizing 70-mm. film have been designed for military reconnaissance, and many have image-motion compensation devices for eliminating blurred negatives at low altitudes.

FIGURE 9-2. A short section of a continuous strip photograph taken from an altitude of 800 feet. The image offset in the direction of flight (indicated by centerline) is the image of the air base. A special viewer is needed for stereoscopic study of this imagery.

The high exposure ratings of new color films make it feasible to obtain positive transparencies of high clarity and sharpness at near tree-top levels. Exposures are triggered by an electronic intervalometer that can send out as many as eight impulses per second. Stereoscopic coverage is derived by the conventional method of obtaining 60 percent overlap along the line of flight. This requires an intervalometer setting of four exposures per second for a photo scale of 50 feet per inch and an indicated airspeed of 100 miles per hour.

Research foresters in the United States and Canada have been quick to realize the potential applications of 70-mm. photography in identifying tree species, detecting insect and disease infestations in timbered areas, and in conducting forest inventories. The Forest Service Remote Sensing Project at Berkeley, California has pioneered in developing one of the most valuable uses of 70-mm. color photography in forestry—the appraisal of forest insect damage by detailed interpretation of large-scale photography with photo-derived information supplemented by ground check points *(Figure 9-3)*. Forest inventory applications of 70-mm. photography are being conducted both at Berkeley and by the Forest Research Branch of the Canada Department of Forestry (Sayn-Wittgenstein, 1965).

The two principal unsolved problems in the use of large-scale, low-altitude aerial photography are (1) the inability to determine photographic scale accurately without costly ground work, and (2) poor camera stabilization, resulting in photographic distortions caused by tip and tilt. Although the use of 70-mm. film is stressed in this section, other formats are suitable when cameras with fast shutter speeds are available. The 70-mm. format has been especially popular in the past, because such cameras have fast shutters, rapid cycling rates, and they are relatively low in cost.

Other attributes favoring 70-mm. cameras are (1) their small size and light weight allow versatility in small aircraft camera systems, (2) they have interchangeable lenses that are easily changed in flight, (3) their narrow angles of view reduce effects of tilt on parallax measurements, (4) 70-mm. film is easy to process with consistent results, and (5) the 2¼ by 2¼-inch format of 70-mm. photography makes it possible to view uncut film rolls with a lens stereoscope *(Figure 9-4)*.

FIGURE 9-3. Stereogram illustrating dead balsam fir trees (white crowns) killed by the spruce budworm near Ely, Minnesota. These 70-mm. panchromatic exposures, printed from original color transparencies, are shown at a scale of about 132 feet per inch. Courtesy of U.S. Forest Service Remote Sensing Project, Berkeley, California.

FIGURE 9-4. Illuminated viewer for stereoscopic study of 70-mm. color transparencies. Courtesy of U.S. Forest Service Remote Sensing Project, Berkeley, California.

Low-Altitude Helicopter Photography

The fact that helicopters are capable of horizontal flight at low airspeeds makes them particularly useful for taking large-scale airphotos of spot locations such as mining operations, forest inventory plots, or urban centers. Sharp negatives are feasible at ordinary shutter speeds, and camera recycling time is not so critical as with faster moving, conventional planes. The principal restriction is the high hourly cost of helicopter operation. Contract rates for helicopter and pilot are often several times that charged for fixed-wing aircraft.

Among technical difficulties peculiar to low-altitude helicopter photography are (1) limitations of weight and space for photographer and pilot, (2) aircraft vibrations, and (3) difficulty in precisely determining altitudes above ground. Weight problems can be partially alleviated by using lightweight cameras, vibrations may be minimized by taking photographs in horizontal flight rather than from a hovering position, and exact flight altitudes (i.e., photo scales) can be computed from known ground distances or with special ground markers.

The feasibility of taking large-scale helicopter photographs of cereal crops was first demonstrated by Colwell (1956). In 1957, the author devised a simple box mount for holding two identical reflex cameras and used the device to obtain helicopter stereograms from a single air exposure station. Camera lenses were separated by 36 inches, the maximum air base practical for the hand-held, manually operated device *(Figure 9-5)*. Photographs made during this experiment were roughly comparable to that previously shown in *Figure 9-3*.

Additional studies of low-altitude, helicopter stereo-photography have been conducted by Lyons (1961, 1964). This work demonstrates the feasibility of obtaining blur-free photographs by use of two cameras mounted on opposite ends of a 15-foot boom and suspended beneath a small helicopter. Resultant photographs have proved useful for (1) forest inventory classifications and measurements, and (2) determining flying height above ground from the photo-measured base length of the two cameras mounted on the boom.

FIGURE 9-5. **Above:** Stereo-camera mount devised by the author for holding two conventional reflex cameras. The thumb-actuated bar trips both shutters simultaneously.
Below: Orientation of dual-camera mount for helicopter photography. To avoid vibration, the mount was lifted off the strut in making exposures. Courtesy of U.S. Forest Service.

Multiband Spectral Reconnaissance

As illustrated by earlier examples of panchromatic and infrared photography, a greater amount of information is made available to the interpreter when two or more aerial photographic sensors are used, each adapted to sensing in a particular region of the electromagnetic spectrum. The simultaneous use of two or more sensors designed to produce imagery from different parts of the electromagnetic spectrum is often referred to as multiband spectral reconnaissance or spectrozonal photography (Colwell, *et al.,* 1966).

The amount of energy which an object reflects or emits in a given spectral band determines the brightness (tone) in which the object registers on a photograph or other image-forming medium. At any one moment in time, two or more features may reflect or emit exactly the same amount of energy in a selected spectral band; when this happens, the two features cannot be distinguished solely on the basis of tone by the interpreter. By selecting another spectral band or a different diurnal period, however, it is probable that the two features *could* be readily differentiated by their "tone signatures."

It follows that if imagery is obtained of cultural or terrain features by sensing in two or more spectral bands at the proper time of day, it is likely that they can be easily distinguished. Also, it is often valuable to know that certain objects produce similar tonal renditions in one spectral band while displaying different characteristics in another portion of the spectrum. As pointed out by Colwell (1963), it is the tone signature of an object that permits it to be identified, and the more complete the signature, the more positive will be the identification. As a general rule, tonal characteristics assume greater and greater importance as image scales become smaller. Because multispectral tone signatures of rocks, soils, and vegetation can sometimes indicate their composition, image tones rather than pattern and texture are likely to be most important in interpreting natural terrain features from small-scale imagery.

Capabilities of Remote Sensors

Multiband spectral reconnaissance encompasses more than improved cameras, sharper lenses, or faster films. In addition to conventional aerial photographs, interpreters are analyzing images from manned space flights, from orbiting satellites, and from thermal infrared and radar systems. Such imagery may be obtained from portions of the electromagnetic spectrum several million times wider than that available to ordinary camera systems (Leonardo, 1964).

Electromagnetic energy is generated as waves whose lengths are microscopically small at one end of the spectrum and very, very long at the other end. The visible spectrum (Figure 6-1) utilizes only a small fragment of the total energy available—about 0.4 to 0.7 micron. Infrared radiations span a range of about 0.7 to 1,000 microns, and microwaves (including radar) encompass wavelengths of about one centimeter to three meters long. These are the portions of the electromagnetic spectrum of greatest interest to the image interpreter. Each type of remote sensor reacts only to energy bands of specific frequency and wavelength. For example, radar receivers cannot detect visible light, and transmitted microwaves are invisible to infrared scanners.

Aerial cameras produce their best imagery on cloudless, hazefree days, but with new techniques and equipment they do obtain reasonably good imagery on clear nights. *Figure 9-6* shows that radar and infrared systems can overcome adverse weather limitations. In-

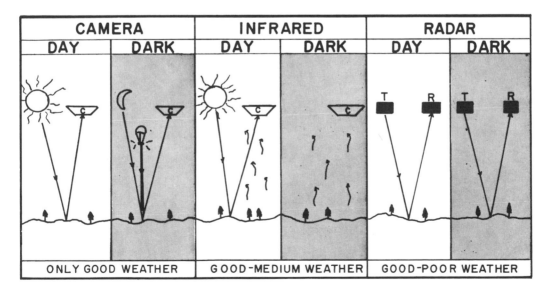

FIGURE 9-6. The effects of time and weather on the capabilities of remote sensors. Adapted from Leonardo, 1964.

frared systems also produce good daytime imagery. However, since they respond to energy radiated from beyond the visible spectrum, night infrared missions with middle and far infrared sensitivity yield excellent results. For many purposes, far infrared data flights obtain their best imagery after dark when there is no interference from solar insolation. Military needs for nighttime operations are obvious.

Infrared radiation may penetrate dust and haze, depending on the size of the aerosol particles, but clouds, high surface winds, and rain greatly reduce image quality. Radar, an active sensor, provides its own source of energy. Therefore, it too is independent of time-of-day. Its longer wavelengths penetrate fog, haze, and clouds with minimum signal loss. Rains attenuate the signal, but the extent depends on system wavelength and rainfall rate. Thick, moisture-laden clouds, however, can effectively block transmitted waves. To what extent these factors affect radar imagery depends on several system parameters.

All three systems can be "tuned" to be more selective to specific frequencies within their operational bands. Narrow band film-filter combinations enable cameras to record spectral responses of one color. Filters are often added to infrared systems to eliminate effect of solar reflection below the middle or far infrared range, depending on the system (Leonardo, 1964).

The Nature of Infrared Radiation

Infrared-sensing or "thermal mapping" refers to the detection of remote objects by recording the amount of infrared energy (heat radiation) emitted from various surfaces. Infrared energy is emitted by any material substance having a temperature above absolute zero (−273° C.). Therefore, all solid objects from animal life to trees and rocks are sources of infrared radiations.

Temperature and surface characteristics are the primary factors that govern the emission of infrared radiation; i.e., the radiation emitted by a body at a given temperature is proportional to the characteristics of its surface. This leads to the concept of "emissivity" which is a ratio expression of the energy radiated from an object in relationship to a "black body." A black body is by definition an object which completely absorbs all radiation incident upon it. The emissivity of a black body is unity. A highly polished surface is an extremely poor radiator and absorber; its emissivity is close to zero. Most surfaces in thermal mapping lie between these two extremes in emissivity. Some materials (e.g., silicon) that are opaque to visible light are relatively transparent to infrared; conversely, bodies of water act as a screen that blocks infrared radiation.

Transmission characteristics of the atmosphere must be considered, since they attenuate the energy radiated from the scene. The major cause of attenuation is water vapor, and this is proportional to the amount of precipitable water in the path. *Figure 9-7* illustrates the transmission characteristics of the atmosphere. Most infrared sensing systems are designed to operate in the spectral bands corresponding to the "infrared windows" (nonshaded areas), i.e., within the approximate ranges of 2-5 or 8-14 microns.

Variations in infrared radiation emitted by various terrain features are due to differences in either emissivity or temperature or combinations of both. Emissivity is a basic physical property (often varying with wavelength) which may be determined once and for all. Actual temperature variation is caused by many factors, including the following:

1. Wind
2. Heat capacity
3. Thermal conductivity
4. Surface to volume ratio

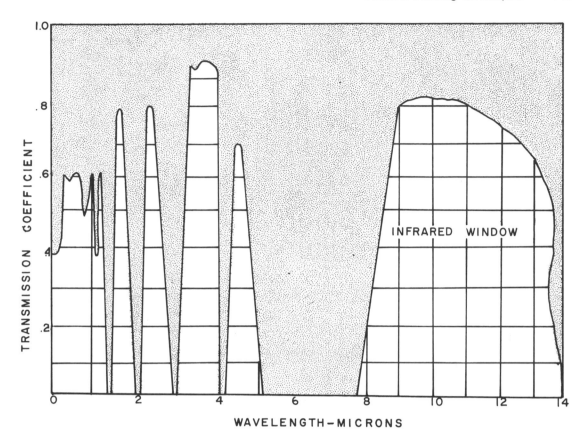

FIGURE 9-7. Transmission spectra of the atmosphere. Although actual transmission varies from time to time, most radiation is transmitted in the nonshaded spectral bands.

5. Moisture content and the evaporation process
6. Sky cover and its effect on radiation exchange
7. Topography and solar history
8. Elevational differences
9. Metabolism of plants
10. Dewfall and precipitation

For solid, nontransparent substances, the sum of reflectivity plus emissivity is unity, so every surface in nature reflects a certain amount of radiation from the surroundings which should be taken into consideration.

Infrared Line-Scanning System

Although the shorter infrared wavelengths can be recorded by conventional photography, highly specialized sensing devices are required for registration of infrared wavelengths longer than 1.0 micron. An infrared sensor is a scanning device that functions somewhat like a television receiver by producing a near-continuous image from a series of line scans *(Figure 9-8)*. Because the terrain is not photographed directly, the term "infrared imagery" is used to describe the final image that is printed onto photographic film.

The line-scanning function is accomplished by means of a rotating mirror that scans the terrain in continuous strips perpendicular to the line of flight. The image from the mirror

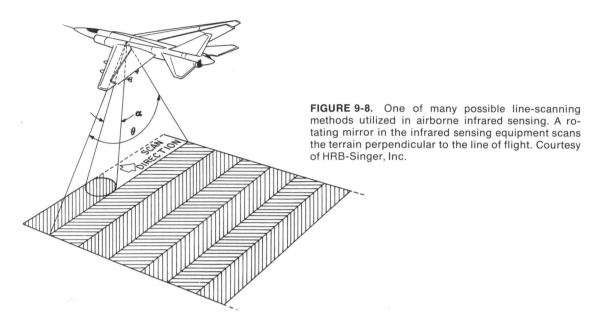

FIGURE 9-8. One of many possible line-scanning methods utilized in airborne infrared sensing. A rotating mirror in the infrared sensing equipment scans the terrain perpendicular to the line of flight. Courtesy of HRB-Singer, Inc.

strikes an element sensitive to infrared radiation (such as indium antimonide or mercury-doped germanium). The signal from the sensitive element is electronically amplified and produces a visual image on a cathode ray tube or by means of a glow tube. A final photographic record is made from this visual image *(Figure 9-9)*.

The film moves across the exposure station at a rate proportional to the aircraft speed-to-altitude ratio, and the result after photographic development is a thermal radiation image of the area flown over. Film density represents effective radiation temperature. Dark areas depict cool thermal signals and light areas warm or hot areas on a positive print. The width of the scanned strip in the direction of flight is directly proportional to the altitude of the aircraft above the terrain and the total scan angle.

Distortions Inherent in Infrared Imagery

Infrared images often bear strong resemblances to conventional photographs, but they have inherent geometric distortions due to the nature of line scanning. For example, the scanning mirror sweeps an angle on either side of the vertical. Hence, except along the nadir line directly beneath the flight line, the final image is an oblique view of the terrain and the scale varies with distance from the nadir line. Because the scale along the line of flight may differ appreciably from that across the flight path, precise *measurements* of images may not be feasible. Infrared imagery may therefore be regarded as more suitable for making *identifications* than for purely mensurational uses, and they should be regarded as supplements to, rather than replacements for, conventional aerial photographs.

It is common practice to correct infrared imagery for roll, but usually no correction is used for pitch or yaw. If there is a crosswind at the time the imagery is made, the aircraft heading and aircraft track do not coincide. Because of this, all points except those at the nadir are skewed in the direction of the aircraft crab. Any turns of the aircraft during the imagery run will cause straight roads parallel to the flight track to appear curved, and straight roads that cross the flight path at oblique angles may appear to be S-shaped (Hirsch, 1965).

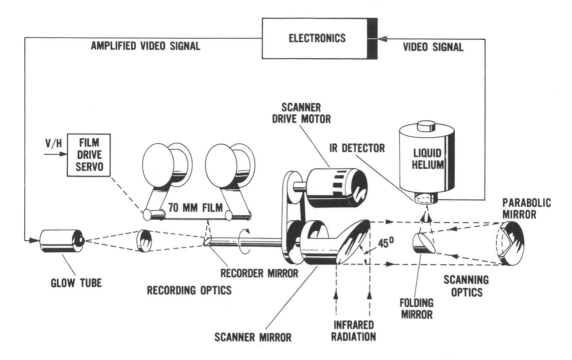

FIGURE 9-9. Schematic representation of airborne infrared detecting system. Courtesy of HRB-Singer, Inc.

Interpretation of Infrared Imagery

Because infrared imagery is presented on standard photographic film, there is an immediate attempt on the part of interpreters to compare infrared imagery with visual photography. It should be remembered, however, that the information recorded on this imagery is based on thermal radiation characteristics of surfaces rather than their light-reflective photographic qualities. The amount of infrared energy transmitted is proportional to the object's emissivity and temperature. Unless these factors are understood, the unique advantages of infrared reconnaissance cannot be gained, and some interpreters may decide that an infrared image is nothing but aerial photography with poor resolution qualities *(Figure 9-10)*.

Solar radiant energy provides the principal source of infrared emissions. In daylight, surfaces with a high absorbence for sunlight store up large amounts of heat, while surfaces having high reflectivity for solar radiation absorb little heat. The temperature that results depends both on the color and on the physical structure of surfaces. A concrete highway will absorb heat at a rapid rate, for example, but its temperature may rise very slowly. This is because the heat capacity of concrete is quite high, and the thermal connection between a highway and the earth is well established. By contrast, grass and other low vegetation heats up quickly, but their capacity for storing heat is limited. As a result, temperatures of such vegetation tend to closely follow diurnal changes in thermal conditions.

Bodies of water have high capacities for storing heat. Water surfaces heat up much more slowly than adjacent soil and rock surfaces, and they also release heat at a much slower rate during a cooling period. In general, cooler surfaces such as water and trees will appear dark in an infrared photograph, while warmer surfaces (e.g., highways, industrial plants, thermal springs) will appear brighter in tone.

FIGURE 9-10. Night infrared imagery of an agricultural area in the Imperial Valley of California. Courtesy of HRB-Singer, Inc.

The reader should bear in mind that imagery shown in this volume does not necessarily illustrate the true capability of infrared sensors currently in use. Because new and sophisticated techniques in remote sensing have a high strategic value, military and defense agencies have been largely responsible for their development and operational use. As a result, many aspects of remote sensing — and the images produced therefrom — are screened from civilian scrutiny by security classifications. All imagery reproduced in this book is unclassified.

Uses of Thermal Imagery

Infrared imagery is ideally suited to the detection and mapping of forest fires because of the great contrasts in surface temperatures that accompany such fires. Studies at the Northern Forest Fire Laboratory of the U.S. Forest Service (Hirsch, 1965) have shown that infrared line scanners are readily adaptable to the detection of spot fires. Infrared images obtained during hours of total darkness clearly indicated the positions of incipient fires, some of which were located beneath a forest overstory. In another instance, the perimeter and relative intensity of a fire, along with the locations of separated spot fires, were discernible in daylight when normal vision from the air was obscured by heavy smoke *(Figure 9-11)*. Distinct patterns of water courses evident on infrared images are also worthy of mention, because such knowledge is often of critical value in organizing the suppression of wildfires.

An entirely different application of infrared sensing has been reported by The Bendix Corporation. Their experiments have indicated that plant leaves, especially the leaves of many trees, appear to be rather similar to black body emitters in the wavelength region of 3.69 to 5.5 microns. As a result of this, leaf temperatures can be remotely measured, or their relative temperatures inferred. Such knowledge could lead to potential applications in determining various aspects of plant health, age, and relative water supply or degree of irrigation. In addition, large area-coverage sensors appear to offer the hope of early detection of thermal damage or frost damage to fruit groves.

In the field of geology, infrared imagery is valuable for mapping seismic fault lines, identifying rocks and minerals, conducting oil surveys, and maintaining a surveillance of volcanoes *(Figure 9-12)*. In agriculture, thermal images have been utilized for the identification of crop species and soil types, for detecting crop diseases, for making animal censuses, and for determining the relative moisture content of various soils.

Infrared scanning systems can extract a considerable amount of information from bodies of water. Hot effluents that result in water pollution when discharged into streams or lakes are easily detected because of temperature gradients. In like fashion, cool underground springs that empty into warmer bodies of water may also be discovered through thermal mapping techniques. Critically needed freshwater sources have been found in Hawaii by detailed analysis of thermal surveys conducted by the U.S. Geological Survey *(Figure 9-13)*.

Military applications of thermal mapping are varied, and often classified, but at least one example may be cited. Aerial reconnaissance laboratories have been built aboard converted transport planes for surveillance of enemy territory. Equipped with both conventional cameras and infrared sensors, these aircraft collect necessary imagery for making thermal maps showing heat emission patterns of forested areas in southeast Asia. Once the normal emission pattern of an area has been established, interpreters are able to quickly pinpoint any thermal changes on the ground — changes that might be attributed to heat radiated from unusual concentrations of troops, weaponry, or military vehicles.

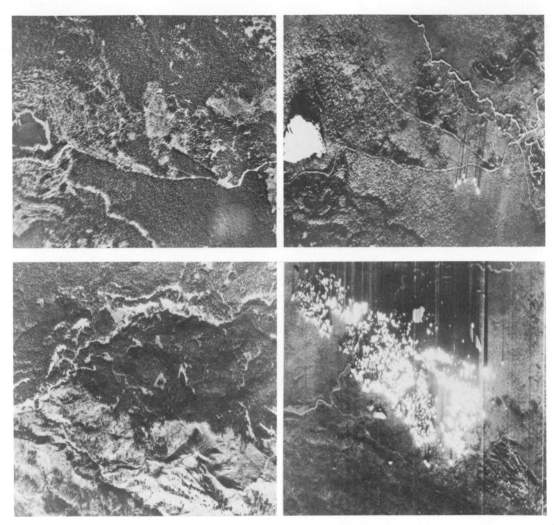

FIGURE 9-11. Panchromatic aerial photographs (left) and corresponding infrared images (right) of forested areas in western United States. In the upper right image, made in total darkness, eight simulated incipient fires in a dense spruce stand can be seen. In the lower right image, the perimeter and relative intensity of a forest fire, along with the location of small spot fires outside of the main fire perimeter, are easily discernible. The area was obscured to normal vision by dense smoke at the time the image was made. Courtesy of U.S. Forest Service.

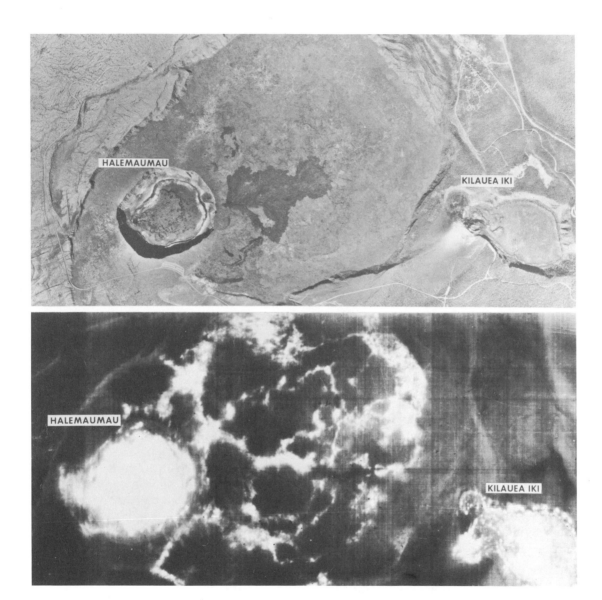

FIGURE 9-12. Panchromatic photograph (above) and infrared image (below) of Kilauea Volcano, Hawaii. The infrared image shows high temperature areas in the crater and flanks of the volcano. Courtesy of U.S. Department of the Interior, Geological Survey.

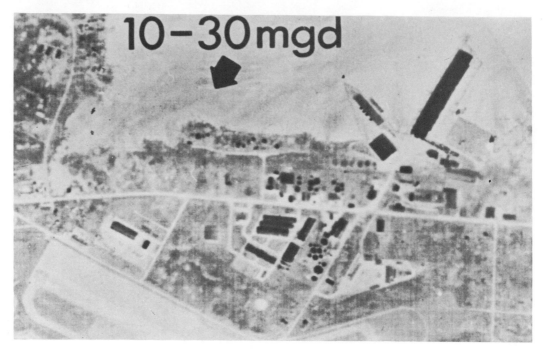

FIGURE 9-13. Infrared image of the Hilo, Hawaii, coastline taken in the spectral band of 4.5-5.5 microns from an altitude of 3,000 feet. Dark areas in the ocean are believed to represent cool water discharged by springs. Numerals indicate estimated rates of flow of springs in millions of gallons per day. Courtesy of U.S. Department of the Interior, Geological Survey.

Capabilities of Radar Systems

The need for obtaining terrain information accurately under cover of darkness and during all weather conditions has been established during the course of wartime operations. This requirement is largely fulfilled by radar, a remote sensor that can be used in all weather and around-the-clock. Radar systems are capable of resolving field patterns and of producing tonal renditions relative to vegetation, drainage, and shoreline features. They can also provide subsurface information and produce the rough equivalent of a photo-reconnaissance mosaic in a single image. All of this is accomplished, however, at the expense of the resolution provided by most types of aerial photography and with a dependence on data from other sources before positive analyses can be made *(Figure 9-14)*. Thus radar photographs constitute a supplement to, rather than a replacement for, conventional aerial photographs.

Radar systems utilize that portion of the electromagnetic spectrum in which wavelengths are approximately one centimeter to three meters long. According to Feder (1960), there are seven unique radar capabilities that control display interpretations. These are as follows:

1. Compositions and conditions below visual rock and soil surfaces can be "read" by analysis of absorbed or modified signal returns.

2. Vegetation can be penetrated to detect subsurface information, such as the presence of water under marsh grass.

3. The texture of terrain-surface materials down to small gravel size (i.e., as small as one-half the wavelength used) can be read directly on radar displays. Assuming a radar

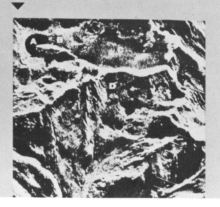

◀ SEPTEMBER 1965: INFRARED EKTACHROME PHOTOGRAPH RECORDS DETAILS OF ICE, SNOW, AND FIRN, NEAR END OF SUMMER MELTING SEASON

OCTOBER 1965: RADAR PENETRATES FIRST SNOWFALL OF WINTER SEASON, REVEALING GROSS CHARACTER OF SURFACE BENEATH ▼

A. LAKE AT TERMINUS OF GLACIER

B. GLACIER ICE; CLEARLY SHOWN ON RADAR IMAGE BY STRONG REFLECTION THROUGH LIGHT SNOW COVER

C. OLD SNOW AND FIRN AREA OF GLACIER; ON THE COLOR INFRARED PHOTO SNOW (WHITE) CAN BE DISTINGUISHED FROM FIRN (GRAY).

D. BEDROCK SURFACE, COVERED BY LIGHT SNOW AT THE TIME OF RADAR (OCTOBER) IMAGE.

FIGURE 9-14. Comparison of photographic and radar images of the South Cascade glacier area. Note that the oblique photograph was originally exposed on infrared Ektachrome film. Courtesy of U.S. Department of the Interior, Geological Survey.

system that transmits a signal of 0.875 cm. wavelength, it is possible to resolve gravel particle interface spacings of half 0.8 cm. or 0.4 cm. (approximately one-quarter inch).

4. The moisture content of terrain can be determined when temperature data are available.

5. Surface temperature can be determined when the moisture content of terrain materials is known.

6. Selected radar bands can be used to read the metallic content of surface and near-surface features. With refined equipment, it may one day be possible to selectively filter a radar indicator in exploring for iron, bauxite, and the highly ferruginous magnetite sands that commonly also bear titanium, rare earths, and radioactive minerals.

7. Terrain properties of snow cover or of features beneath a snow cover can be determined. Also, the ability of some radar systems to penetrate clouds and atmospheric haze makes them especially valuable for obtaining imagery on overcast or stormy days. As a rule, radar imagery can be obtained whenever aircraft can be sent aloft.

Plan Positive Indicator Radar

Radar images are obtained through microwave energy that is transmitted to the ground by antennas designed to concentrate the energy in a specific beam pattern. The terrain is scanned by the beam, and a portion of the energy is reflected back to an airborne receiver. These echoed signals are displayed on a cathode ray tube or "scope" for direct visual interpretation; images may also be continuously recorded on photographic film for later interpretation on the ground. The two principal types of radar displays that have been used in the past are referred to as "plan positive indicator" (PPI) and "side-looking airborne radar" (SLAR).

PPI provides a circular sweep-type display, with the center of the scope representing the position of the aircraft. Images shown in the circle represent terrain features located at varying distances from the transmitter—in all directions to a specified range limit. This range setting is chosen by the operator, or established by the design of the equipment. The antenna rotates in a clockwise direction as the transmitted energy is reflected by the terrain features, and detail is recorded on the phosphor-coated scope face by a synchronized electronic trace that duplicates the antenna movement.

The phosphor has a controlled image decay, and the initial portion of the scan retains its characteristics to some extent until the entire 360° rotation is completed. Thus the whole picture is continually visible. This rotation requires a number of seconds depending on the type of equipment. The aircraft is moving forward during this operation, so each consecutive scan represents a slightly different presentation of detail. Distances can be measured on the presentation by reference to the circular range markers which electronically appear on the indicator. An azimuth ring is mounted around the circumference of the scope so that approximate direction can be determined. Manual controls are provided so that the operator can regulate the general appearance of the PPI scope (Hoffman, 1958).

Side-Looking Airborne Radar

With SLAR equipment, a continuous strip image of terrain is presented for recording on photographic film. By means of two antennas, energy is transmitted to either side of the aircraft at right angles to the flight path. The reflected energy produces individual single-line image traces on two scopes, one for each side. These traces are photographed side-by-side on the same film to present a continuous presentation of the collected data. *Figure 9-15* and *9-16* illustrate SLAR images recorded on panchromatic film.

Because of the increased power of SLAR equipment and the design of the antennas, the resolution of terrain features in this presentation is greater by a significant factor than that provided by most PPI radar sets. This improves the opportunities for interpretation, although it must be recognized that the resolution quality of a radar image is decidedly inferior in direct comparison with a conventional aerial photograph. In many instances, however, the all-weather capability of radar more than offsets the lower resolution of terrain features presented.

Radar Image Interpretation

Radar photographs such as those illustrated here exhibit many qualities that are similar to conventional photography. Strong or bright signal returns (light tones) are usually indicative of prominent cultural features or man-made structures. Intermediate energy returns (medium gray tones) may indicate areas of open country or areas of "no return," e.g., the flat and smooth terrain of an airfield. Weaker returns, denoted by black images, commonly indicate the presence of water and hydrologic features.

Refinements in the identification process may be accomplished by consideration of such photographic qualities as size, shape, pattern or arrangement, tone, texture, shadows, and relation of images to environment, i.e., location. In a detailed study of image texture, for example, the interpreter might rely upon the patchwork appearance of cultivated field patterns, the characteristic shading effect of bright and dark areas of relief features, and the

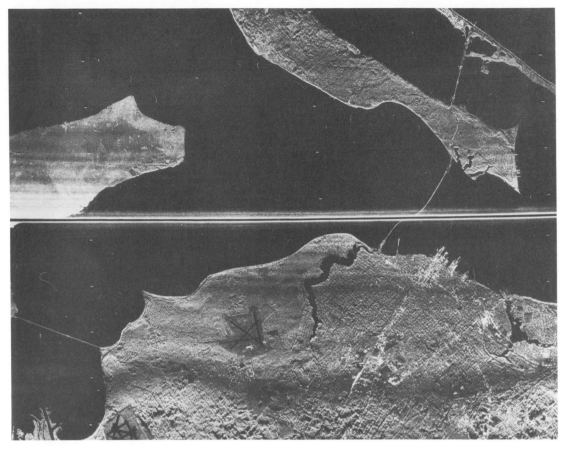

FIGURE 9-15. Side-looking airborne radar image of Pensacola, Florida, and vicinity, 1958. Altitude is 2,500 feet; sweep range is 5 nautical miles to each side. Courtesy of Westinghouse Electric Corp.

"cardinal point" effect of increased brightness of returns from areas where cultural features are predominantly aligned along perpendicular axes. Although rough measurements of area and distance can be made on SLAR imagery, precise determinations are dependent on corrections of certain distortions inherent to all radar systems.

Space Photographs and Related Imagery

Man's ability to place men and instruments in orbit about the earth and other planets presents many new vistas in the field of remote sensing. The military significance of orbiting satellites for photo reconnaissance is obvious; thus the sections that follow are largely devoted to nonmilitary applications, e.g., the evaluation of earth terrain features. Unmanned orbital satellites that regularly monitor cloud patterns and weather conditions by transmitting television pictures back to earth are already operational. The resolution capabilities of such instruments have now been improved to the point where they can be used for ice-pack reconnaissance, measurement of snow cover, and evaluation of hydrologic features *(Figure 9-17).*

To some degree, aerial photographs taken from space platforms can probably duplicate the type of coverage obtained from high-altitude aircraft. Presuming the use of a camera with a focal length of about 10 feet and a lens resolving power of 100 lines per millimeter, a

FIGURE 9-16. Side-looking airborne radar image of Baltimore Harbor, Maryland, 1959. Altitude is 5,000 feet; sweep range is 5 nautical miles to each side. Courtesy of Westinghouse Electric Corp.

FIGURE 9-17. Nimbus television satellite imagery of Great Salt Lake, Utah. Courtesy of U.S. Department of the Interior, Geological Survey.

photograph taken from 150 miles up would produce a ground resolution of 2 to 3 feet (Lowman, 1965). Ignoring the matter of duplication, however, space photography from orbiting satellites has several unique advantages over aircraft photography. These are (1) greater perspective of view, (2) wider coverage, and (3) greater speed in obtaining comparative coverage.

The perspective provided by space photography makes it possible to study large physiographic zones and drainage basins at a glance *(Figure 9-18)*. A single image can provide an effective mosaic that would normally require many hours to assemble from ordinary contact prints *(Figure 9-19)*. By use of polar-orbiting spacecraft, the entire surface of the world could be photographed within a week or less. Sequential coverage at short time intervals is therefore feasible for such critical activities as monitoring ice packs during spring thaws or estimating seasonal agricultural crop yields in food-deficient regions.

FIGURE 9-18. Gemini IV view east over the Nile Delta to the Suez Canal, Red Sea, and Dead Sea in background from an altitude of 110-120 miles. Broad perspectives such as this one provide geographers with new insight into mankind's use of the earth's surface. Courtesy of U.S. Department of the Interior, Geological Survey.

FIGURE 9-19. This Gemini photograph of southwestern United States covers as much land area in a single view as 500 or more conventional aerial photographs. Courtesy of U.S. Department of the Interior, Geological Survey.

Earth Resources Observation Satellite

The U.S. Geological Survey, in cooperation with the National Aeronautics and Space Administration, has developed a program aimed at gathering facts about the natural resources of the earth from earth-orbiting satellites that will carry sophisticated, remote-sensing observation instruments. According to the Department of the Interior, "Project EROS" will be dedicated to the task of assembling regional and continental planning data on the distribution of needed minerals, water supplies and the extent of water pollution, agricultural crops and forests, and human habitations.

The earth-orbiting resources satellite will likely be equipped with television cameras at the beginning, with the satellite flown in an orbit that will cover the entire surface of the earth under nearly identical conditions of illumination *(Figure 9-20)*. Later on, sensing systems may utilize infrared sensors to monitor the earth's volcanoes and search for sources of geothermal power, radar equipment that will "see" beneath the clouds, and cameras with sufficient resolving power to permit timely updating of the national topographic map series.

From such space vehicles as EROS, it may be possible in the future to determine rates of reservoir sedimentation, measure the movement of glaciers, check on the effluents of major rivers, monitor the levels of lakes and reservoirs, and assess the growth of deltas. Photographic techniques already available should make it possible to construct maps showing land use and vegetation. Other remote sensors may yield measurements of ground-surface temperature and ground-moisture content useful in a variety of engineering and agricultural problems. Even population counts and measurements of daily fluctuations in the traffic flow of people and vehicles appear to be within the capability of improved space sensors.

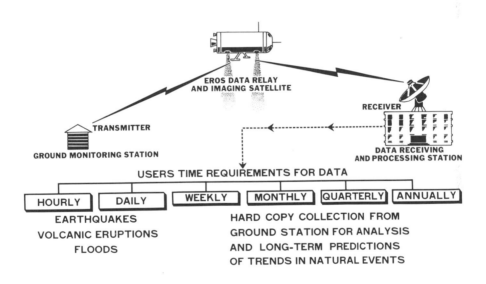

FIGURE 9-20. Potential capabilities of an earth resources orbiting satellite. Courtesy of U.S. Department of the Interior, Geological Survey.

References

Aldrich, Robert C.
   1966. Forestry applications of 70-mm. color. Photogram. Engineering 32:802-810, illus.

_____, Bailey, W. F., and Heller, R. C.
   1959. Large scale 70-mm. color photography techniques and equipment and their application to a forest sampling prob-lem. Photogram. Engineering 25:747-754, illus.

Avery, T. Eugene.
   1959. Photographing forests from helicopters. Jour. Forestry 57:339-342, illus.

_____.
   1958. Helicopter stereo-photography of forest plots. Photogram. Engineering 24:617-625, illus.

Batson, Raymond M., and Larson, Kathleen B.
1967. Compilation of survey or television mosaics. Photogram. Engineering 33: 163-173, illus.

Cantrell, John L.
1964. Infrared geology. Photogram. Engineering 30:916-922, illus.

Claveloux, Bernard A.
1960. Sketching projector for side-looking radar photography. Photogram. Engineering 26:644-646, illus.

Colwell, Robert N.
1963. Basic matter and energy relationships involved in remote reconnaissance. Photogram. Engineering 29:761-799, illus.

——————.
1956. The taking of helicopter photography for use in photogrammetric research and training. Photogram. Engineering 22:613-621, illus.

——————, Draeger, William C., Lent, Jerry D., and Thorley, Gene A.
1966. A multispectral photographic experiment based on statistical analysis of spectrometric data. NASA Report, University of California, Berkeley. 3 parts, illus.

Feder, Allen M.
1960. Interpreting natural terrain from radar displays. Photogram. Engineering 26: 618-630, illus.

Fiore, C.
1967. Side-looking radar restitution. Photogram. Engineering 33:215-220, illus.

Frost, Robert E.
1960. The program of multiband sensing research at the U.S. Army Snow, Ice, and Permafrost Research Establishment. Photogram. Engineering 26:786-792.

Gosling, L. A. Peter.
1966. *Spacecraft in Geographic Research.* National Academy of Sciences — National Research Council, Washington, D.C. Publication 1353, 107 pp.

Harris, David E., and Woodbridge, Caspar L.
1964. Terrain mapping by use of infrared radiation. Photogram. Engineering 30: 134-139, illus.

Heller, Robert C.
1965. Aerial remote sensing in forestry. Proceedings of Society of American Foresters, Detroit, Mich., 162-168, illus.

——————, Aldrich, R. C., and Bailey, W. F.
1959. An evaluation of aerial photography for detecting southern pine beetle damage.

Photogram. Engineering 25:595-606, illus.

Hirsch, Stanley N.
1965. Infrared line scanners — a tool for remote sensing of forest areas. Proceedings of Society of American Foresters, Detroit, Mich. 169-172, illus.

Hoffman, Pamela R.
1958. Photogrammetric applications of radarscope photographs. Photogram. Engineering 24:756-764, illus.

Lancaster, Charles W., and Feder, Allen M.
1966. The multisensor mission. Photogram. Engineering 32:484-494, illus.

Lattman, Laurence H.
1963. Geologic interpretation of airborne infrared imagery. Photogram. Engineering 29:83-87, illus.

Lent, Jerry D.
1966. Cloud cover interference with remote sensing of forested areas from earth-orbital and lower altitudes. NASA Report, University of California, Berkeley, 47 pp., illus.

Leonardo, Earl S.
1964. Capabilities and limitations of remote sensors. Photogram. Engineering 30: 1005-1010, illus.

——————.
1959. An application of photogrammetry to radar research studies. Photogram. Engineering 25:376-380, illus.

——————— and Tolliver, Robert A.
1960. A photographic method for transformation of a black-and-white radar map into a full-color presentation. Photogram. Engineering 26:647-650, illus.

Lowman, Paul D.
1965. Space photography — a review. Photogram. Engineering 31:76-86, illus.

Lyons, E. H.
1964. Recent developments in 70-mm. stereophotography from helicopters. Photogram. Engineering 30:750-756, illus.

——————.
1961. Preliminary studies of two camera, low-elevation stereo-photography from helicopters. Photogram. Engineering 27:72-76, illus.

Lyytikainen, H. E.
1960. An analysis of radar profiles over mountainous terrain. Photogram. Engineering 26:403-412, illus.

Meier, Hans.
1959. The use of Doppler radar in present and future mapping operations. Photo-

gram. Engineering 25:632-635, illus.

Merifield, Paul M., and Rammelkamp, James.
1966. Terrain seen from TIROS. Photogram. Engineering 32:44-54, illus.

Mignery, Arnold L.
1951. Use of low-altitude continuous-strip aerial photography in forestry. U.S. Forest Serv., Southern Forest Expt. Sta., Occas. Paper 118, 19 pp., illus.

Newbry, L. E.
1960. Terrain radar reflectance study. Photogram. Engineering 26:630-637, illus.

Ockert, Donn L.
1960. Satellite photography with strip and frame cameras. Photogram. Engineering 26:592-596, illus.

Olson, Charles E., Jr.
1964. Infrared sensors and their potential applications to forestry. Mich. Acad. Science, Arts, and Letters, Vol. L, 39-47, illus.

Rosenberg, Paul.
1960. Utility of manned space operations for photogrammetry and for a physics laboratory in space. Photogram. Engineering 26:455-457.

Sayn-Wittgenstein, L.
1965. Large scale aerial photography—plans and problems. Proceedings of Society of American Foresters, Detroit, Mich., 178-179.

Scheps, Bernard B.
1960. To measure is to know—geometric fidelity and interpretation in radar mapping. Photogram. Engineering 26:637-644, illus.

Stephan, Joachim G.
1967. Mapping the ocean floor. Photogram. Engineering 33:312-317, illus.

Suits, G. H.
1960. The nature of infrared radiation and ways to photograph it. Photogram. Engineering 26:763-772, illus.

Thompson, Morrell.
1965. The utilization of an infrared thermal mapping system for urban planning. Paper presented at the third annual conference on urban planning information systems and programs. Ameri-can Society of Planning Officials and Northwestern University, Chicago, Ill.

U.S. Department of the Interior.
1966. Earth resources observation satellite. Geological Survey, Washington, D.C., 19 pp., illus.

University of Michigan.
1962. Proceedings of the first symposium on remote sensing of environment. Institute of Science and Technology, Ann Arbor, 110 pp., illus.

———.
1963. Proceedings of the second symposium on remote sensing of environment. Institute of Science and Technology, Ann Arbor, 459 pp., illus.

———.
1964. Proceedings of the third symposium on remote sensing of environment. Institute of Science and Technology, Ann Arbor, 821 pp., illus.

———.
1966. Proceedings of the fourth symposium on remote sensing of environment. Institute of Science and Technology, Ann Arbor, 871 pp., illus.

———.
1966. Peaceful uses of earth-observation spacecraft. Infrared and Optical Sensor Laboratory, Institute of Science and Technology, Ann Arbor, 3 volumes, illus.

Wear, John F.
1960. Interpretation methods and field use of aerial color photos. Photogram. Engineering 26:805-808, illus.

Willingham, J. W.
1959. Obtaining vertical aerial photographic coverage with a 35 mm. camera. Jour. Forestry 57:108-110, illus.

Wilson, Richard C.
1966. Space photography versus aerial photography as applied to forestry. Paper presented at annual meeting of American Society of Photogrammetry, Washington, D.C., 11 pp.

Wohl, Martin, and Sickle, Stephen M.
1959. Continuous strip photography—an approach to traffic studies. Photogram. Engineering 25:397-403, illus.

CHAPTER 10

Agricultural and Land-Use Patterns

Monitoring of Crop Acreages

Agricultural information that is often extracted from various types of aerial imagery includes the measurement of crop acreages, identification of specific crops or types of farming, evaluation of soil characteristics from terrain indicators, and analysis of significant changes in land-use patterns. Techniques of measuring areas have been discussed in Chapter 5. However, it is worthy of mention that one of the principal reasons for the existence of the Agricultural Stabilization and Conservation Service in the U.S. Department of Agriculture is that agency's responsibility for the monitoring of crop acreages.

Maintaining up-to-date checks of each farmer's annual planting allotment would be virtually impossible today without some form of aerial reconnaissance. Accordingly, almost all sizable agricultural areas of conterminous United States are rephotographed for ASCS at scheduled intervals of about three to seven years. Photographic enlargements, rectified to an exact scale by ground checks, are used to determine each owner's acreage planted to price-supported crops such as cotton, wheat, peanuts, and tobacco. Although a few citizens have professed to resent this "spy method" of crop monitoring, it remains the most efficient technique for the detection of overplanted areas and the maintenance of equitable allotments for a majority of the nation's farmers.

Classes of Agricultural Land

The first step in the classification of agricultural land is that of learning to recognize broad categories that are easily separable on conventional photographs *(Figure 10-1)*. In most of the United States and Canada, the following six types can be identified: seasonal row crops; continuous cover crops; improved pasture lands; fallow or abandoned fields, including unimproved grazing lands; orchards; and vineyards. It is also usually feasible to differentiate between irrigated and dry-farming areas. And with special types of aerial imagery, crop vigor and the presence of unhealthy or diseased plants may be effectively assessed. A generalized map of major farming regions in conterminous United States is shown in *Figure 10-2*.

Identifying Farm Crops

Identification of individual farm crops is heavily dependent on the exact dates of photographic coverage available. During early phases of the growing season, spring-planted crops are almost identical in tone and general appearance. After harvesting begins in late summer, crop differentiation is again difficult, especially for small grains. In a study of

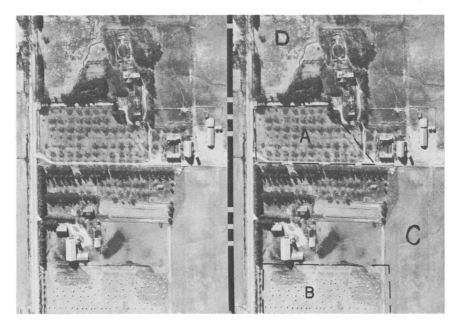

FIGURE 10-1. Agricultural land classes easily recognized on this Wisconsin farm include an orchard (A), shocks of grain (B), field used for annual row crops (C), and pasture (D). Scale is 600 feet per inch.

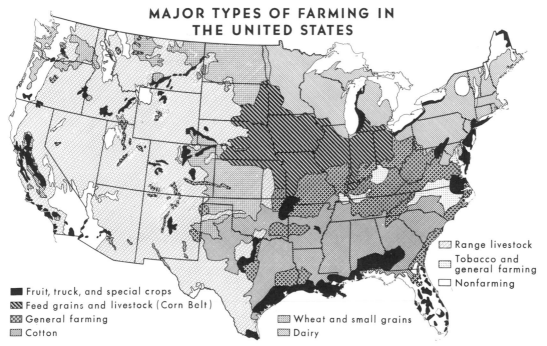

FIGURE 10-2. Specialized agricultural production areas are largely an indication of the effects of climate, soil type, and site. Proximity to markets is also a contributing factor in the location of fruit, vegetable, and dairy industries. Courtesy of U.S. Department of Agriculture.

farm crop identification in northern Illinois, the optimum conditions for recognizing crops on panchromatic photographs were found to occur between July 15 and July 30 (Goodman, 1959). During this brief period, cultivated crops including alfalfa, wheat, corn, barley, oats, and soybeans were identified. Several of these crops are pictured in *Figure 10-3*.

Photographic tone and texture are the most important factors to be considered in recognizing individual crops on black-and-white prints. Local variations in farm practices, methods of plowing, and harvesting techniques have proved to be of limited value in the identification process. Tones may range from nearly black, in the case of oats and alfalfa fields, to almost white, as exhibited by stands of ripe wheat. Corn and soybeans are intermediate in tone by comparison with these extremes.

After corn and soybeans have begun to mature, they may be separated on the basis of texture and differences in height. The mottled texture (light and dark spots) seen on many photographs of agricultural land is usually due to differences in soil moisture. The drier portions of fields, i.e., higher elevations, tend to show up in light tones on panchromatic prints. When soil moisture is of primary concern to the interpreter, however, infrared photography is preferred over panchromatic film.

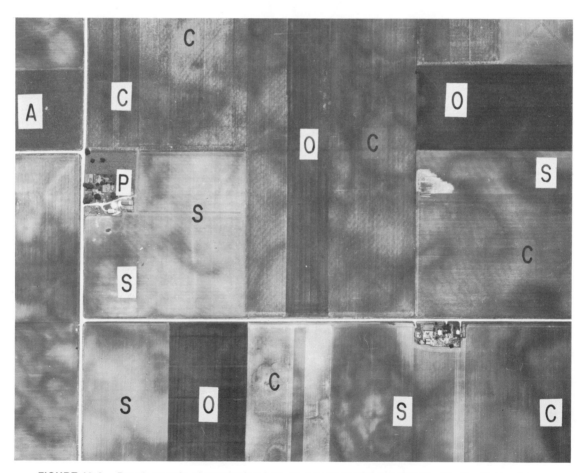

FIGURE 10-3. Panchromatic photograph taken on July 15 in McLean County, Illinois. Crops shown are alfalfa (A), corn (C), oats (O), pasture (P), and soybeans (S). Scale is about 600 feet per inch. Courtesy of University of Illinois.

Irrigated or flooded crops such as rice are easily recognized by the presence of low, wavy terraces that show up as irregular lines on panchromatic film *(Figure 10-4)*. Pasture lands can be detected by the presence of farm stock ponds or well-trodden lanes leading to and from barns or across roads that bisect fenced lands. Detailed studies of farmsteads and ranches on large-scale prints may also reveal the presence of dairy barns, horse stables, tent-shaped hog houses, and similar animal structures *(Figure 10-5)*.

Orchards and Vineyards

As a rule, orchards are characterized by uniformly spaced rows of trees that give the appearance of a grid pattern. Orchards planted in regions of level terrain (e.g., pecans or citrus trees) are usually laid out in squares so that the same spacing exists between rows as between individual trees in the same row. On rolling to hilly terrain, tree rows may follow old cultivation terraces or land contours (e.g., peaches or apples). In such instances, the sinuous lines of trees tend to somewhat resemble fingerprints when viewed on small-scale photographs.

Vineyards present a uniformly linear pattern on aerial photographs. Because of the localization of grape cultivation and the wider spacings between individual rows, vineyards are not likely to be confused with corn or other row crops of similar height and texture *(Figure 10-6)*. Grapes are grown locally over much of the eastern United States, but the largest production areas in Anglo-America are found in north-central California.

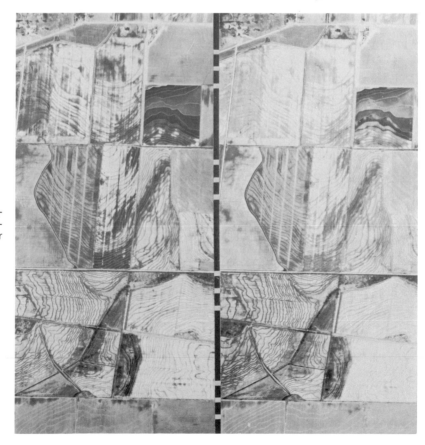

FIGURE 10-4. Rice cultivation near Pine Bluff, Arkansas. Scale is 2,000 feet per inch.

FIGURE 10-5. Cattle farm in eastern Tennessee. Note cattle grazing in improved pasture (A) and large stock pond (B). Scale is 450 feet per inch.

Seasonal Changes in Farm Patterns

Photographic comparisons of the same area taken during the four seasons show pronounced differences in the tones of soils, vegetation, and erosional features. Seasonal contrasts are particularly significant in mid-latitude regions that have humid-temperate climates. Where such areas are under intensive cultivation, changes can be detected not only in vegetation and soil moisture but also in the outlines of the fields. These periodic changes may be summarized as follows:

Spring: Field patterns are sharp and distinct due to differences in the state of tillage and crop development. Mottled textures due to differences in soil moisture content are very distinct. High topographic positions, even those only a few inches above adjacent lower sites, tend to photograph in light tones. Low topographic positions photograph dark because of large local variations in soil moisture. Recently cultivated fields exhibit very light photo tones which imply good internal soil drainage.

Summer: Photographs are dominated by dark tones of mature growing crops and heavily foliaged trees. Soil moisture content is normally low; therefore, bare soil tends to photograph light gray. Field patterns are subdued because of the predominance of green vegetation.

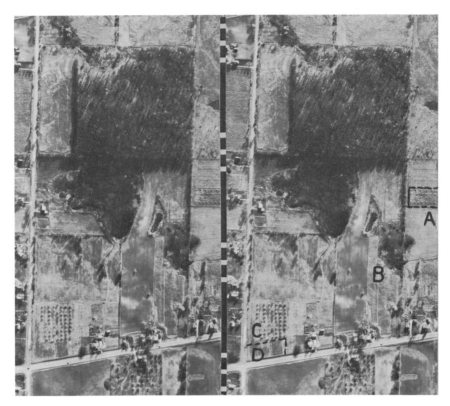

FIGURE 10-6. Haystacks (A), corn stubble (B), orchard (C), and small vine-yard (D) as seen in December on a southern Michigan farm. Scale is about 800 feet per inch.

Autumn: Field patterns are relatively distinct because of various stages of crop development and harvesting. Differences in tone resulting from variations in soil moisture content are subdued.

Winter: Photographic tones are drab and dull, with some field patterns indistinct. Mottling due to variations in soil moisture is practically nonexistent, and bare ground tends to photograph in dark tones because soil moisture content is uniformly high. Low angle of incident light causes sharp shadow patterns in wooded areas, producing a distinctive form of flecked texture. Gullies are usually more pronounced during winter than in summer, because the low winter sun casts denser shadows and dormant, leafless vegetation does not mask the surface.

Detection of Diseased Plants

There is no universal technique for evaluating crop vigor or detecting disease-infected plants on aerial photographs. The presence of certain diseases such as stem rusts on wheat or oats and blight on potatoes may be detected by use of photographs taken in the near-infrared band of the electromagnetic spectrum, i.e., between 0.7 and 0.9 micron. On positive infrared prints, diseased plants register in abnormally dark tones. Although individually affected plants may not be discernible on small-scale prints, it is often possible to delineate patches of diseased plants. In the case of orchards, separate tree crowns that are infected may be pin-pointed.

Infrared color or camouflage-detection film (Chapter 6) has been successfully used to locate unhealthy forest trees that have been attacked by various pathogens and insect enemies. It appears likely that this same film emulsion will prove valuable in assessing the vigor of certain agricultural crops.

Soil Characteristics from Terrain Indicators

Terrain elements are the features, attributes, and materials that comprise a landscape. The more important factors to be considered in the evolution of landscapes are topography, drainage patterns, local erosion, natural vegetation, and the works of man. Topography is the result of the interaction of erosional and depositional agents, the nature of the rocks and soils, the structure of the earth's crust, and the climatic regime. The topographic surface is, in effect, a synthesis of all environmental elements into a single expression. As such, it plays an important role in soil surveys, because it provides a key for deducing the soil-forming processes at work in a given region.

A number of attempts have been made to classify drainage patterns into specific regional groupings *(Figure 10-7)*. When this can be done, much can be inferred with regard to soil

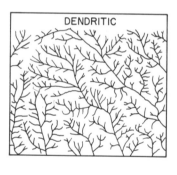

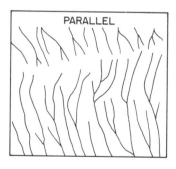

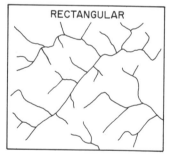

FIGURE 10-7. Diagrammatic presentation of several drainage patterns that can be recognized on aerial photographs.

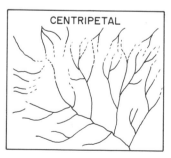

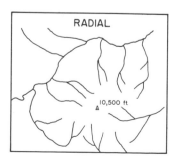

type, geologic structure, amount and intensity of local precipitation, and the land tenure history. However, stream patterns are almost infinitely variable, and the various types often grade into one another so that no single pattern appears to predominate. In some instances, a large drainage system may display several sub-types of drainage simultaneously. For example, the gross drainage pattern of a region may be dendritic, while associated lesser stream patterns may be pinnate. This situation is quite common in areas of deep loess deposits.

Wind Erosion

Features produced by wind and water erosion are important aids in photo interpretation because they are diagnostic of surface soil textures, soil profile characteristics, and soil moisture conditions. Specific implications of each type are discussed in the following paragraphs.

Evidences of wind erosion include blowouts, which are smoothly rounded and irregularly shaped depressions; sand streaks, which are light-toned but poorly defined parallel streaks; and sand blotches, which are light-toned and poorly defined patches. Evaluation of such features depends on a knowledge of prevailing wind direction, wind velocity, and the general climatic regime. Climate is important because it provides some indication of probable soil moisture conditions. Any surface unprotected by vegetation and not continuously moist may be eroded by the wind. Both local and regional topographic configurations should be kept in mind in evaluating eolian action, because mountains, hills, or other features may channel air movements in such a way that erosion is severe in one locality and insignificant in another.

Plowed fields, beaches, alluvial fans, and floodplains are examples of surfaces especially susceptible to wind erosion *(Figure 10-8)*. In general, the finer the grain size the greater the distance surface material is transported. As a result, a blowout with evidence of immediate deposition downwind implies relatively coarse-grained material, whereas a blowout without such evidence implies fine-grained material.

Many small erosional forms resulting from wind action are difficult to identify on airphotos. As a rule, only the larger blowouts are readily picked out. Evidence of deposition is more easily detected, because resulting dunes or sheets present distinctive shapes or light-toned streaks and blotches. These are of considerable significance in regional land-use studies. In any given locality, wind-deposited materials tend to be of uniform size, resulting in homogeneous soils. This implies that agricultural conditions in any one locality will be approximately uniform, provided slope, vegetation, and moisture conditions are similar.

Water Erosion

Moving water is the major active agent in developing surface configuration of the earth. Despite its awesome power in the form of floods and tidal waves, moving water is delicately responsive to variations in environment, and modest changes in the material being eroded or the climatic regime can profoundly modify the surface expressions produced. Therefore, the landscape patterns produced through the action of moving water are of great importance to the photo interpreter *(Figure 10-9)*. However, the interpreter should have a basic knowledge of the interrelations between climate, surface materials, surface configuration, and vegetation.

FIGURE 10-8. Cultivated portion of a dissected loess plain in Harrison County, Iowa. The fine-grained eolian soils, deposited from glacial outwash areas to the north, are easily eroded by wind and water. Corn is the leading crop in this rolling plains area, with livestock providing the bulk of the farm income. Scale is about 1,667 feet per inch. Courtesy of U.S. Department of Agriculture.

The relative importance of various factors influencing runoff varies according to specific environmental conditions that occur in a given area. Surface runoff is governed by the following general considerations:

1. The amount and intensity of rainfall determine the degree of runoff. A heavy rainfall of short duration may produce more runoff than the same amount over a longer period of time.

2. The amount of runoff is dependent upon the moisture in the soil prior to rainfall. A given rainfall on wet soil will produce more runoff than the same rainfall on dry soil. A proportion of the incident water will be stored by the dry soil, whereas the wet soil has less available storage capacity.

3. A noncohesive soil is eroded more readily than a cohesive soil.

4. The greater the permeability of a soil, the less the surface runoff.

5. In general, the greater the density of vegetation, the less the runoff for a given quantity of incident water.

6. The steeper the slope, the greater the surface runoff.

Vegetation as an Indicator of Terrain

In some instances, native vegetation can be used as a guide in evaluating soil types and moisture relationships. Although individual plant species are not easily identified except at very large scales, there are some notable exceptions in regions where pure stands of perennial vegetation occur naturally.

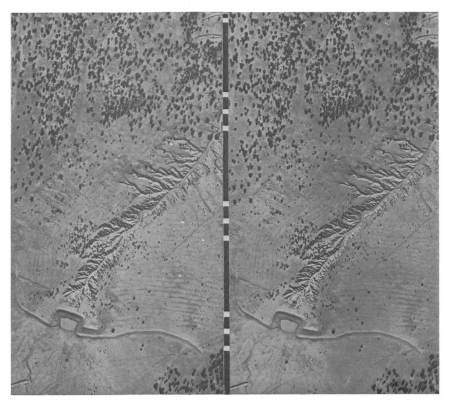

FIGURE 10-9. Dendritic drainage pattern formed in soft sediments near the Rio Grande in New Mexico. Scale is 500 feet per inch. Courtesy of Abrams Aerial Survey Corp.

For example, distinctive crown shapes may permit identification of individual long-leaf pines growing on sandy ridges of the Atlantic and Gulf Coastal Plain. When individual species cannot be recognized, however, the interpreter must rely on composite patterns formed by aggregates of tree crowns. Some general relationships between natural plant indicators and soil conditions have been summarized by Rula, Grabau, and Miles (1963):

1. There is a marked tendency for certain plants to be concentrated along desert washes, indicating a slightly more persistent soil moisture than in surrounding uplands.

2. There are concentric zones of vegetation around lakes and ponds, especially in cold-humid regions. For example, a common zonation around lakes in Quebec Province of Canada is, from the water outward, the sedge zone, heath zone, and spruce zone. This zonation indicates successive reductions in waterlogging of the soil, and it is also a measure of the amount of organic material in the soil. The sedges may actually be floating, the heaths normally rest on peat, and the spruce grow in highly organic, silty soils.

3. In the Lower Mississippi Valley floodplain, a heavily forested area indicates a high water table and extreme susceptibility to flooding. This is often an indicator of clayey or silty soils with poor internal drainage and high organic content *(Figure 10-10)*.

4. A combination of tall grass or sedges and a roughly rectangular drainage pattern indicates fine-grained, highly organic soils subject to repeated tidal flooding.

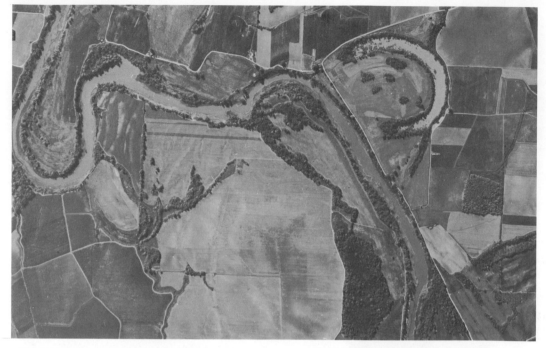

FIGURE 10-10. Portion of the Mississippi alluvial plain in Sunflower County, Mississippi. Dark-toned forest areas, river meander scars, and oxbow lakes are evident in this fertile area devoted primarily to cotton farming. Scale is about 1,667 feet per inch. Courtesy of U.S. Department of Agriculture.

5. In the hardwood forest belt, the oaks that hold their leaves in winter are indicative of dry soils such as sands. Stands of poplar, birch, maple, walnut, and red and white oaks indicate moist, fine-textured soils; sycamore, cottonwood, and willow indicate wet soils.

6. In coastal plain areas, wet soils generally show dense tree growth of hydrophytic types, whereas dry soils are likely to exhibit sparse tree growth.

7. Muck and peat bogs that are waterlogged can readily be differentiated by the contrast in vegetation as compared to surrounding forested or cultivated land.

Measurement of Land-Use Changes

In analyzing the economic development of any area, land utilization provides one of the more valuable indicators of rural, urban, and industrial growth. Sequential aerial photography makes it feasible for a trained interpreter to evaluate land-use patterns at two or more distinct points in time *(Figure 10-11)*. To illustrate the basic methodology of evaluating land-use changes from standard USDA contact prints, a case study made in Clarke County, Georgia is summarized here.

Panchromatic photography taken in 1944 and 1960 for the Agricultural Stabilization and Conservation Service was available for this project. Six land-use classes were chosen after preliminary interpretation and ground verification checks. While greater refinements in land delineations might have been desirable, several proposed categories had to be rejected, because they could not be consistently recognized. The restrictions imposed on the selection of such classes are obvious when one realizes that accurate field checks cannot be made for 16 to 20-year-old photographs. An example of the 1944 and 1960 photography appears in *Figure 10-12*.

FIGURE 10-11. Urban area photographed in 1954 (above) and again in 1961 (below). Note addition of shopping center and new residences on the lower stereogram. Courtesy of Abrams Aerial Survey Corp.

Trial-and-error experimentation resulted in the selection of six definitive classifications:

Cultivated land: Land used for growing agricultural crops or apparently cultivated during the growing season preceding photography. Also included were improved pasture lands, because such lands were not always distinguishable from cropland on the photographs available.

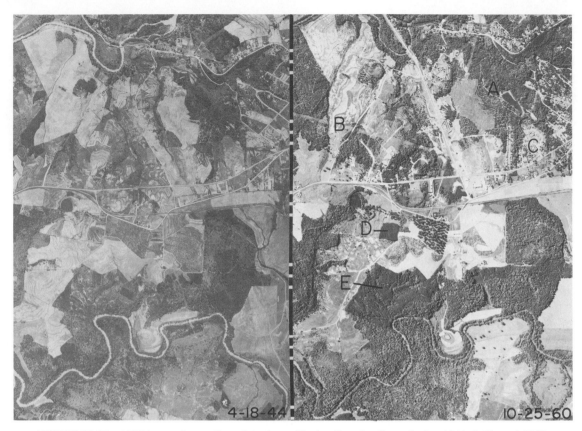

FIGURE 10-12. USDA panchromatic prints from Clarke County, Georgia for 1944 (left) and 1960 (right). Among changes evident on the 1960 print are a new pond (A), cleared right-of-way (B), new residential area (C), pine plantation (D), and reversion of an abandoned field to forest land (E). Scale is about 1,667 feet per inch.

Pine forest: Woodlands having a tree crown density of 10 percent or more, with pine species comprising 51 percent or more of the dominant (visible) crown canopy.

Hardwood forest: Woodlands having a tree crown density of 10 percent or more, with deciduous tree species comprising 51 percent or more of the dominant (visible) crown canopy.

Urban land: All residential and industrial areas within the city limits of incorporated towns were included in this category.

Idle land: All open wild lands having a tree crown density of less than 10 percent and not classed as cultivated. Also included were unimproved pastures, i.e., unfenced grazing areas not sown with forage crops.

Water: Lakes and ponds larger than three acres and river channels 200 feet wide or more were included in this classification.

Land-Use Areas

Areas of each land-use class were obtained by dot grid counts on 9 by 9-inch contact prints. With a grid having 16 dots per square inch, each dot represented approximately four acres at the nominal photo scale of 1:20,000. However, because of slight scale differences in the 1944 and 1960 prints, acreages of each classification were determined proportionally by the following relationship:

$$\text{Type acreage} = \frac{\text{No. of dots in type}}{\text{Total dots counted}} \times \text{County area in acres}$$

Acreages and percent of county area occupied by each type during 1944 and 1960 are shown in *Table 10-1*. The area of cultivated land decreased by 13,600 acres during the 16-year interval; all other classifications increased in size, with the largest gains evident in urban areas and pine forest land. In summary, the economy of this county in the Piedmont Plateau of Georgia changed from rural-agricultural to an urban-industrial base during the period spanned by sequential photography.

**TABLE 10-1. Summary of land-use changes in
Clarke County, Georgia, 1944-1960**

Land use	1944		1960	
	Acres	Percent	Acres	Percent
Cultivated land	44,000	55.0	30,400	38.0
Pine forest	12,000	15.0	19,200	24.0
Hardwood forest	12,560	15.7	13,840	17.3
Urban land	5,680	7.1	8,400	10.5
Idle land	5,600	7.0	7,600	9.5
Water	160	0.2	560	0.7
Totals	80,000	100.0	80,000	100.0

Significance of Land-Use Patterns

The varieties of tones, patterns, and spatial arrangements depicted on aerial photographs reflect the combined works of nature and the cultural patterns of man. Man's activities in settling, cultivating, mining, and exploiting various land resources have left characteristic marks upon the earth's surface. Many of the telltale markings are unattractive, undesirable, or completely out of phase with the concept of natural resources conservation. Still, much can be learned from studies of these indelible footprints, for certain land-use patterns are repeated wherever man vies with natural forces in shaping his environment.

In the early days on the American frontier, travel was usually by wagon road or along navigable streams; hence, the first settlements were found along these natural highways. The advent of systematic land surveys and the development of railroad networks resulted in new settlement patterns and methods of land exploitation. Today, rural populations are migrating to expanding urban centers, and transportation systems are dominated by private automobiles, multi-lane highway networks, and commercial aircraft. When these kinds of changes are recorded on film, the aerial photograph becomes a historical document of considerable value. Examples of interesting and unusual land-use patterns found in the United States are presented in *Figures 10-13* to *10-20*. Unless otherwise specified, all are USDA panchromatic photographs at a scale of about 1,667 feet per inch.

FIGURE 10-13. Active sand dunes along the Lake Michigan shore in Porter County, Indiana. Much of the stabilizing native vegetation has been removed to make room for expanding residential properties.

FIGURE 10-14. This quilt-like pattern of small land clearings connected by roads is an oil field in McKean County, Pennsylvania. Two pumping stations are encircled. The difference between older and newer drillings is shown by the regrowth of vegetation.

FIGURE 10-15. Springtime patterns of cultivated land in the rolling hills of Carroll County, Maryland. Light-toned strips indicate recently plowed fields. The principal crops in this area are corn, wheat, barley, and oats.

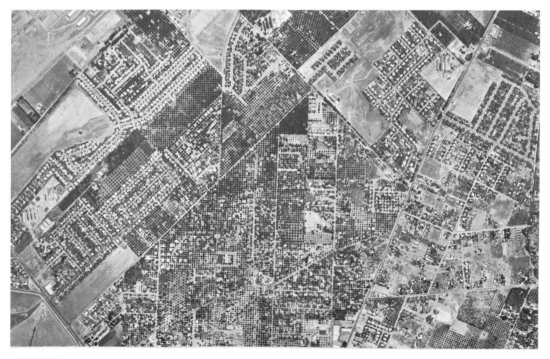

FIGURE 10-16. Encroachment of residential properties upon orchard lands in Contra Costa County, California.

FIGURE 10-17. French long-lot patterns in Assumption Parish, Louisiana. This pattern, found in several European countries, was brought over by early colonists who depended on river transportation; each landowner thus had river frontage. Roads and dwellings are concentrated on artificial levees on either side of the river. The principal crops grown here are sugar cane, cotton, and rice.

Automatic Image Interpretation

Technological advances that permit electronic scanning of both conventional imagery and digitized pictorial data will eventually lead to automated systems of image interpretation. Tests of automatic scanning and pattern recognition equipment have already indicated a reliability of about 80 percent in recognizing four basic terrain classes, viz., water, cultivated lands, trees, and urban areas. Further developments in optics-electronics research may permit the image interpreter to shift many routine tasks such as land-use classifications to analytically programmed scanning-recording devices. When one considers the single task of analyzing imagery from repetitive coverage of military target areas, the potential value of automatic interpretation systems becomes obvious.

Automatic extraction of information from aerial imagery may be based on (1) scanning systems that search for images having specific shapes and sizes, or (2) measurements of textural parameters that indicate density contrasts in the photographic image. Objects such as vehicles, airfields, or storage tanks possess characteristics that are conducive to the use of recognition systems based on size and shape. Terrain types, agricultural crops, and land-use patterns are features that are more likely to be classified according to textural differences, i.e., differences in density as "read" from scanning records of photographic images.

Automatic size and shape recognition is sometimes accomplished by matching the photographic image with a selected physical or mathematical template to produce a specific electronic signal at points that correspond to locations of images having a given shape.

FIGURE 10-18. Sugar-cane fields and processing plant in Lafayette Parish, Louisiana. Plantation fields are interlaced with irrigation ditches that are fed by an elaborate canal system. The enclosed area is the plantation nucleus, with storage sheds at (A) and the processing plant at (B).

An advantage of this direct matching system is that it selects and recognizes the given-shaped images in a single operation; it does not require that portions of the photograph first be selected and then tested to determine whether or not they have the given shape. This approach has the disadvantage of being sensitive to the relative orientation of the photograph and template. However, it can be performed for all possible orientations at fairly high speeds (Rosenfeld, 1962).

In recognizing terrain types through an automated analysis of image texture, an obvious requirement is that differences in tone or image contrast *between* terrain classes should be greater than differences occurring *within* a given category. As a result, elementary scanning experiments are generally aimed toward the differentiation of such obvious features as water, cultivated fields, pastures, and forests. Among devices that show promise for land-use classification is an automatic scanning "microdensitometer." As outlined by Doverspike, Flynn, and Heller (1965), the technique of microdensitometry involves measuring either the reflection or transmission density of microscopically small image areas. Automatically recorded results may be presented graphically on a chart or in digitized form for computer reduction and analysis.

FIGURE 10-19. Typical pattern of an old masonry-walled Spanish fort near Clinton, Tennessee. Scale is 800 feet per inch.

The Outlook for Automated Scanning

Even though tests of the microdensitometer and similar scanning systems show great promise, there is no immediate prospect of the human photo interpreter becoming obsolete. Certain scientific image interpretation problems which involve simple images may have practical solutions at today's level of recognition technology. But the fully automatic interpretation of reconnaissance imagery has yet to be achieved to any practical degree. When new breakthroughs are made, the initial functions of robot interpreters are likely to include such mundane chores as (1) automatically "screening" imagery for priority of examination by human interpreters, (2) automatically performing tentative detections and attracting the human interpreter to them for verification, (3) aiding in the decision process by computer-analyzing human observations, and (4) performing measurements of images identified by a human interpreter.

References

Avery, T. Eugene.
  1965. Measuring land use changes on USDA photographs. Photogram. Engineering 31:620-624, illus.

  —————————— and Richter, Dennis.
  1965. An airphoto index to physical and cultural features in eastern United States. Photogram. Engineering 31:896-914, illus.

Brunnschweiler, Dieter H.
  1957. Seasonal changes of the agricultural pattern: a study in comparative airphoto interpretation. Photogram. Engineering 23:131-139, illus.

Dill, Henry W., Jr.
  1959. Use of the comparison method in agricultural airphoto interpretation. Photogram. Engineering 25:44-49, illus.

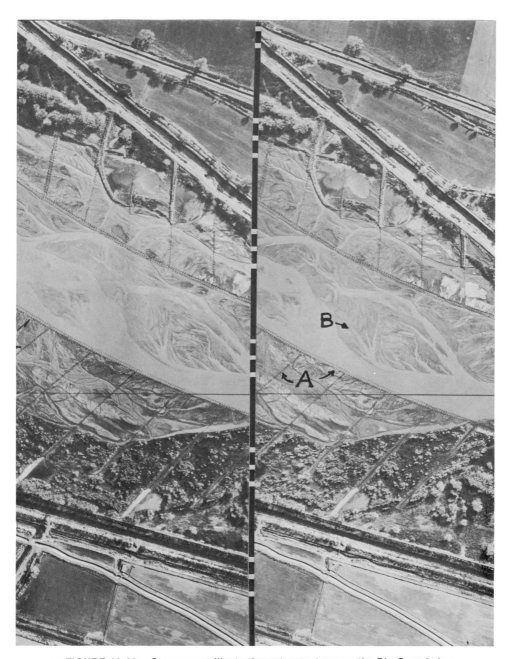

FIGURE 10-20. Stereogram illustrating a transect across the Rio Grande in New Mexico. Note the intricate layout of stabilizing revetments (A) and the braided stream pattern (B). Scale is 500 feet per inch. Courtesy of Abrams Aerial Survey Corp.

Doverspike, George E., Flynn, Frank M.,
and Heller, Robert C.
  1965. Microdensitometer applied to land use classification. Photogram. Engineering 31:294-306, illus.

Goodman, Marjorie Smith.
  1964. Criteria for the identification of types of farming on aerial photographs. Photogram. Engineering 30:984-990, illus.

_____.
  1959. A technique for the identification of farm crops on aerial photographs. Photogram. Engineering 25:131-137, illus.

Hawkins, J. K., and Munsey, C. J.
  1963. Automatic photo reading. Photogram. Engineering 29:632-640, illus.

Langley, P. G.
  1965. Automating aerial photo-interpretation in forestry — how it works and what it will do for you. Proceedings of Society of American Foresters, Detroit, Mich., 172-177, illus.

Marschner, F. J.
  1959. Land use and its patterns in the United States. U.S. Department of Agriculture Handbook 153, Government Printing Office, Washington, D.C., 277 pp., illus.

Olson, David P.
  1964. The use of aerial photographs in studies of marsh vegetation. Bull. 13, Tech. series, Maine Agri. Expt. Sta., 62 pp., illus.

Rosenfeld, Azriel.
  1965. Automatic imagery interpretation. Photogram. Engineering 31:240-242.

_____.
  1962. Automatic recognition of basic terrain types from aerial photographs. Photogram. Engineering 28:115-132, illus.

_____.
  1962. An approach to automatic photographic interpretation. Photogram. Engineering 28:660-665, illus.

Rula, A. A., Grabau, W. E., and Miles, R. D.
  1963. Forecasting trafficability of soils — airphoto approach. U.S. Army Engineer Waterways Experiment Station, Vicksburg, Miss., 218 pp., illus. (two volumes).

Steiner, Dieter.
  1967. Index to the use of aerial photographs for rural land use studies. Commission on Interpretation of Aerial Photographs, International Geographical Union, Bad Godesberg, Germany, 232 pp.

_____.
  1965. Tone distortion for automated interpretation. Photogram. Engineering 31:269-280, illus.

U.S. Department of Agriculture.
  1958. Land: the Yearbook of Agriculture. Government Printing Office, Washington, D.C., 605 pp., illus.

CHAPTER 11

Forestry Uses of Aerial Photographs

Introduction

Today, almost all foresters use aerial photographs in preparing cover-type maps, locating timber-access roads and property boundaries, determining bearings and distances to field sample plots, and measuring areas. Skilled interpreters may also be adept in recognizing individual tree species and appraising fire, insect, or disease damage by means of special photography. In addition to these applications, aerial photographs have proved valuable for watershed and wildlife habitat management, for making outdoor recreation surveys, and for determining counts or volumes of standing trees and cut forest products.

In this chapter emphasis is placed on identifying and mapping forest cover types, recognizing tree species on large-scale prints, forest inventory techniques, and photo stratifications for ground cruising. Although photo interpretation can make the forester's job easier, there are limitations which must be recognized. Accurate measurements of such items as tree diameter, form class, and stem defect are possible only on the ground. Aerial photographs are therefore used to complement, improve, or reduce field work rather than take its place.

Identifying Forest Cover Types

The degree to which forest cover types and tree species can be recognized depends on the quality, scale, and season of photography, the type of film used, and the interpreter's background and ability. The shape, texture, and tone of tree crowns as seen on vertical photographs may also be influenced by stand age or topographic site. Furthermore, such images may be distorted by time of day, sun angle, atmospheric haze, clouds, or inconsistent processing of negatives and prints. In spite of insistence on rigid specifications, it is often impossible to obtain uniform imagery of extensive timber holdings. Nevertheless, experienced interpreters *can* reliably distinguish cover types in diverse forest regions when photographic flights are carefully planned to minimize the foregoing limitations.

A general map of forest regions in the United States is shown in *Figure 11-1*. The tree species listed provide the first step in identification, i.e., the elimination of those cover types not likely to occur in a given locality. The second step is to establish which types may logically be encountered. Here, a general knowledge of forest ecology is helpful, and field experience in the specific area to be mapped is even more valuable. The occurrence and distribution of vegetative cover in a given locality are governed by such elements as (1) annual or seasonal rainfall, (2) latitude or elevation above sea level, (3) length of the growing season, (4) solar radiation and temperature regimes, (5) soil type and drainage conditions, (6) topographic aspect and slope, (7) prevailing winds, (8) salt spray, and (9) air pollutants.

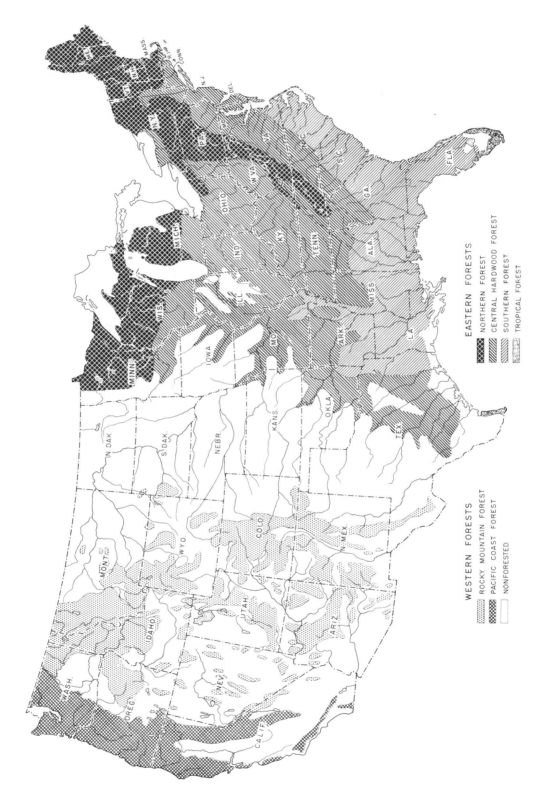

FIGURE 11-1. Forest regions of the United States.

PRINCIPAL TREES OF THE FOREST REGIONS

NOTE. — The order indicates the relative importance or abundance of the trees

ROCKY MOUNTAIN FOREST

Northern Portion (Northern Idaho and Western Montana):

Lodgepole pine
Douglas-fir
Western larch
Engelmann spruce
Ponderosa pine
Western white pine
Western redcedar
Grand and alpine firs
Western and mountain hemlocks
Whitebark pine
Balsam poplar

Eastern Oregon, Central Idaho, and Eastern Washington:

Ponderosa pine
Douglas-fir
Lodgepole pine
Western larch
Engelmann spruce
Western redcedar
Western hemlock
White, grand, and alpine firs
Western white pine
Oaks and junipers (in Oregon)

Central Montana, Wyoming, and South Dakota:

Lodgepole pine
Douglas-fir
Ponderosa pine
Engelmann spruce
Alpine fir
Limber pine
Aspen and cottonwoods
Rocky Mountain juniper
White spruce

Central Portion (Colorado, Utah, and Nevada):

Lodgepole pine
Engelmann and blue spruces
Alpine and white firs
Douglas-fir
Ponderosa pine
Aspen and cottonwoods
Pinyons
Rocky Mountain and Utah junipers
Bristlecone and limber pines
Mountain-mahogany

Southern Portion (New Mexico and Arizona):

Ponderosa pine
Douglas-fir
White, alpine, and corkbark firs
Engelmann and blue spruces
Pinyons
One-seed, alligator, and Rocky Mountain junipers
Aspen and cottonwoods
Limber, Mexican white, and Arizona pines
Oaks, walnut, sycamore, alder, boxelder
Arizona cypress

PACIFIC COAST FOREST

Northern Portion (Western Washington and Western Oregon):

Douglas-fir
Western hemlock
Grand, noble, and Pacific silver firs
Western redcedar
Sitka and Engelmann spruces
Western white pine
Port Orford cedar and Alaska cedar
Western and alpine larches
Lodgepole pine
Mountain hemlock
Oaks, ashes, maples, birches, alders, cottonwoods, madrone

Southern Portion (California):

Ponderosa and Jeffrey pines
Sugar pine
Redwood and giant sequoia
White, red, grand, and Shasta red firs
California incense-cedar
Douglas-fir
Lodgepole pine
Knobcone and Digger pines
Bigcone-spruce
Monterey and Gowen cypresses
Sierra and California junipers
Singleleaf pinyon
Oaks, buckeye, California-laurel, alder, madrone

SOUTHERN FOREST

Pine Lands:

Shortleaf, loblolly, longleaf, slash, and sand pines
Southern red, black, post, laurel, cherrybark, and willow oaks
Sweetgum
Winged, American, and cedar elms
Black, red, sand, and pignut hickories
Eastern and southern redcedars
Basswoods

Alluvial Bottoms and Swamps:

Sweetgum and tupelos
Water, laurel, live, overcup, Texas, and swamp white oaks
Southern cypress
Pecan, water and swamp hickories
Beech
River birch
Ashes

Alluvial Bottoms and Swamps:

Red and silver maples
Cottonwoods and willows
Sycamore
Hackberry
Honeylocust
Holly
Redbay and sweetbay
Southern magnolia
Pond and spruce pines
Atlantic white-cedar

CENTRAL HARDWOOD FOREST

Northern Portion:

White, black, northern red, scarlet, bur, chestnut, and chinquapin oaks
Shagbark, mockernut, pignut, and bitternut hickories
White, blue, green, and red ashes
American, rock, and slippery elms
Red, sugar, and silver maples
Beech
Pitch, shortleaf, and Virginia pines
Yellow-poplar
Sycamore
Chestnut
Black walnut
Cottonwoods
Hackberry
Black cherry
Basswoods
Ohio buckeye
Eastern redcedar

Southern Portion:

White, post, southern red, blackjack, Shumard, chestnut, swamp chestnut, and pin oaks
Sweetgum and tupelos
Mockernut, pignut, southern shagbark, and shellbark hickories
Shortleaf and Virginia ("scrub") pines
White, blue, and red ashes
Yellow-poplar
Black locust
Elms
Sycamore
Black walnut
Silver and red maples
Beech
Persimmon
Dogwood
Cottonwoods and willows
Eastern redcedar
Osage-orange

Texas Portion:

Post, southern red, and blackjack oaks
Eastern redcedar, Ashe juniper

FLORIDA AND TEXAS FOREST – TROPICAL

Mangrove, false mangrove
Royal and thatch palms; palmettos
Florida yew
Wild figs
Seagrapes ("pigeon plum")
Blolly
Bahama lysiloma ("wild tamarind")
Wild-dilly
Gumbo-limbo
Poisontree
Inkwood
Holly
Button-mangrove
False-mastic ("wild olive")
Fishpoison-tree ("Jamaica dogwood")

NORTHERN FOREST

Northern Portion:

Red, black, and white spruces
Balsam fir
Eastern white, red ("Norway"), jack, and pitch pines
Hemlock
Sugar and red maples
Beech
Northern'red, white, black, and scarlet oaks
Yellow, paper, sweet, and gray birches
Quaking and bigtooth aspens
Basswoods
Black cherry
American, rock, and slippery elms
White and black ashes
Shagbark and pignut hickories
Butternut
Northern white-cedar
Tamarack

Southern Portion (Appalachian Region):

White, northern red, chestnut, black, and scarlet oaks
Chestnut
Hemlock
Eastern white, shortleaf, pitch, and Virginia ("scrub") pines
Sweet, yellow, and river birches
Basswood
Sugar and red maples
Beech
Red spruce
Fraser fir
Yellow-poplar
Cucumber magnolia
Black walnut and butternut
Black cherry
Pignut, mockernut, and red hickories
Black locust
Tupelos ("blackgums")
Buckeye

ALASKA FOREST

Coast Forest:

Western hemlock (important)
Sitka spruce (important)
Western redcedar
Alaska cedar
Mountain hemlock
Lodgepole pine
Black cottonwood
Red and Sitka alders
Willows

Interior Forest:

White (important) and black spruces
Alaska paper (important) and Kenai birches
Black cottonwood
Balsam poplar
Aspen
Willows
Tamarack

The chief diagnostic features used by the interpreter in recognizing forest cover types are photographic texture (smoothness or coarseness of images), tonal contrast, relative sizes of tree images at a given photo scale, and topographic location or site. Most of these characteristics constitute rather weak clues when observed singly, but together they may comprise the final link in the chain of "identification by elimination." Several important cover types occurring in the United States and Canada are illustrated in *Figures 11-2* through *11-7*.

Identifying Individual Tree Species

Recognition of individual tree species, often feasible only on very large-scale photography, is normally the culmination of intensive study. It is obvious that the forest interpreter must be familiar with branching patterns and crown shapes of all important species in his particular region. Mature trees in sparsely stocked stands can often be recognized by the configuration of their crown shadows falling on level ground *(Figure 11-8)*. Many foresters have found the study of oblique photographs of trees helpful as an identification aid.

The identification of individual trees on vertical photographs also requires a familiarity with tree crowns as seen in overhead views *(Figure 11-9)*. While such image characteristics are not always apparent at scales of 1:12,000 to 1:20,000, they can be of invaluable

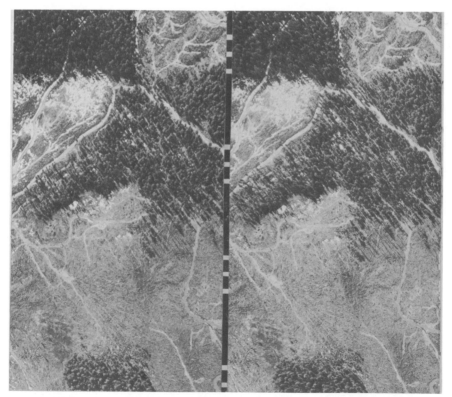

FIGURE 11-2. Panchromatic stereogram of a recently logged stand of Douglas-fir in Lewis County, Washington. Scale is about 500 feet per inch. Courtesy of Northern Pacific Railroad.

assistance when working with large-scale stereograms. Photo scales as large as 50 feet per inch are sometimes used for tree species identifications by foresters in the United States and Canada.

As outlined in Chapter 5, photo interpretation keys are useful aids to the recognition of tree species, especially when such keys are well illustrated with high-quality stereograms. A sample elimination key for identifying northern conifers is reproduced here by courtesy of the Canada Department of Forestry. In its original form, this tree species key was supplemented by descriptive materials and several illustrations.

KEY TO THE NORTHERN CONIFERS

1. Crowns small, or if large then definitely cone-shaped.

   2. Crown broadly conical, usually rounded tip, branches not prominent. . . . . *cedar*

   2. Crowns have a pointed top, or coarse branching, or both.
   —crowns narrow, often cylindrical, trees frequently
   grow in swamps . . . . *swamp type black spruce*

   —crowns conical, deciduous, very light-toned in fall, usually associated with black spruce . . . . *tamarack*

   —crowns narrowly conical, very symmetrical, top pointed, branches less prominent than in white spruce . . . . *balsam fir*

   —crowns narrowly conical, top often appears obtuse on photograph (except northern white spruce), branches more prominent than in
   balsam fir . . . . *white spruce, black spruce (except swamp type)*

   —crowns irregular, with pointed top, has thinner foliage and smoother texture than spruce and balsam fir . . . . *jack pine*

1. Crowns large and spreading, not narrowly conical, top often not well defined.

   3. Crowns very dense, irregular or broadly conical.

      4. Individual branches very prominent, crown usually irregular . . . . *white pine*

      4. Individual branches rarely very prominent, crown usually conical . . *eastern hemlock*

   3. Crowns open, oval (circular in plan view) . . . . *red pine*

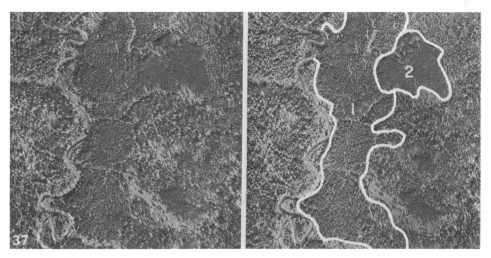

FIGURE 11-3. Summer panchromatic stereogram of (1) balsam fir and (2) black spruce in Ontario. Scale is 1,320 feet per inch. Courtesy of V. Zsilinszky, Ontario Department of Lands and Forests.

FIGURE 11-4. Summer panchromatic stereogram of (1) aspen-white birch and (2) young beech stand in Ontario. Scale is 1,320 feet per inch. Courtesy of V. Zsilinszky, Ontario Department of Lands and Forests.

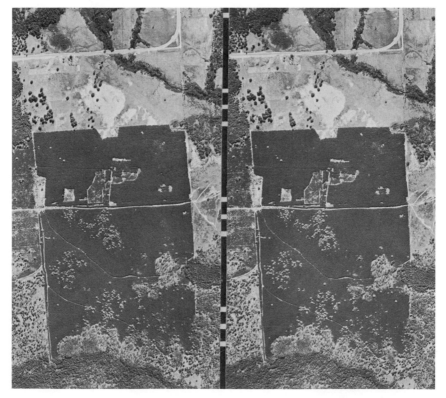

FIGURE 11-5. Summer panchromatic stereogram of red pine plantation (dark crowns) in the lower peninsula of Michigan. Scale is 1,667 feet per inch. Courtesy of Abrams Aerial Survey Corp.

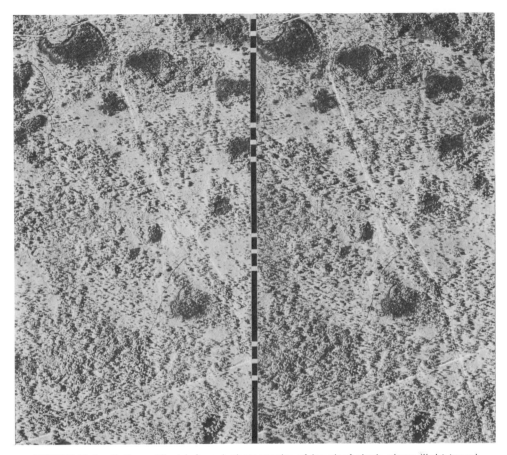

FIGURE 11-6. Fall modified infrared photography of longleaf-slash pines (light-toned crowns) in the Georgia coastal plain. The dark-toned, water-filled depressions are "ponds" of southern cypress. Scale is 1,320 feet per inch.

Vegetation keys for Anglo-American species are most easily constructed in northern and western forests where conifers predominate. In these regions, there are relatively few species to be considered and crown patterns are rather distinctive for each important group. By contrast, few reliable keys are available for the highly variable hardwood forests of southern and eastern United States. An excellent selective key to tree species in Ontario has been prepared by Zsilinszky (1966). Another high-quality key, designed for use with large-scale color photographs, has been compiled by Heller, Doverspike, and Aldrich (1964). Selected examples of tree species that may be identified on panchromatic stereograms are shown in *Figures 11-10* through *11-13.*

Preparing Forest Cover-Type Maps

The first step in the preparation of a forest cover map is the selection or compilation of a suitable planimetric base map. These procedures have been summarized in Chapter 8. The base map should be drawn to the approximate scale of the aerial photographs used for interpreting cover types; in this way, the subsequent transfer of detail from photographs to the map will be greatly simplified. All drainage and cultural features should be shown by use of standard mapping symbols *(Figure 11-14).*

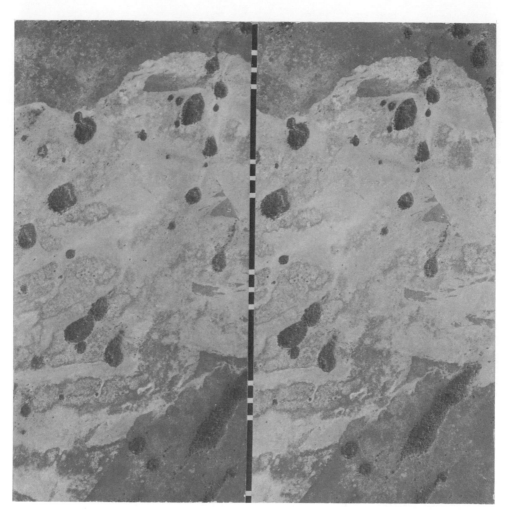

FIGURE 11-7. Panchromatic stereogram from the Everglades in Dade County, Florida. Occasional "hammocks" of hardwood trees on higher ground appear as dark-toned islands in the great "river of grass." The lightest tones here are water areas, and the smooth, medium-gray tones represent sawgrass. Scale is 800 feet per inch. Courtesy of U.S. Department of Agriculture.

Forested areas are usually defined as those having a tree crown density of 10 percent or more. Areas of lower tree stocking, including windbreaks and timbered strips less than 100 feet wide, may be classed as plantable, nonstocked, or idle land. Other land classes often recognized are cultivated cropland, improved pasture, abandoned or fallow fields, orchards, vineyards, and open water. The minimum area typed may range from 3 to 20 acres, depending on photographic scale and value of the vegetative cover.

Cover-type classifications should first be delineated on contact prints with water-soluble ink or a china-marking pencil. Forest types are preferably designated according to numerical codes such as those recommended by the Society of American Foresters or the U.S. Forest Service. Tree height and stand density classes may also be recognized within each major cover-type group. As an alternative, timber stand sizes may be merely designated as sawtimber, cordwood, or seedling-saplings (*Figure 11-15*).

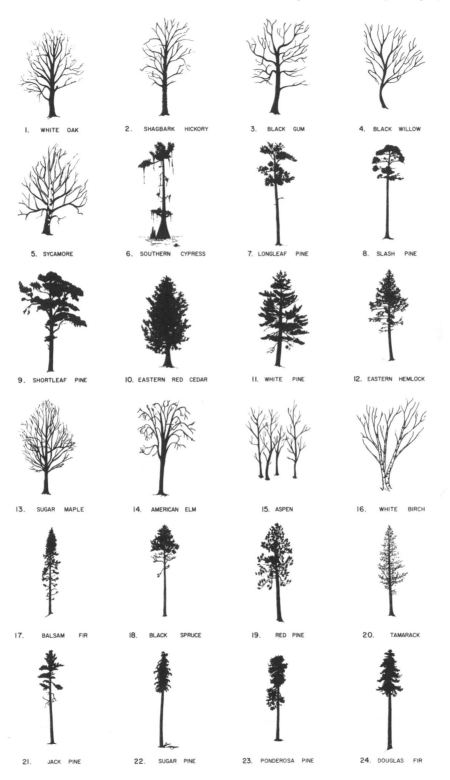

FIGURE 11-8. Silhouettes of 24 forest trees. When tree shadows fall on level ground, they often permit identification of individual species.

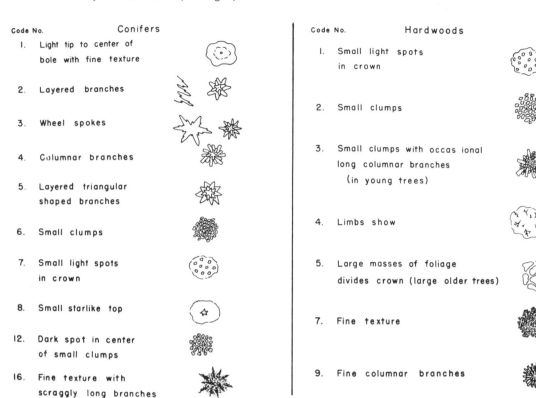

FIGURE 11-9. Sketches of overhead views of tree crowns for 14 boreal tree species. Courtesy of U.S. Forest Service Remote Sensing Project, Berkeley, California.

Where two-storied stands are regularly encountered, the fractional coding scheme suggested by Bernstein (1962) for Douglas-fir provides a ready solution. By this technique, codes designating the overstory comprise the numerator of the fraction, while understory descriptions are placed in the denominator. After all type lines and identifications have been verified by field checks, the transfer of detail to the base map can be accomplished with an instrument such as the vertical sketchmaster or Stereotope, as outlined in earlier sections.

The appearance of a finished cover-type map is improved by using lightly shaded colors or black-and-white tonal patterns to designate each cover type. The completed map is preferably drawn in black ink on good-quality vellum or frosted cellulose acetate at a scale approximating that of the contact prints. An inked border should be placed inside the trimmed edges of the sheet. Lettering and symbols should be neat, well-proportioned, and correctly placed for easy reading. The map should be oriented so that the top of the sheet represents due North.

Tree Crown Diameter

For most coniferous species and many hardwoods, tree crown diameter is related to stem diameter. It is a useful photographic measurement when estimating individual tree volumes or stand-size classes. Actual determination of crown diameter is simply a distance measurement, but it is somewhat complicated by the small sizes of tree images and the effects of crown shadows.

Crown diameters are measured with either wedges or dot-type scales reading in thousandths of an inch. With a crown wedge, the diverging lines are placed tangent to both sides of the crown for making the reading. Dot-type scales have circles of graduated sizes for direct comparison with the tree crowns *(Figure 11-16)*. For converting measurements, the scale of photography is calculated in feet per thousandth of an inch. At 1:20,000, each 0.001 inch of crown measure equals 1.667 feet. A reading of 0.010 inch would therefore imply a crown diameter of 17 feet *(Table 11-1)*.

Tree crowns are rarely circular, but, because individual limbs are often invisible on aerial photographs, they usually appear roughly circular or elliptical. Since only the portions visible from above can be evaluated, photo measures of crown diameter are often lower than ground checks of the same trees. Nevertheless, most interpreters can determine average crown diameter with reasonable precision if they take several readings and avoid bias in measurement.

TABLE 11-1.   Actual crown widths for various photo-crown widths and photo scales

Photo crown width (thousandths of an inch)	1:7,920 or 660 ft./in.	1:10,000 or 883 ft./in.	1:12,000 or 1,000 ft./in.	1:15,840 or 1,320 ft./in.	1:18,000 or 1,500 ft./in.	1:20,000 or 1,667 ft./in.
	- Feet -					
2.5	2	2	3	3	4	4
5.0	3	4	5	7	8	8
7.5	5	6	8	10	11	13
10.0	7	8	10	13	15	17
12.5	8	10	13	17	19	21
15.0	10	12	15	20	23	25
17.5	11	15	18	23	26	29
20.0	13	17	20	26	30	33
22.5	15	19	23	30	34	38
25.0	17	21	25	33	38	42
27.5	18	23	28	36	41	46
30.0	20	25	30	40	45	50
32.5	21	27	33	43	49	54
35.0	23	29	35	46	53	58
37.5	25	31	38	50	56	63
40.0	26	33	40	53	60	67
42.5	28	35	43	56	—	—
45.0	30	37	45	59	—	—
47.5	31	40	48	63	—	—
50.0	33	42	50	66	—	—

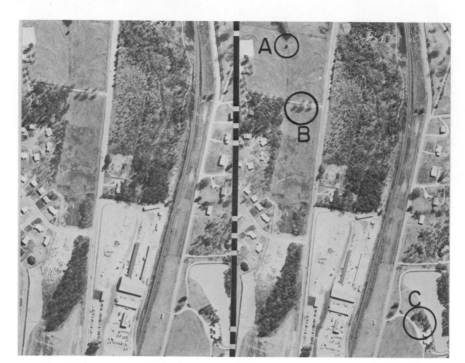

FIGURE 11-10. Winter stereogram taken near Charlotte, North Carolina showing distinctive tree shadows of eastern redcedar (A), oaks devoid of foliage (B), and shortleaf pines (C). Compare with drawings in Figure 11-8. Scale is about 1,320 feet per inch.

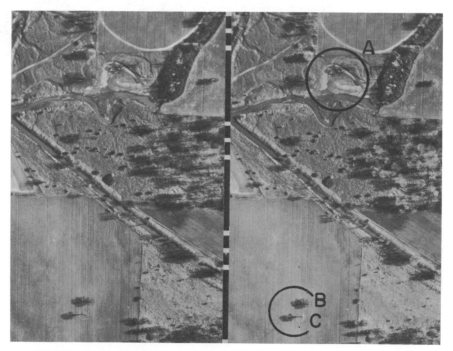

FIGURE 11-11. Winter stereogram taken near Grandville, Michigan picturing distinctive tree shadows of American elm (A and C), and oak (B). Compare with drawings in Figure 11-8. Scale is about 500 feet per inch.

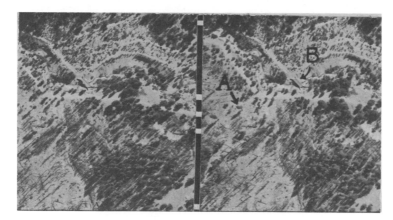

FIGURE 11-12. Stereogram from the Plumas National Forest, California illustrating the shadow pattern of a sugar pine (A). Compare with drawing in Figure 11-8. At "B" is an abandoned bridge with roadway approaches washed out by severe erosion. Scale is about 425 feet per inch.

Obviously, crown diameter measurements of individual trees are most accurate in open-grown stands. In dense stands, measurements are generally confined to determination of an average for the dominant trees. Crowns of mature conifers can usually be classified by 2 or 3-foot classes on large-scale photos (1:10,000 and larger) and by 5-foot classes on smaller scale prints.

Tree Crown Closure

Crown closure percent, also referred to as crown density, is the proportion of the forest canopy occupied by trees. The term may refer to all crowns in the stand regardless of canopy level or only to the dominants. Estimates are purely ocular, and stands are commonly grouped into 10-percent density classes. Comparative stereograms illustrating various levels of estimated crown densities have proved useful as training aids for inexperienced interpreters *(Figure 11-17)*.

Evaluation of crown closure is much more subjective than the determination of tree height or crown diameter. Actual measurement is virtually impossible on small-scale photographs, and accuracy is dependent on the interpreter's judgment. Inexperienced interpreters tend to overestimate closure by ignoring small stand openings or including portions of crown shadows. Devices for checking closure on the ground fail to provide estimates that are truly comparable to those made on vertical photographs. Thus the neophyte must rely on practice and checks by skilled interpreters as a means of developing his own proficiency.

Crown closure is useful because of its relation to stand volume per acre. It is applied in lieu of basal area or number of trees per acre, as these variables often cannot be determined on available photography. Measurements of crown diameter and estimates of closure should always be made under the stereoscope.

Complete numerical tallies of individual trees can seldom be made on small-scale photographs. In dense stands, suppressed trees and many intermediate stems cannot be seen. Clumps of two or three trees often appear as single crowns, and ragged individual crowns may look like two trees. Only in even-aged, open-grown forests can all trees in a stand be separated. Counting all trees on a plot is tedious, and this measure of density is seldom used. Where large-scale photographs are available, individual-tree counts may be much more reliable.

FIGURE 11-13. Stereo-triplet on 70mm. panchromatic film from the Superior National Forest, Minnesota. Species encircled are (1) balsam fir, (2) trembling aspen, (3) paper birch, (4) red maple, (5) white spruce, (6) red pine, and (7) white pine. Scale is about 132 feet per inch. Courtesy of U.S. Forest Service Remote Sensing Project, Berkeley, California.

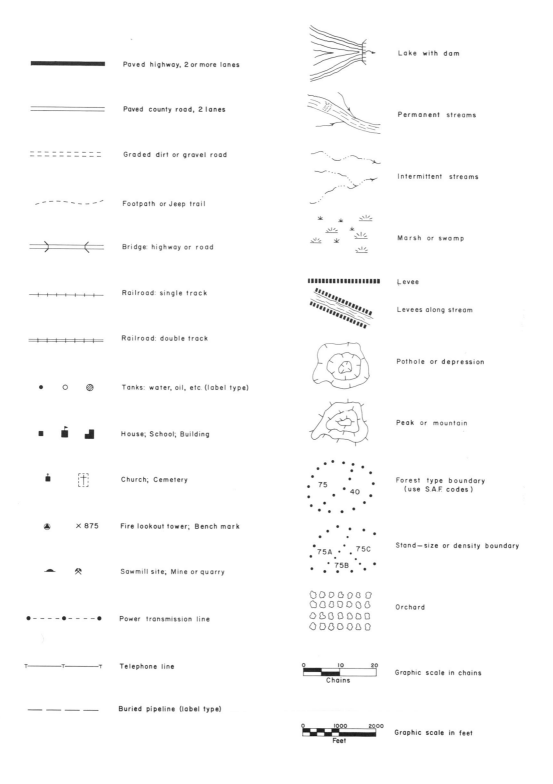

FIGURE 11-14. Mapping symbols commonly used by foresters.

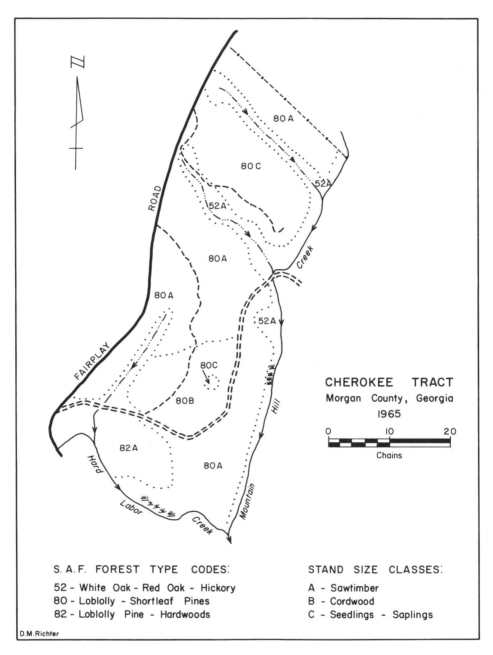

FIGURE 11-15. Simplified forest cover-type map compiled from aerial photographs.

FIGURE 11-16. Dot-type scale for measuring crown diameters. Such scales are usually printed on transparent film. Courtesy of U.S. Forest Service.

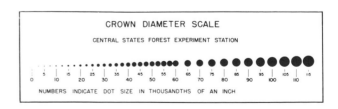

FIGURE 11-17. Infrared stereo-triplet from central Alaska showing estimates of tree crown closure. Scale is about 420 feet per inch; each circle represents approximately 0.25 acre. The solid black line indicates the path of the aircraft.

Individual Tree Volumes

Ordinary tree volume tables can be easily converted to aerial volume tables when correlations can be established between tree crown diameters and stem diameters. In applying this technique, photographic determinations of crown diameter and total tree height are merely substituted for the usual field measures of stem diameter (d.b.h.) and merchantable height, respectively *(Figure 11-18)*. Photographic measurements are usually limited to well-defined, open-grown trees, and crown counts are required to obtain total volume for a given stand of timber.

The construction and application of aerial tree volume tables depends on a well-established relationship between photographic measures of crown diameter and ground determinations of tree d.b.h. Such relationships can often be established for individual tree species or species groups, notably even-aged conifers in the middle diameter classes. By contrast, stem-crown diameter correlations rarely have been used for estimating volumes of individual hardwoods.

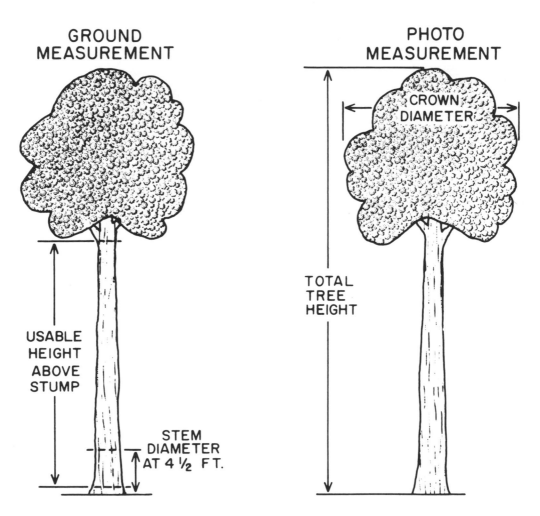

FIGURE 11-18. Comparison of ground and photographic measurements in the determination of individual tree volumes.

The aerial tree table included here *(Table 11-2)* provides volumes in terms of gross cubic feet. In making an aerial cruise, photographic measurements may include all trees on 0.2 to 1-acre circular plots, or stands may be delineated according to height classes for determination of the average tree per unit area. In the latter instance, a tree count must be made for obtaining the total stand volume.

In general, the individual-tree approach to aerial cruising is of limited value when the interpreter is restricted to photo scales smaller than 1:12,000. In such instances, images are usually too small to permit accurate assessment of individual trees.

Stand Volume Per Acre

If recent photographs and reliable aerial stand-volume tables can be obtained, average stand volume per acre can be estimated with a minimum of field work. Estimates are made in terms of gross volume, as amount of cull or defect cannot be adequately evaluated. Even-aged stands of simple species structure are best suited for this type of estimating, especially if gross and net volumes are essentially identical. All-aged stands of mixed hardwoods are

TABLE 11-2. Individual tree volume table for second-growth southern pines[1]

Crown diameter class (feet)	Total tree height in feet						
	50	60	70	80	90	100	110
	Tree volume in cubic feet						
10	9.5	11.5	12.5	15.0	17.5	19.5	
12	12.5	14.5	16.5	18.0	20.5	22.5	
14	15.0	17.0	19.0	23.5	25.0	27.5	30.5
16	17.5	20.5	24.0	27.5	30.5	33.0	36.0
18		23.5	27.0	30.5	34.5	38.0	42.5
20		28.0	33.5	36.0	40.0	45.5	49.0
22		32.5	37.0	42.5	46.5	52.0	57.5
24		37.0	42.5	48.5	54.5	60.0	66.0
26		42.5	47.5	54.0	61.0	67.5	75.5
28			53.0	60.5	70.5	76.0	83.0
30			60.5	68.0	78.0	85.5	94.5

[1] Based on 324 trees in Arkansas, Louisiana, and Mississippi. Gross volumes are inside bark and include the merchantable stem to a variable top averaging 6 inches i.b.

more difficult to assess, but satisfactory results can be obtained where field checks are made to adjust the photographic estimate of stand volume per acre and to determine allowance for defect. Though photo volumes cannot be expressed by species and diameter classes, total gross volumes for areas as small as 40 acres may be estimated within 10 to 15 percent of volumes derived from conventional ground cruises.

Most aerial stand-volume tables for mixed species are constructed in terms of cubic feet per acre. Tables for species occurring naturally in pure stands, such as Douglas-fir, may be expressed either in board feet or cubic feet per acre. Three photographic measurements of the dominant stand are generally required for entering an aerial stand volume table: average total height, crown diameter, and crown closure percent.

As indicated by the references following this chapter, aerial volume tables have been constructed for many of the important timber associations in the United States. Included here are composite tables for northeast Mississippi *(Table 11-3)* and for northern Minnesota *(Table 11-4)*. In the Minnesota table, crown diameter has been eliminated as a variable, and only measurements of stand height and crown density are required. One of several procedures for making aerial volume estimates is as follows:

1. Outline tract boundaries on the photographs, utilizing the effective area of every other print in each flight line. This assures stereoscopic coverage of the area on a minimum number of photographs and avoids duplication of measurements.

2. Delineate all forest types. Except where type lines define stands of relatively uniform stocking and total height, they should be further broken down into homogeneous units so that measures of height, density, and crown diameter will apply to the entire unit. Generally, it is unnecessary to recognize stands smaller than 5 to 10 acres.

3. Determine the acreage of each condition class with dot grids. This determination can often be made on contact prints.

4. By stereoscopic examination, measure the variables for entering the aerial stand volume table. From the table, obtain the average volume per acre for each condition class.

5. Multiply gross volumes per acre from the table by condition class areas to determine gross volume.

6. Add class volumes for the total gross volume on the tract.

Adjusting Photo Volumes by Field Checks

When aerial volume tables are not sufficiently reliable for acceptance of pure photo estimates and allowance must be made for defective trees, some of the plots interpreted should be selected for field measurement. For example, if 350 plots were interpreted and every tenth plot selected, 35 plots would be visited in the field. If the field volumes averaged 600 cubic feet per acre as opposed to 800 cubic feet per acre for the photo plots, the adjustment ratio would be $600 \div 800$ or 0.75. If the 35 field plots are representative of the total, the ratio can be applied to the average photo volume per acre to determine the adjusted volume. It is desirable to compute ratios by forest types, because hardwoods are likely to require larger adjustments than conifers.

The accuracy of aerial cruises depends not only upon the volume tables but on the availability of recent photographs and the interpreter's ability to make photo measurements correctly. This last item may be the greatest single source of error. It is advisable to measure each photo variable twice for an average, or two interpreters should assess each plot.

**TABLE 11-3.   Composite aerial volume table for northeast Mississippi
(In cubic feet per acre[1])**

Average stand height (feet)	Crown closure percent								
	15	25	35	45	55	65	75	85	95
10-FOOT AVERAGE CROWN DIAMETER									
30	190	310	430	560	690	810	940	1,060	1,180
40	230	380	530	690	840	990	1,140	1,300	1,450
50	260	440	620	800	980	1,150	1,330	1,510	1,680
60	300	500	690	890	1,090	1,290	1,490	1,680	1,880
70	340	570	800	1,030	1,260	1,490	1,720	1,950	2,180
80	380	640	890	1,140	1,400	1,650	1,910	2,160	2,420
15-FOOT AVERAGE CROWN DIAMETER									
30	210	350	500	640	780	930	1,070	1,220	1,360
40	260	430	610	780	950	1,130	1,300	1,480	1,650
50	310	510	730	930	1,140	1,350	1,550	1,770	1,970
60	360	590	930	1,070	1,300	1,550	1,780	2,030	2,260
70	400	660	940	1,200	1,460	1,740	2,000	2,280	2,540
80	440	740	1,040	1,330	1,620	1,930	2,220	2,530	2,820
90	480	800	1,140	1,450	1,770	2,100	2,420	2,760	3,070
20-FOOT AVERAGE CROWN DIAMETER									
40	270	450	630	820	1,000	1,190	1,370	1,550	1,720
50	320	540	750	970	1,190	1,410	1,630	1,840	2,040
60	360	610	860	1,110	1,360	1,600	1,850	2,100	2,330
70	410	680	960	1,240	1,520	1,800	2,080	2,360	2,610
80	450	760	1,070	1,380	1,690	2,000	2,310	2,620	2,900
90	500	840	1,190	1,530	1,870	2,220	2,560	2,900	3,220
100	540	920	1,290	1,670	2,040	2,410	2,790	3,160	3,500
25-FOOT AVERAGE CROWN DIAMETER									
50	320	550	770	1,000	1,220	1,450	1,670	1,900	2,120
60	370	620	880	1,130	1,390	1,650	1,900	2,160	2,410
70	410	700	980	1,270	1,550	1,840	2,130	2,410	2,700
80	460	780	1,100	1,420	1,740	2,060	2,380	2,700	3,020
90	510	860	1,220	1,570	1,930	2,280	2,640	2,990	3,350
100	550	940	1,320	1,710	2,090	2,480	2,860	3,250	3,630

[1] Based on Girard form class 77. Gross volumes are inside bark and include the merchantable stem to a variable top not smaller than 3 inches i.b.

TABLE 11-4. Composite aerial volume table for northern Minnesota[1]
(In cubic feet per acre[2])

Average total height (feet)	Crown closure, in percent									
	5	15	25	35	45	55	65	75	85	95
30	40	120	200	280	360	440	520	600	680	760
35	80	190	300	410	520	630	740	850	960	1,070
40	180	310	440	570	700	830	960	1,090	1,220	1,350
45	460	590	720	850	980	1,110	1,240	1,370	1,500	1,630
50	740	870	1,000	1,130	1,260	1,390	1,520	1,650	1,780	1,910
55	1,020	1,150	1,280	1,410	1,540	1,670	1,800	1,930	2,060	2,190
60	1,300	1,430	1,560	1,690	1,820	1,950	2,080	2,210	2,340	2,470
65	1,580	1,710	1,840	1,970	2,100	2,230	2,360	2,490	2,620	2,750
70	1,860	1,990	2,120	2,250	2,380	2,510	2,640	2,770	2,900	3,030
75	2,140	2,270	2,400	2,530	2,660	2,790	2,920	3,050	3,180	3,310
80	2,420	2,550	2,680	2,810	2,940	3,070	3,200	3,330	3,460	3,590
85	2,700	2,830	2,960	3,090	3,220	3,350	3,480	3,610	3,740	3,870
90	2,980	3,110	3,240	3,370	3,500	3,630	3,760	3,890	4,020	4,150
95	3,260	3,390	3,520	3,650	3,780	3,910	4,040	4,170	4,300	4,430
100	3,540	3,670	3,800	3,930	4,060	4,190	4,320	4,450	4,580	4,710

[1] Based on fifty 1-acre plots in Carlton County, Minn. Heavy lines indicate limits of basic data.

[2] Gross volumes are inside bark and include all trees 5.0 inches d.b.h. and larger from stump to a variable top diameter not less than 4.0 inches i.b. Volumes may be converted to rough cords per acre by dividing by 80.

Photo Stratification for Ground Cruising

A photo-controlled ground cruise combines the features of aerial and ground estimating, offering a means of obtaining timber volumes with maximum efficiency. Photographs are used for area determination, for allocation of field samples by forest type and stand-size classes, and for designing the pattern of field work. Tree volumes, growth, cull percents, form class, and other data are obtained on the ground by conventional methods. A photo-controlled cruise may increase the efficiency and reduce the total cost of an inventory on tracts as small as 100 acres.

The approach to an inventory of this kind is largely dependent on the types of strata recognized and the method of allocating field samples. The total number of field sample units to be measured is determined by cost considerations or by the statistical precision required. Once the number has been determined, there are several ways in which the samples may be distributed among various photo classifications:

1. By area of each class. Though sometimes used, this method is often unsatisfactory because stands of low value occupy the greatest acreage, while high-value stands may be insufficiently sampled. The opposite extreme may result if value alone (volume-per-acre classes) is used.

2. By applying different cruising intensities to each class. A 20-percent cruise might be used for high-value stands, 10 percent for medium value, and 5 percent or less for low-value areas. This arbitrary method is better than using acreage alone, but it may not be the most economical and efficient.

3. By statistical methods. A preliminary cruise or a good estimate of the variability within each class must be made before the required number of plots per class can be computed. This approach is the best to use for large tracts, but it may be costly or unwieldy for small woodland areas.

4. By a combination of area and value (volume). This is the preferred approach for small areas. A suggested procedure follows:

Plot Allocation by Area and Volume

Assume that the tract area is 1,600 acres and that 400 field plots are to be distributed among three forest types (pine, pine-hardwood, and hardwood), and three volume classes within each type (5, 8, and 12 cords per acre).

1. Stratify each forest type into volume-per-acre classes on the basis of personal experience or with aerial stand-volume tables. Precision is not required, as the volume classes are used only as a guide. Tabulate by type and acreage:

Cords per acre	Pine (Acres)	Pine-hardwood (Acres)	Hardwood (Acres)
5	120	200	100
8	100	500	350
12	80	100	50
Totals	300	800	500

2. Multiply the number of acres in each class by the cord volume per acre. The product is the number of cords per class:

Pine	Pine-hardwood	Hardwood
$5 \times 120 = 600$	$5 \times 200 = 1,000$	$5 \times 100 = 500$
$8 \times 100 = 800$	$8 \times 500 = 4,000$	$8 \times 350 = 2,800$
$12 \times 80 = 960$	$12 \times 100 = 1,200$	$12 \times 50 = 600$
Totals $= 2,360$	$6,200$	$3,900$

3. Add the cordage in each class to get the total for the entire area: $2,360 + 6,200 + 3,900 = 12,460$ cords. Divide by the number of plots to get the number of cords to be represented by each plot: $\dfrac{12,460}{400} = 31.15$ cords per plot

4. Divide the volume for each class (Item 2) by the cord volume per plot to get the number of plots assigned to each class. Round to the nearest whole number. Add the plots for each class to make sure the total (400) is correct.

Pine	Pine-hardwood	Hardwood
$\dfrac{600}{31.15} = 19.26 \ (19)$	$\dfrac{1,000}{31.15} = 32.10 \ (32)$	$\dfrac{500}{31.15} = 16.05 \ (16)$
$\dfrac{800}{31.15} = 25.68 \ (26)$	$\dfrac{4,000}{31.15} = 128.41 \ (128)$	$\dfrac{2,800}{31.15} = 89.88 \ (90)$
$\dfrac{960}{31.15} = 30.82 \ \underline{(31)}$	$\dfrac{1,200}{31.15} = 38.52 \ \underline{(39)}$	$\dfrac{600}{31.15} = 19.26 \ \underline{(19)}$
Plot totals (76)	(199)	(125)

Arrangement of Ground Samples

If type boundaries have been accurately delineated and stands are homogeneous within the recognized classes, field plots can sometimes be taken along routes of easy travel without introducing much bias. Usually, though, it is necessary to lay out line-plot or strip cruises at right angles to topography. The cruise lines should be drawn to scale on a type map in such a way that the required number of samples within each class can be obtained. The number of plots or chains of strip that a crew can complete per day is the basis for calculating the lengths of the lines. To minimize travel, lines may be triangular or U-shaped, beginning and ending near the same starting point on a road or trail. Compass bearings and distances can be determined on the map to avoid location bias in the field. The cruise lines can then be placed on the photographs for use in the field, if desired.

Field measurements are taken by conventional procedures. Cumulative tally sheets or point-sampling may be employed to speed up the tree tally. After the cordage per acre for each volume class has been determined by field sampling, the values are multiplied by the appropriate stand acreages. The result is the total volume on the tract, by forest types:

PINE TYPE

Assumed volume class (cords per acre)	Field plots (number)	Field volumes per acre (cords)	Type area (acres)	Volume per class (cords)
5	19	3.9	120	468.0
8	26	8.2	100	820.0
12	31	11.3	80	904.0
Totals	76		300	2,192.0

PINE-HARDWOOD TYPE

5	32	5.8	200	1,160.0
8	128	7.7	500	3,850.0
12	39	14.1	100	1,410.0
Totals	199		800	6,420.0

HARDWOOD TYPE

5	16	4.7	100	470.0
8	90	8.6	350	3,010.0
12	19	13.5	50	675.0
Totals	125		500	4,155.0

Special Uses of Photographic Coverage

Foresters have long used aerial photographs in various activities related to the prevention and control of wildfires. The potential fire danger in a given locality can be predicted by intensive analyses of seasonal changes in plant cover. These "forest fuels" are readily mapped by timing special photographic flights at known periods of critical fire danger.

Presuppression activities include aerial photo searches for reliable sources of water during expected drought periods. Advance photographic coverage also provides information on existing fire lines and makes it feasible to lay out new lines and timber access routes prior to the occurrence of wildfires *(Figure 11-19)*. Woodlands subject to heavy use by

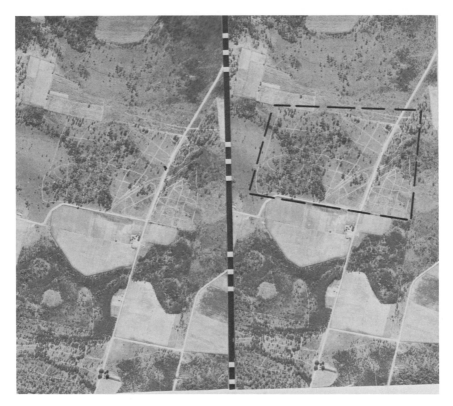

FIGURE 11-19. Irregular pattern of plowed fire lines designed to protect a stand of southern pines in the Georgia coastal plain. Scale is 1,320 feet per inch.

recreationists, campers, hunters, and fishermen are sometimes critical fire danger spots, and these areas can be regularly monitored by means of up-to-date aerial photographs. The detection of wildfires by thermal imagery techniques has been previously discussed in Chapter 9.

Special-purpose photography may also be used to advantage by foresters in estimating timber volumes removed during harvesting operations or in assessing logging damage to residual stands of timber. In *Figure 11-20,* for example, individual tree stumps may be counted and merchantable logs that were removed may be estimated by measuring photo distances between paired stumps and undisturbed tree tops. The shadows reveal that stumps were cut rather high—probably an indication of the predominace of swell-butted bottomland hardwood species. It will also be noted that the stand was rather heavily cut and that subsequent flooding of the river flat will probably result in severe soil erosion.

Inventories of Floating Roundwood

Cut roundwood being rafted down rivers, towed in booms, or stored in ponds can be inventoried with fair success from large-scale aerial photographs. A sampling technique for counting floating pulpwood sticks has been reported by Young, Laverty, and Stoeckeler (1956). The recommended procedure consisted of counting individual sticks of wood on a number of sample "plots" randomly located in water storage areas. A Kelsh plotter was then used to delineate the water storage areas, and acreages were determined by planimetry

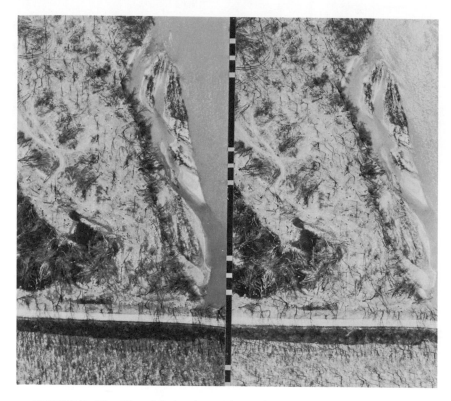

FIGURE 11-20. Site of timber-harvesting operation near Newcomerstown, Ohio. Individual tree stumps and residual tops are discernible. It is also evident that the river flat has been subjected to periodic flooding in the past. Scale is 250 feet per inch. Courtesy of Abrams Aerial Survey Corp.

to permit expansion of the plot estimates. As a result of the study, it was concluded that the clarity or sharpness of the photographic image was the major factor affecting the precision of pulpwood stick counts.

Photography flown especially for making inventories of floating roundwood should be taken when water areas are calm and when floating timber is spread out in a single layer. When roundwood is piled high in several layers or covered by snow and ice, reliable counts are virtually impossible. The extremes in seasonal photographic coverage of floating roundwood are illustrated by *Figures 11-21* and *11-22*.

References

Avery, T. Eugene.
> 1967. *Forest Measurements.* McGraw-Hill Book Co., New York, N.Y., 290 pp., illus.

_____.
> 1966. Identifying forest vegetation on aerial photographs. Sixth World Forestry Congress, Madrid, Spain, 7 pp.

_____.
> 1960. Identifying southern forest types on aerial photographs. U.S. Forest Serv., Southeastern Forest Exp. Sta., Station Paper 112, 12 pp., illus.

_____.
> 1958. Composite aerial volume table for southern pines and hardwoods. Jour. Forestry 56: 741-745, illus.

_____ and Meyer, Merle P.
> 1959. Volume tables for aerial timber estimating in northern Minnesota. U.S. Forest Serv., Lake States Forest Expt. Sta., Station Paper 78, 21 pp., illus.

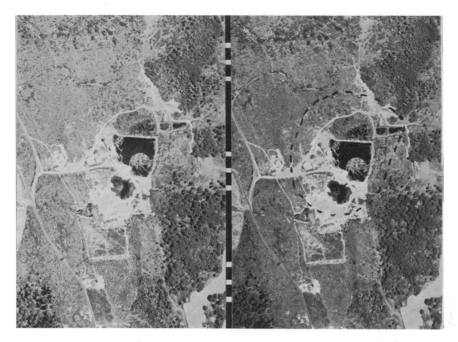

FIGURE 11-21.   Sawmill storage pond for logs in Lewis County, Washington. Average log length and a reliable log count can be determined from such photography. Scale is 500 feet per inch. Courtesy of Northern Pacific Railroad.

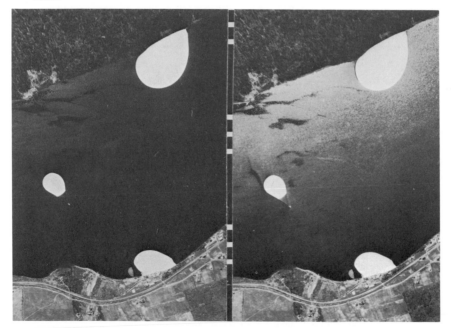

FIGURE 11-22.   Storage of floating roundwood along river banks in Aroostook County, Maine. A boom of wood is also being towed across the river. The mantle of snow and ice on the wood prohibits a reliable inventory. Scale is about 1,667 feet per inch. Courtesy of U.S. Department of Agriculture.

Bernstein, David A.
1962. Guide to two-story forest type mapping in the Douglas-fir subregion. U.S. Forest Serv., Pacific Northwest Region, 15 pp., illus.

Bonner, G. M.
1966. Provisional aerial stand volume tables for selected forest types in Canada. Forest Research Branch, Canada Dept. of Forestry, Pub. 1175, 24 pp., illus.

_____.
1964. A tree volume table for red pine by crown width and height. Forestry Chron. 40:339-346.

Carnegie, David M., Draeger, William C., and Lauer, Donald T.
1966. The use of high altitude color and spectrozonal imagery for the inventory of wildland resources. NASA report, University of California, Berkeley. Vol. I, 41 pp., Vol. II, 23 pp., Vol. III, 42 pp., illus.

Croxton, Ralph J.
1966. Detection and classification of ash dieback on large-scale color aerial photographs. U.S. Forest Service, Pacific Southwest Forest and Range Expt. Sta., Res. Paper PSW-35, 13 pp., illus.

Dill, Henry W.
1963. Airphoto analysis in outdoor recreation: site inventory and planning. Photogram. Engineering 29:67-70, illus.

Heller, Robert C.
1966. The use of multispectral sensing techniques to detect ponderosa pine trees under stress from insect or pathogenic organisms. NASA report, U.S. Forest Serv., Pacific Southwest Forest and Range Expt. Sta., 60 pp., illus.

_____, Doverspike, G. E., and Aldrich, R. C.
1964. Identification of tree species on large-scale panchromatic and color aerial photographs. U.S. Department of Agriculture Handbook 261, Government Printing Office, Washington, D.C., 17 pp., illus.

Hindley, Earle, and Smith, J. Harry G.
1957. Spectrophotometric analysis of some British Columbia conifers. Photogram. Engineering 23:894-895.

Jurdant, Michel.
1964. Photo interpretation and forest land classification. Forest Research Branch, Canada Dept. of Forestry, 7 pp., illus.

Kippen, F. W., and Sayn-Wittgenstein, L.
1964. Tree measurements on large-scale, vertical 70-mm. air photographs. Forest Research Branch, Canada Dept. of Forestry, Pub. 1053, 16 pp., illus.

Lauer, Donald T.
1966. The feasibility of identifying forest species and delineating major timber types in California by means of high altitude small scale aerial photography. NASA report, University of California, Berkeley, unpaginated, illus.

Lutz, H. J., and Caporaso, A. P.
1958. Indicators of forest land classes in airphoto interpretation of the Alaska Interior. U.S. Forest Serv., Alaska Forest Research Center, 31 pp., illus.

Minor, C. O.
1951. Stem-crown diameter relations in southern pine. Jour. Forestry 49:490-493, illus.

Moessner, Karl E.
1964. Two aerial photo basal area tables. U.S. Forest Serv., Intermountain Forest and Range Expt. Sta., Res. Note INT-23, 7 pp.

_____.
1957. Preliminary aerial volume tables for conifer stands in the Rocky Mountains. U.S. Forest Serv., Intermountain Forest and Range Expt. Sta., Res. Paper 41, 17 pp., illus.

_____.
1951. Aerial volume tables for hardwood stands in the Central States. U.S. Forest Serv., Central States Forest Expt. Sta., Tech. Paper 122, 15 pp., illus.

Pope, Robert B.
1962. Constructing aerial photo volume tables. U.S. Forest Serv., Pacific Northwest Forest and Range Expt. Sta., Res. Paper 49, 25 pp., illus.

Sayn-Wittgenstein, L.
1967. Tree volumes from large-scale photos. Photogram. Engineering 33:69-73, illus.

_____.
1961. Phenological aids to species identification on air photographs. Forest Research Branch, Canada Dept. of Forestry, Tech. Note 104, 26 pp., illus.

_____.
1960. Recognition of tree species on air photographs by crown characteristics. Forest Research Branch, Canada Dept. of Forestry, Tech. Note 95, 56 pp., illus.

Seely, H. E.
1964. Canadian forest inventory methods. Forest Research Branch, Canada Dept. of Forestry, Pub. 1068, 11 pp., illus.

Smith, J. Harry G.
1957. Problems and potential uses of photomensurational techniques for estimation of volume of some immature stands of Douglas-fir and western hemlock. Photogram. Engineering 23:595-599.

Society of American Foresters.
1954. Forest cover types of North America, exclusive of Mexico. Committee on Forest Types, Washington, D.C., 68 pp., illus.

Tomlinson, Roger F., and Brown, W. George.
1962. The use of vegetation analysis in the photo interpretation of surface material. Photogram. Engineering 28: 584-592, illus.

Wear, John F.
1966. The development of spectro-signature indicators of root disease on large forest areas. NASA report U.S. Forest Serv., Pacific Southwest Forest and Range Expt. Sta., 24 pp., illus.

Weber, F. P.
1966. Multispectral imagery for species identification. NASA report, U.S. Forest Serv., Pacific Southwest Forest and Range Expt. Sta., 37 pp., illus.

Wile, B. C.
1964. Crown size and stem diameter in red spruce and balsam fir. Forest Research Branch, Canada Dept. of Forestry, Pub. 1056, 9 pp., illus.

Young, H. E., Laverty, R. E.,
and Stoeckeler, E. G.
1965. Airphoto inventory of pulpwood in water storage. Photogram. Engineering 22:696-702, illus.

Zsilinszky, Victor G.
1966. Photographic interpretation of tree species in Ontario, 2nd ed., rev. Ontario Dept. Lands and Forests, 86 pp., illus.

_____.
1964. The practice of photo interpretation for a forest inventory. Paper presented at International Congress of Photogrammetry, Lisbon, Portugal. Photogrammetria 19(5), 18 pp., illus.

CHAPTER 12

Landforms and Physiographic Features

Applications of Photogeology

The use of aerial photographs to obtain both qualitative and quantitative geologic information is referred to as photogeology. Geologists commonly use photographs for structural mapping, fuel and mineral exploration, and general engineering surveys. Geologic interpretation is based on the fundamental recognition elements of photographic tone, color, texture, pattern, relationships of associated features, shape, and size. Although oblique photographs are often of value to the photogeologist, most detailed analyses make use of vertical photography.

The quantity of geologic information that can be obtained from aerial photographs is dependent on the type of terrain, climatic environment, and stage of the geomorphic cycle. Because features are more readily recognized where strong differences exist in the erosional resistance of adjacent rocks, sedimentary terrain may be expected to yield the greatest amount of information from aerial photographs. Metamorphic terrain may yield the least information, because metamorphic processes tend to destroy differences that may have existed in the unmetamorphosed rocks.

In petroleum exploration, aerial photographs provide a wealth of information with regard to potential structural traps. Folds may be interpreted from a study of strike and dip of bedding or from stream patterns. Anomalous stream characteristics, such as deflections, may suggest subsurface structures. The variety of photographic criteria that suggests faults permits aerial photographs to be of particular use in ore-deposit studies. Analysis of soil patterns yields information regarding permeability of the surficial materials that are a concern of the engineering geologist (Ray, 1960).

Although detailed analyses of geomorphology and stratigraphy require professional training in geology, skilled interpreters may develop a high degree of proficiency in recognizing broad lithologic units and identifying distinctive landforms or surface features *(Figure 12-1)*. Thus the objective of this chapter is to provide the nongeologist with a simple introduction to the study of landforms and physiographic features through a series of aerial photographic examples. The serious student of photography should supplement this material by studying additional texts on physiography and geomorphology, such as those listed at the end of this chapter.

Lithologic Units

It is usually valuable for the interpreter to be able to classify rock with respect to its general geologic type; that is, whether the rock was formed directly from a molten mass

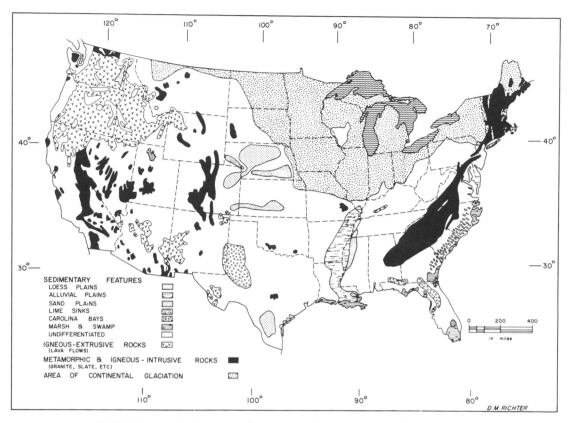

FIGURE 12-1. Distinctive surface features in conterminous United States.

(igneous), by deposition of rock grains transported by water or wind (sedimentary), or by the action of heat or pressure on previously existing rock (metamorphic). Landforms composed of these rock classes often show up with striking clarity on aerial photographs; in many instances, key physiographic signatures will reveal their lithologic composition to the practiced interpreter.

Igneous surface materials that may be directly recognized or identified by inference include granite, basalt, lava flows, volcanic glass (obsidian), and pumice. In the case of sedimentary materials, it may be possible to recognize gypsum sand, quartz sand, sandstone, dolomite, and limestone deposits. Shale is the principal metamorphic rock that is commonly observed, although the presence of such rocks as marble may be detected in open quarries. Simple inferences regarding surficial deposits can be of considerable economic importance to the engineering geologist in search of materials such as sand or gravel for construction purposes *(Figure 12-2)*.

Strike and Dip Determinations

Patterns of fractures, faults, and dikes, usually discernible on aerial photographs, are important in mineralogical exploration. Inclined beds of sedimentary rock may also reveal structural anomalies that indicate possible mineral deposits. On good-quality photographs of the proper scale, it is possible to obtain quantitative information on tilted sedimentary beds by direct measurements of dip (the angle of a geologic surface with respect to the horizontal) and strike (the bearing of the line of intersection of an inclined geologic surface

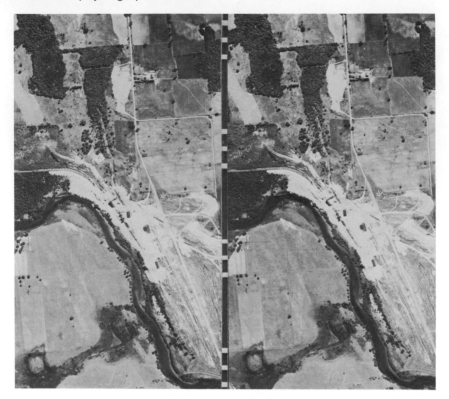

FIGURE 12-2. A knowledge of the depositional characteristics of flowing streams led to the discovery of this sand deposit along a Michigan river. Scale is about 1,667 feet per inch.

with the horizontal). Stated in another way, dip is the *angle* in which the inclined bed disappears beneath the ground, and strike is the *true compass bearing* of a line along the edge of the exposed dipping bed *(Figure 12-3)*.

In some instances, the direction of the dip angle is also required for a complete description of the plane of contact between rock bodies. As stated by Dort (1964), "Dip is the angle and direction down which a mine would be excavated in order to follow a layer of coal. The strike is the direction along which that layer of coal would be exposed across a flat field."

When bedding surfaces coincide with topographic surfaces, the dip angle can be determined by measuring the height difference between two points, one directly downslope from the other. Such height differences can be derived from measurements of stereoscopic parallax as described in Chapter 4. After determining the horizontal distance between the same two points, the dip angle can be computed by this trigonometric relationship:

$$\frac{\text{Vertical distance}}{\text{Horizontal distance}} = \text{tangent of dip angle}$$

If relief in an area is low, the horizontal distance may be scaled directly from a single photograph without significant error in computing the dip. However, when relief is moderate or high, a correction for the relief displacement of the upper point with respect to the lower point should be made. In the unique circumstance where the strike is radial from a photograph center, or the surface on which the dip to be measured is near a photograph center, there is little or no relief displacement in the dip direction, and no correction in scaling the horizontal distance need be made (Ray, 1960).

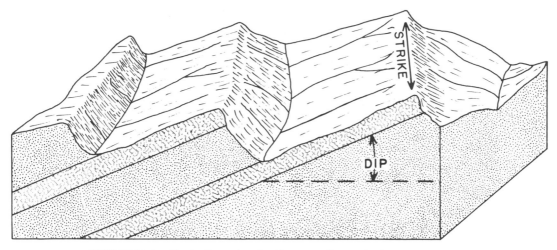

FIGURE 12-3. Illustration of strike line and dip angle for gently dipping beds of sedimentary rocks.

The strike line generally can be determined with a protractor by inspecting the stereo-scopic model and noting two points of equal altitude on a bed. Where dips are low, however, tilt in the photographs will affect the direction of strike. The lower the dip, the greater the effect on the change in azimuth of the strike line.

Analysis of Drainage Patterns

As pointed out in Chapter 10, the type of drainage pattern prevailing on a given land-form surface is often indicative of the kind of soil, parent material, and underlying lithologic structure. The absence of an integrated drainage system also provides information of significance. For example, the lack of a well-defined drainage network might indicate the presence of porous rock, such as basaltic lava, where surface water percolates downward to the water table through cracks and cavities. In other instances, soluble rocks such as limestone may absorb runoff through sinkholes and underground solution channels. And there are minor watersheds, such as dikes and drumlins, that may be too small to collect enough water for the establishment of a drainage pattern. Generally speaking, however, large landforms develop some detectable drainage system that approximates one of the types pictured earlier in *Figure 10-7*.

The dendritic or treelike pattern is a well-integrated pattern formed by the tributaries of a main stream as it branches and rebranches freely in all directions. This type of pattern implies that the area was originally flat and is composed of relatively uniform materials. Flat-lying beds of sedimentary rocks tend to develop dendritic drainage, along with glacial till, tidal marshes, and localized areas in sandy coastal plains. The difference in texture (density) of a dendritic pattern may aid in identifying the surficial material; granitic areas, for example, exhibit a fine-textured dendritic pattern with repetitious curving tributaries outlining circular, domelike hills. The tributaries, as a result of steep slopes in granite hills, join each other at right angles. They appear pincerlike on photographs.

The trellis pattern, which resembles a vine trellis, is characteristic of folded or dipping rocks. The trellis pattern is developed over tilted sedimentary beds, and results from rocks originally folded in parallel waves and then dissected. Parallel patterns are comprised of streams flowing side by side in the direction of the regional slope. The greater the slope, the more nearly parallel the drainage and the straighter the flow. Local areas of lava flows often have parallel drainage, even though the regional pattern may be radial. Alluvial fans may also exhibit parallel drainage, but the pattern may be locally influenced by faults or jointing. And coastal plains, because of their slope toward the sea, develop parallel drainage over broad regions.

Rectangular patterns, characterized by abrupt bends in streams, develop where a tree-like drainage pattern prevails over a broad region, but the pattern is locally influenced by faults, joints, or folds of rock. Metamorphic rock surfaces, particularly those comprised of schist and slate, commonly have rectangular drainage. Slate possesses a particularly fine-textured system. Its drainage pattern is extremely angular and has easily recognizable short gullies that are locally parallel.

Radial and centripetal patterns are characteristic of domes or depressions. For example, the sides of a dome or volcano might have a radial drainage system, while the pattern inside a volcanic cone or a dry lakebed (playa) might be centripetal, i.e., converging toward the center of the depression. Granitic dome drainage channels may follow a circular path around the base of the dome when it is surrounded by tilted beds. These channels form an annular pattern, which is a modified form of radial drainage.

No system of landform grouping or lithologic classification is perfectly suited for photo-geologic study. Any given photograph is likely to show two or more rock types, drainage patterns, structures, or depositional features. Therefore, it should be recognized that the classification scheme which follows is somewhat arbitrary and that other methods of grouping may also be appropriate:

Flat-Lying Sedimentary Rocks
Tilted Sedimentary Rocks
Igneous Rocks
Metamorphic Rocks
Fluvial Landforms

Beach Ridges and Tidal Flats
Glacial Landscapes
Eolian Features
Miscellaneous Landscapes

Flat-Lying Sedimentary Rocks

Sedimentary rocks are the most widely distributed surface materials in the world; as a result, they comprise the principal lithologic features seen on aerial photographs. Sedimentary rocks are originally deposited as horizontal beds, but they may later become tilted or inclined as a result of folding and faulting. As used in this section, flat-lying beds refer to those sedimentary deposits that are tilted no more than a few degrees. Sedimentary rocks are of three basic types: sandstone, limestone, and shale. Such materials were formed from water-deposited materials associated with lakes or oceans. Almost all igneous or metamorphic landforms are in contact with one or more kinds of sedimentary rock (*Figure 12-4*).

Sand grains originally deposited along shorelines and later cemented together have resulted in sandstone beds up to 20 feet thick in some parts of the world. Sandstone is a weather-resistant but porous material; as a consequence, the rock is a prime source of water in arid regions. The characteristic drainage pattern is dendritic to rectangular, depending on the presence of faults, fractures, and joints. Sandstone boundaries adjacent to lowland areas typically exhibit sharp, vertical cliffs because of the jointed but resistant qualities of the beds. When sandstone borders other sedimentary formations, the contact is commonly linear, because the more weather-resistant sandstone becomes a cap rock. Sandstone deposits photograph in light tones on panchromatic photographs due to the development of a thin mantle of sand and silt (*Figure 12-5*).

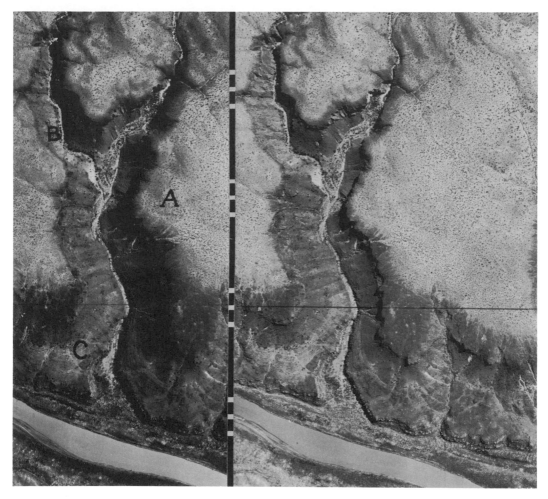

FIGURE 12-4. Basaltic lava flow (darkest tones) overlying gently dipping beds of sedimentary rock in New Mexico. Note semi-desert vegetation (A), joint-controlled rectangular drainage (B), and sedimentary beds in contact with lava cap rock (C). Scale is 500 feet per inch.

Shale is formed from the alternating deposition and compaction of waterborne silts and clays. Shale is an impervious rock, but it has low strength qualities and is easily eroded. Drainage patterns are typically dendritic, and stream courses are meandering. In humid regions, rounded hills are characteristic of shale deposits, and photographic tones are mottled because of variations in moisture and the presence of organic material. Shale topography in arid regions exhibits minutely dissected hills with steep slopes, light photographic tones, and streams that are usually well-entrenched in valley floors. Shale is commonly found as horizontal layers interbedded with sandstone or limestone *(Figure 12-6)*. Such formations result in a stairstepped topography that appears banded because of selective differences in vegetative growth.

Limestone is a sedimentary rock formed by the consolidation of calcareous shells of marine animals or by the chemical precipitation of calcium carbonate from sea water. Limestone plains are easily recognized by concentrations of circular sinkholes that result from underground solution in stream channels. Where beds of limestone are inclined, sinkholes are somewhat elliptical in shape and may be exposed along bedding planes.

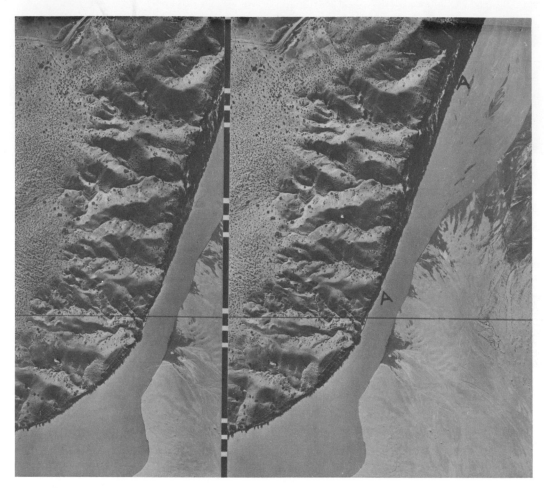

FIGURE 12-5. Rectangular-dendritic drainage pattern on flat-lying sandstone-shale beds along the Rio Grande in New Mexico. The sharp cliffs and unusually straight river channel (A) suggest that the shoreline is structurally controlled. Scale is 500 feet per inch.

Small amounts of water pass through these sinkholes, and, as solution takes place, an underground drainage system is developed. These underground channels are connected by vertical channels which show up as circular depressions on the surface *(Figure 12-7)*. Limestone areas are generally light-toned on photographs, except where sinkholes are water-filled. In well-developed limestone topography, there is little or no local surface drainage pattern, and few major streams are found.

Tilted Sedimentary Rocks

Horizontally deposited beds of sedimentary rock may become tilted or deformed through the development of faults and folds *(Figure 12-8)*. Tilted strata, especially when composed of two or more rock types, show up as a series of near-parallel, continuous or broken ridges that may be either closely spaced or separated by valleys. Ridges may be of any height, and they are likely to exhibit a steeper slope on one side than on the other *(Figure 12-9)*. In terms of weathering and erosion, sandstone appears as sharp ridges, shale is

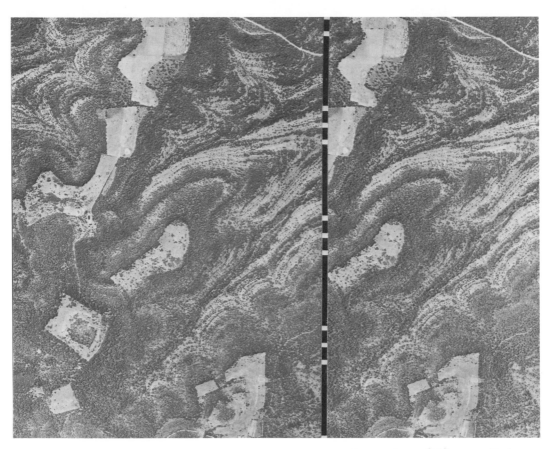

FIGURE 12-6. Flat-lying, interbedded sedimentary rocks in Baxter County, Arkansas. Dark bands supporting heavier vegetation are sandstone; lighter toned bands are mainly shale or limestone deposits. Surface drainage is not well developed, and few gullies are found. The cap rock is principally sandstone here. Scale is about 1,667 feet per inch.

typified by well-dissected valleys, and limestone topography has rounded hills and numerous sinkholes. Drainage systems usually form a trellis pattern, and large streams occur mainly in areas of shale deposits.

Alternating anticlines and synclines, along with parallel banding of rocks, are the chief identifying features of inclined, interbedded sedimentary rocks *(Figure 12-10)*. In humid climates, massive ridges indicate cap rocks of resistant sandstone; steep sides of ridges are usually covered by forest vegetation *(Figure 12-11)*. As a rule, ridges are more rounded in humid climates. In arid regions, ridge lines have sharper crests, and vegetative cover is confined to stream valleys or sandstone-limestone outcrops.

The contact zone between tilted sedimentary rocks and flat-lying beds takes the form of a transition area where dip angles vary from steep to gentle. By contrast, sedimentary contacts with igneous intrusions or faults are denoted by distinct, linear boundaries.

With flat-lying sedimentary rocks, stratigraphic thicknesses of exposed beds can be determined directly by measurements of stereoscopic parallax. If beds are inclined, however, the angle of dip must first be determined; then corrections must be made for relief displacement and for the effect of dip on the stratigraphic thickness.

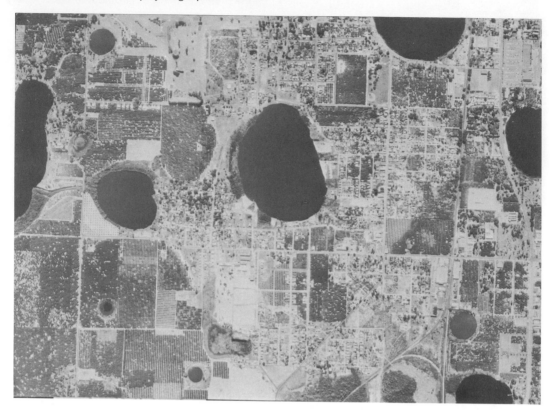

FIGURE 12-7. Rolling upland limestone ridge in Polk County, Florida. Numerous lakes (lime sinks) are found in this humid, sub-tropical "Karst" region devoted to citrus orchards. Scale is about 1,667 feet per inch.

Igneous Rocks

Igneous rocks are classed as being either intrusive or extrusive. Intrusive rocks are formed by molten materials that are slowly cooled and solidified within the earth's crust. These rocks, such as granite, diorite, and gabbro, may later be exposed by erosion of overlain surface materials and often appear as large domes or as narrow belts *(Figure 12-12)*.

Extrusive rocks are formed by the quick cooling and solidification of molten matter after it breaks through the earth's crust. This molten matter may flow over the surface, or it may be explosively ejected as fragments. Common types of extrusive rocks are basalt, rhyolite, andesite, and obsidian. Ejected fragments occur as volcanic ash or volcanic breccia.

Granite is one of the most frequently encountered intrusive rocks. Granitic surfaces, except for impermeable domes or jointed areas, have well-developed dendritic drainage patterns. Photographic tones are light in color, and the absence of stratification prevents confusion of granite with sedimentary rocks.

The most widely distributed extrusive rock is basaltic lava which is emitted from volcanic cones or fissures and flows over the adjacent surfaces as it cools and solidifies *(Figure 12-13)*. A basaltic lava landform was illustrated earlier by *Figure 12-4*; topography may be flat or hilly, and minor surface irregularities are common. Canyon-wall slopes are nearly vertical when breached by rivers, and both stratification and columnar jointing may be encountered. If a lava flow ends at an escarpment face or along a body of water, a distinct outline with serrated or ragged edges denotes the cliff boundary.

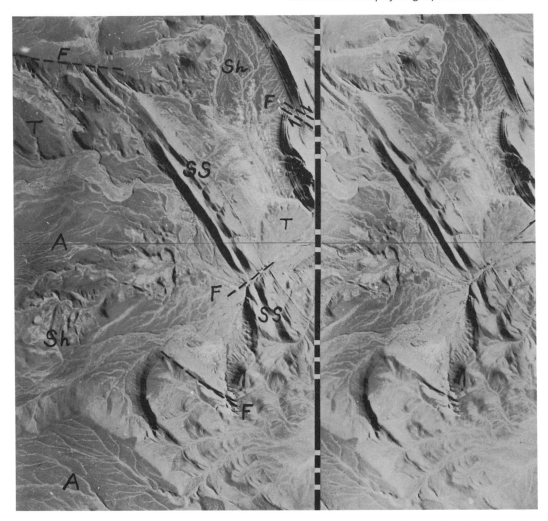

FIGURE 12-8. Inclined sedimentary rocks and fault zones in the Northern Sahara. Clearly discernible are sandstone "hogbacks" (SS), shale deposits (Sh), fault zones (F), alluvial fans (A), and terraces of granular deposits (T). Scale is about 3,300 feet per inch. Courtesy of U.S. Air Force.

On panchromatic aerial photographs, basaltic lava appears in very dark tones; regional drainage patterns are likely to be of the parallel type because of slopes developed during original flows. In areas of predominantly igneous rock, basaltic lava may form resistant dikes or sills that are easily traced on aerial photographs *(Figure 12-14)*.

Metamorphic Rocks

When diastrophic forces of extreme heat and pressure alter the chemical and structural composition of igneous or sedimentary rocks, the resultant materials are known as metamorphic rocks. Among the more common metamorphic rocks are gneiss, schist, and slate.

Gneiss has a chemical composition similar, but not identical, to granite. Component minerals have a laminated arrangement that produces a banded appearance in the rock. Drainage patterns are angularly dendritic as a result of fractures, foliation, and possibly glaciation. Gneiss formations characteristically exhibit highly dissected hills that may occur as roughly parallel ridges *(Figure 12-15)*.

FIGURE 12-9. Oblique view of gently dipping beds of sandstone and shales in the Atlas Mountains of Mauritania, North Africa. Shale valleys are eroded and partially covered with alluvium. Courtesy of U.S. Air Force.

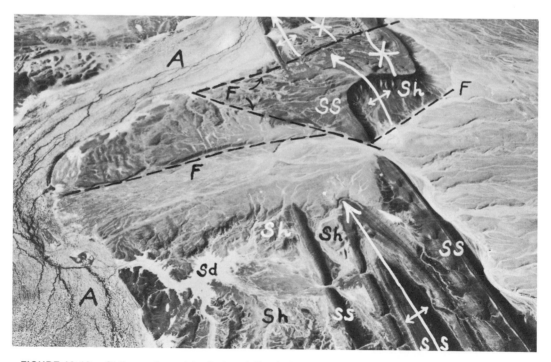

FIGURE 12-10. Oblique view of faulted anticline in North Africa. Note dark sandstone ridges (SS), shale with dendritic drainage (Sh), fault zones (F), alluvium (A), and sand (Sd). Courtesy of U.S. Air Force.

FIGURE 12-11. Escarpment face of a plunging syncline in a humid region (Logan County, Arkansas). Arrows indicate a water gap eroded through the relatively soft sediments by Petit Jean Creek. Scale is about 1,667 feet per inch.

FIGURE 12-12. Stone Mountain, Georgia, a granite exfoliation dome located 15 miles east of Atlanta. The monadnock is about seven miles in circumference and rises 1,200 feet above an ancient peneplain. Arrows indicate the location of an incomplete Civil War carving on the steepest side. Scale is about 1,667 feet per inch.

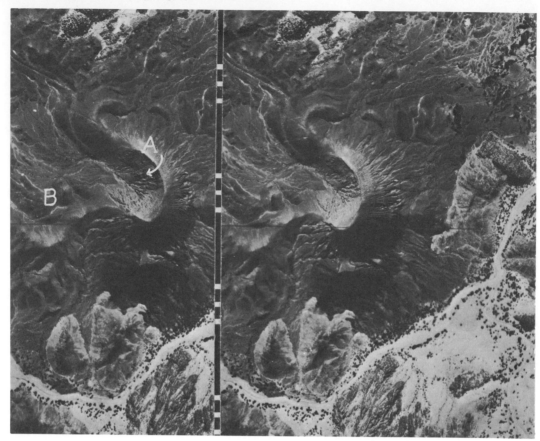

FIGURE 12-13. Inactive volcanic cone (A) breached by a subsequent basaltic lava flow (B). Note radial drainage pattern on side of cone. Location: Africa. Courtesy of U.S. Air Force.

Schist is a laminated rock largely composed of quartz, mica, and hornblende. In arid regions, these rock surfaces are likely to be weathered into jagged outcrops *(Figure 12-16)*. Covering soils may obscure the laminated structure in humid areas, but underlying schist formations may be revealed by a structurally controlled, rectangular drainage pattern. Parallel gullying is common on these easily eroded soils.

Slate is formed from metamorphosed shale. Topography is typically rugged in all climates, and the drainage pattern is rectangular and more highly developed than in shale or schist soils. Slate tends to photograph in a light-gray tone on panchromatic film.

Fluvial Landforms

As defined here, fluvial landforms refer to those features shaped by stream erosional and depositional processes. Included are floodplains, filled valleys, alluvial fans, and deltas.

Earlier illustrations *(Figures 10-10* and *10-17)* have depicted portions of the Mississippi alluvial valley. Meander floodplains are formed by streams subject to periodic flooding. During overflow periods, stream deposits on adjacent surfaces result in the formation of a broad plain of low relief. Such floodplains are characterized by channel scars, oxbow lakes, meander scrolls, slip-off slopes, and cut banks. This plain is composed of coarse materials. Streams flow in single channels during flood stages, but at low water they may flow in braided channels *(Figure 12-17)*.

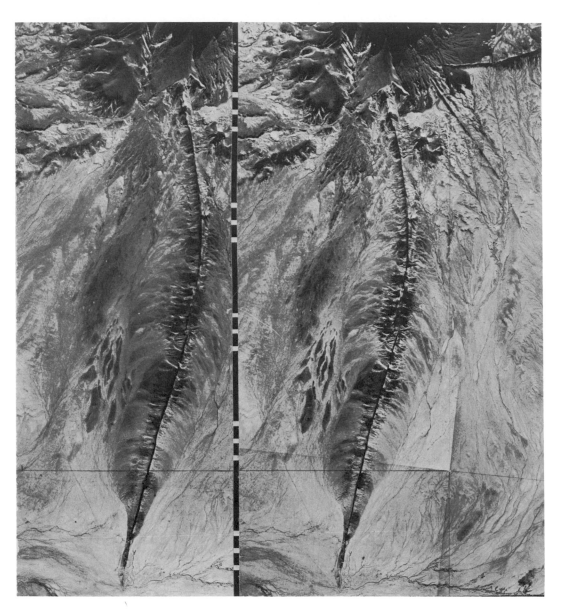

FIGURE 12-14. Large dike of basaltic lava radiating from Shiprock, an ancient volcanic structure in San Juan County, New Mexico. Scale is about 1,700 feet per inch. Courtesy of U.S. Department of Agriculture.

FIGURE 12-15. Oblique view of glaciated gneiss in Canada. Angular drainage, angular water boundaries, and parallel ridges serve to differentiate this metamorphic rock from granite.

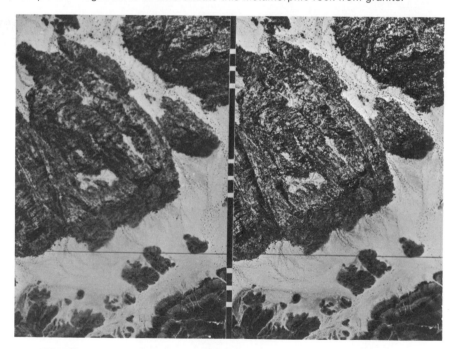

FIGURE 12-16. Dark-toned, laminated pattern of schists in Arabia. The sharp and rugged appearance results from alternating layers of hard and soft materials that are tilted upward, jointed, and weathered. Scale is about 3,300 feet per inch. Courtesy of U.S. Air Force.

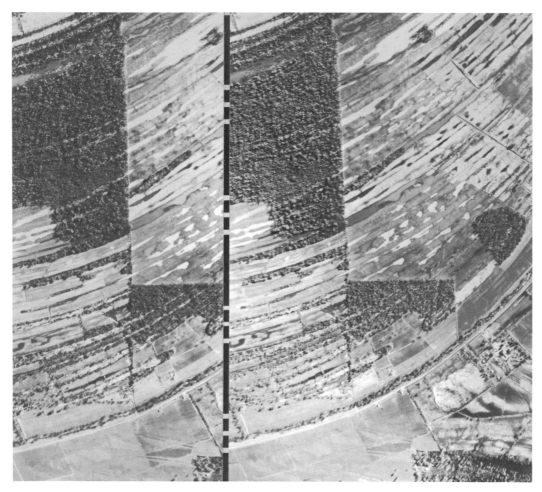

FIGURE 12-17. A series of filled-in river meander scars in Concordia Parish, Louisiana. This is a common pattern in floodplain areas such as the Mississippi Valley. Scale is about 1,850 feet per inch.

Covered plains are constructed by floods which build up deposits, primarily in a vertical dimension, and form natural levees, slack-water deposits, and backswamps. The deposited material is generally fine-grained and thick. The covered plains may form over a meander plain because of a change in flood type of the parent river.

Alluvial fans are formed by the action of running water when the velocity of a loaded stream is reduced and the coarser part of the stream load is deposited. This action results in a sloping, fan-shaped deposit. The head of the fan is at the mouth of the highland stream, and its borders spread out into surrounding flat zones. In arid and semi-arid areas, the texture of fan materials is predominantly coarse due to rapid weathering and torrential flooding. Dry channels are common *(Figure 12-18)*.

Filled valleys are found in arid and semi-arid regions in intermountain lowlands that have accumulated materials washed down from the mountains. They can be identified by light tones, braided stream channels, lack of vegetation, and sharp topographic contrast to surrounding peaks.

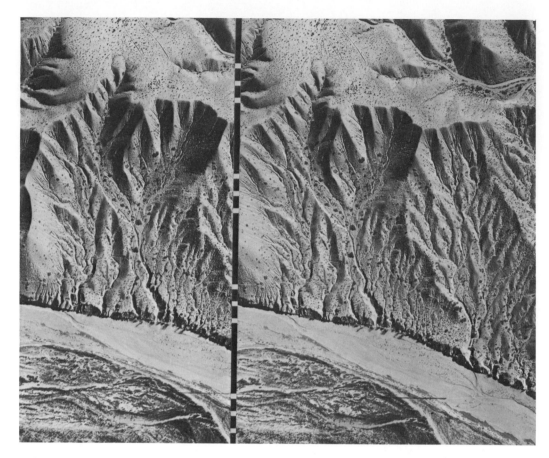

FIGURE 12-18. Dissected alluvial fan with parallel drainage and filled valley floor in New Mexico. Dry streambed has braided channel characteristics. Scale is 500 feet per inch.

Deltas are formed when flowing streams enter calm bodies of water such as lakes or oceans. Reduced stream velocity results in build-ups of sediments at the mouth of the river *(Figure 12-19)*. The arc-shaped (triangular) delta is most commonly observed. The delta of the Nile River is a prime example of this type (refer back to *Figure 9-18*). Stream channels may shift over the sand and silt surface, extending a delta seaward in all directions.

One of the outstanding characteristics of deltas is their level surface. Differences in elevation caused by stream channels, natural levees, lakes, and backswamps are minor when the extent of the delta is considered. Slight slopes may occur in very small deltas or in delta fans that are composed of coarse materials.

Beach Ridges and Tidal Flats

Beach ridges are formed when the level of a lake or an ocean is constant, and wave action sorts and transports granular deposits of material. If the water level is slowly lowered, or if wave action is climatic, a series of ridges may develop. These ridges are usually found along the present-day shoreline but may be far inland if the water level or land surface changes drastically over a period of time.

FIGURE 12-19. Oblique view of a delta forming at Iliamna Lake, Alaska. Note the barrier beach across part of the mouth of the river. Courtesy of U.S. Air Force.

The outline of beach ridges is roughly rectangular and nearly parallels the shoreline. The boundary is smoothly curving to straight on the seaward side, and less distinct or irregular to the landward side *(Figure 12-20)*.

Tidal flats are formed along coastlines that are protected from wave action by sandbars, barrier beaches, or offshore islands *(Figure 12-21)*. Lagoons or bays thus enclosed are filled with sediments and organic matter when streams empty into them. As a consequence, marshes subject to tidal fluctuations are formed. Tidal flats have an imperceptible amount of relief, and they become partially submerged at high tide. Mud flats are almost devoid of vegetation, but marshes may support dense growths of low marsh grass. *Figure 7-1* presented earlier illustrates the intricate drainage pattern characteristic of tidal marsh flats. Beach ridges are also clearly pictured on this photograph.

Glacial Landscapes

The extent of continental glaciation in the United States was shown by *Figure 12-1*. Continental glaciers did not cover Alaska, but there were many local mountain glaciers there. Glaciers exerted great pressure on the land they overrode, profoundly modifying the bedrock landscape. Transported boulders, soil, disintegrated rock, and fresh rock were distributed throughout the glacial mass, especially in the bases of glaciers. As the ice masses melted, "glacial drift" was deposited over the landscape, thereby mantling it with debris.

Glacial drift is an all-inclusive term applied to soil or rock mixtures moved by ice or meltwaters. This drift may or may not be water-sorted. Unsorted mixtures are called glacial till and are composed of a heterogeneous mixture of particle sizes. Water-sorted materials are called stratified drift and are composed of layered sands and gravels.

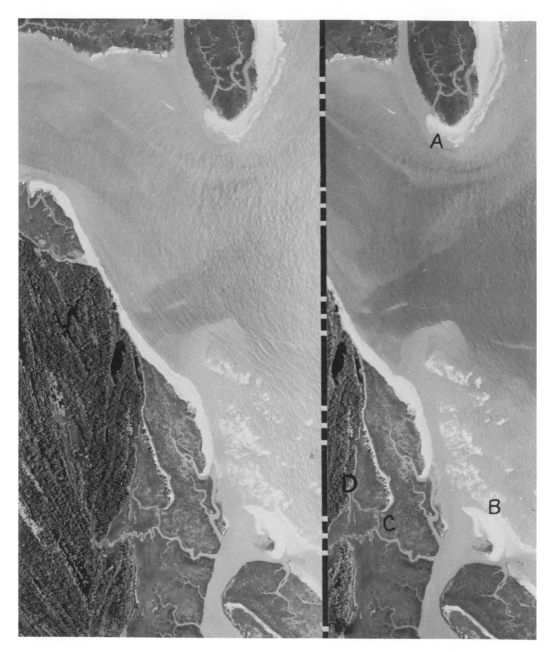

FIGURE 12-20. Littoral features near Beaufort, South Carolina include a sand spit or hook forming (A), barrier beach (B), tidal flat (C), and beach ridges (D). Scale is about 1,667 feet per inch.

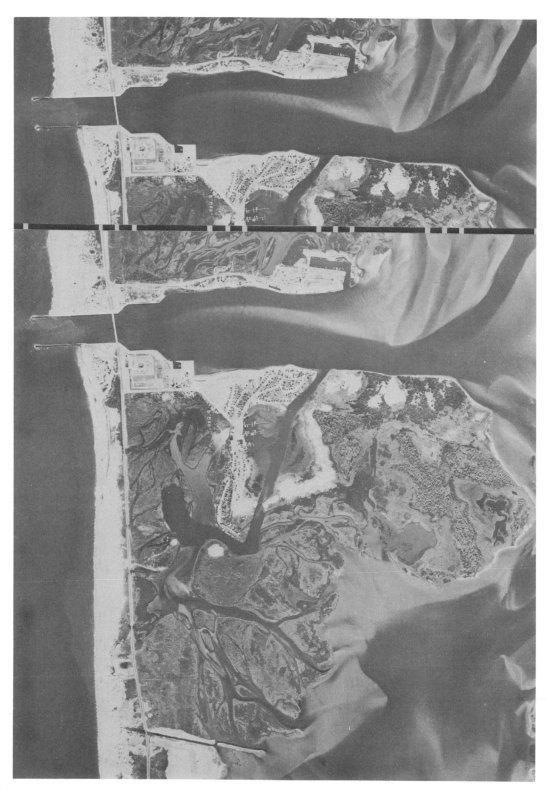

FIGURE 12-21. Barrier beach and tidal flat at Rehoboth Bay, Sussex County, Delaware. Note sand deposits in ship channel. Scale is about 1,667 feet per inch.

There are two distinct types of glaciation: mountain and continental. Certain landforms such as till plains, lakebeds, and drumlins are almost exclusively due to continental glaciation. Erosional features such as cirques, horns, and large U-shaped valleys are exclusively due to mountain glaciers. Three selected glacial features (eskers, till plains, and drumlins) are briefly discussed here.

Eskers are narrow serpentine ridges of sand and gravel that were formed by glacial meltwater streams flowing in tunnels within or under immobile ice, by streams flowing on glacial surfaces, or by deposits in crevasses of glacial ice. They are distinctive and easily recognized on aerial photographs *(Figure 12-22)*.

Till plains are composed of sorted and unsorted stratified glacial materials; the mixture was deposited over the original land surface during a uniform retreat movement of glaciers. The till may be a thin veneer insufficient to obliterate the influence of the bedrock, or it may be thick enough to completely cover the bedrock. Layers of well-sorted sands and gravels may be found in deep vertical cuts of till.

Young till plains have an undulating land surface which appears in mottled tones on panchromatic photographs *(Figure 12-23)*. Other characteristics are field and road patterns that form nearly perfect rectangles. Old till plains have a level land surface and a well-

FIGURE 12-22. Serpentine-shaped esker in Aroostook County, Maine. The esker is discontinuous but various segments are part of the same ridge. Scale is about 1,667 feet per inch.

FIGURE 12-23. Young glacial till plain in La Porte County, Indiana. Light-mottled tones result from soil removal at higher ground elevations. Scale is about 1,667 feet per inch.

developed dendritic drainage system. These areas show a lack of morainic topography and little or no tonal mottling on aerial photographs.

Drumlins are elliptical ridges 50 to 150 feet high, 500 to 1,000 feet wide, and up to a mile in length. They are composed of glacial till and are oriented with their long axes parallel to the direction of glacial movement. Drumlins taper in one direction; the head end usually points northward, and it is steeper and broader than the tail end *(Figure 12-24)*. Generally, there is no drainage development on drumlins. However, there may be a few small gullies and mud-flow scars on the steepest slopes. Cultivated fields on drumlins are parallel to the long axis, and orchards are sometimes planted on these formations. If drumlin side slopes are steep, the formation may be densely timbered or in pasture.

Eolian Features

Wind-deposited materials are commonly classified as either sand dunes or loess deposits. Sand dunes, most often found near shorelines or in desert areas, are formed by wind movement of granular material; the deposits are built up along obstructions or behind the protective cover of rocks and bushes. The three main types of dunes are barchan, longitudinal, and transverse.

Barchan dunes, the most common, are crescent-shaped and are the basic unit for most dunes. They occur most frequently in inland areas where winds are strong and sand supply is meager. All dunes show a tendency to move parallel or perpendicular to the prevailing winds. Barchan dunes with well-developed forms are not common. The horns of distinct barchan dunes point downwind. Longitudinal dunes are ridges which extend downwind from an obstruction. Their length is in line with the direction of the prevailing wind. Transverse dunes, common in arid areas, are formed by gentle winds blowing over areas of abundant sands. These dunes are scalloped ridges perpendicular to the direction of the wind and they tend to migrate forward *(Figure 12-25)*.

Dunes are mostly composed of quartz sand, though gypsum dunes occur in a few regions. Photographic tones are very light, except when dunes are covered by vegetation. Little or no surface drainage is apparent, because dunes are very porous and too small to provide full-fledged watersheds.

Loess is a wind or waterborne deposit of silt normally found to the windward side of deserts and glaciated regions. Windlaid silts that form loess deposits may be suspended in the air as dust and deposited on surfaces far from the silt origin. Deposits of loess may present a rolling or, when adjacent to streams, a highly dissected topography. If the loess mantle is thin, subdued features of the underlying landform will be dominant. Loess deposits provide good soils for agricultural purposes *(Figure 12-26)*.

Vertical bluffs and steep-sided, U-shaped gullies are the prime criteria for recognizing loess deposits on aerial photographs. On a regional basis, the prevailing drainage pattern is dendritic *(Figure 12-27)*. The boundary of loess is insignificant because a wide transitional zone usually exists between loess deposits and adjacent landforms. When these deposits are bounded by streams or floodplains, they form steep cliffs that follow the general outline of valleys.

Miscellaneous Landscapes

Unusual landscapes such as meteor crater in Arizona, Mt. Capulin in New Mexico, and the Everglades of Florida have been illustrated in earlier chapters. Pictured in this section are Carolina bays *(Figure 12-28)* and part of a salt dome *(Figure 12-29)*.

FIGURE 12-24. Control of agricultural patterns by drumlins in Jefferson County, Wisconsin. Scale is about 1,667 feet per inch.

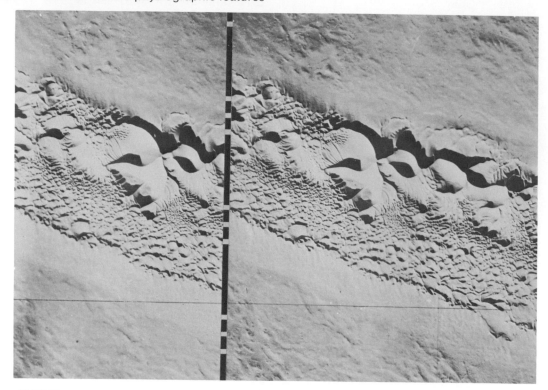

FIGURE 12-25. Transverse sand dunes in Algeria. The dunes are being held in place by an escarpment. Scale is about 3,350 feet per inch. Courtesy of U.S. Air Force.

FIGURE 12-26. Oblique view of a heavily eroded loess deposit near the Ching-Ho River in China. The U-shaped gullies are terraced and intensively cultivated. Courtesy of U.S. Air Force.

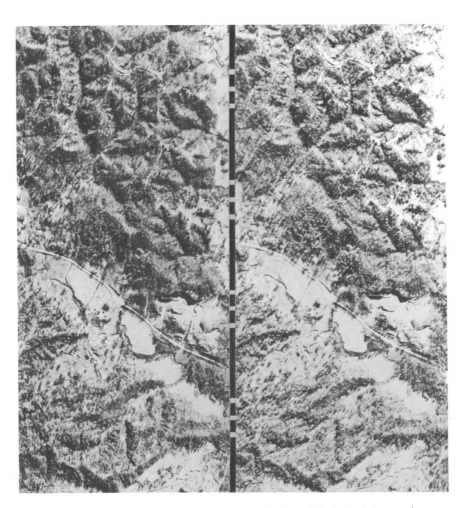

FIGURE 12-27. Eroded loess bluffs near Natchez, Mississippi. Loess deposits border the Mississippi River on the east from Natchez to upper Wisconsin. The source for these fine-textured deposits was alluvial material of glacial origin. In many places, the bluffs rise 200 feet above adjacent alluvial plains. Scale is about 1,850 feet per inch.

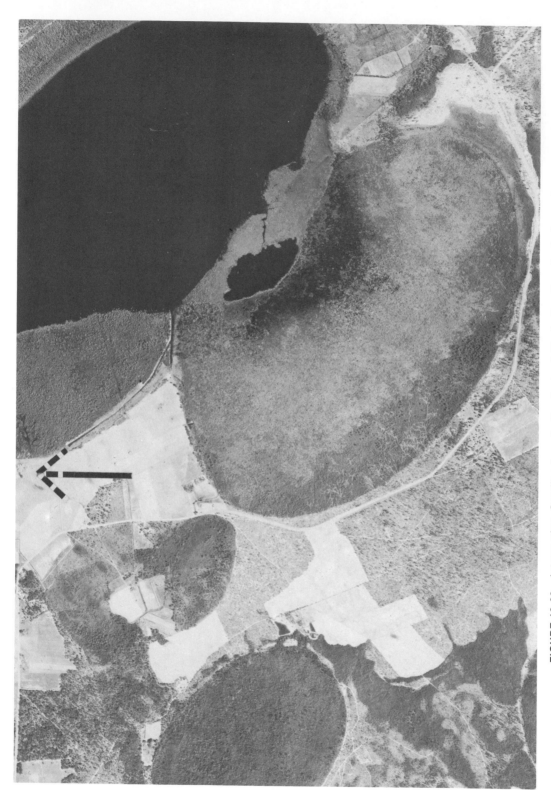

FIGURE 12-28. Intersecting Carolina bays in Cumberland, North Carolina. Such depressions are oriented NW-SE, they are usually deeper at the southeast end, and sandy rims occur along southeastern edges. Arrow indicates north direction. Scale is about 1,667 feet per inch.

FIGURE 12-29. Portion of a large salt dome in Iberia Parish, Louisiana. A processing plant may be seen near the center of the stereoscopic view. Scale is about 1,667 feet per inch.

The Carolina bays are shallow, elliptical depressions of unknown origin that occur at low elevations in a belt of the Atlantic Coastal Plain from New Jersey to Georgia. The greatest concentrations of bays are located in North Carolina and South Carolina; it is estimated that the total number of these oval swamps may exceed one million. Locally, the bays may be referred to as "pocosins," an Indian term denoting a swamp on a hill, i.e., having no external drainage system.

Most of the bays are shallow basins with poor, internal drainage; local relief is normally less than five feet. All are oriented in a northwest-southeast direction, and low, sandy rims are commonly found around the deeper, southeasterly edges. These characteristics have led to speculation that the bays were originally formed by intensive showers of meteorites from the northwest, or by shock waves formed just ahead of meteorites that burned up as they entered the earth's atmosphere.

Most geomorphologists discount the theory of meteoritic origin, however. It is more commonly believed that the bays were originally formed by a series of complex, interacting processes involving underground solution and surface subsidence as found in limestone sink areas. The sinkholes may have been later elongated and rimmed with sand by wave action during interglacial periods. In some instances, the sandy rims may be the result of eolian processes. Regardless of origin, the Carolina bays constitute a unique and dominating feature of the Atlantic Coastal Plain.

In certain parts of the world, salt concentrated in closed-off basins reaches such high levels that it is precipitated along with other chemicals found in sea water. These deposits can attain large proportions, and they assume the shape of irregular subsurface patches along coastlines of emergence. Salt deposits are covered by impermeable clays or shales which prevents solution by rain and sea water. In some cases, structural processes result in the formation of "salt plugs;" when these plugs appear near the surface, a domelike landform may be observed.

Radial drainage patterns are characteristic of salt domes. Various anomalies in stream patterns as seen on aerial photographs have led to the discovery of deep-seated salt domes along the Gulf Coast of the United States. The salt dome pictured here is one of the largest in North America.

References

Bascom, Willard.
    1960. Beaches. Scientific American reprint, W. H. Freeman and Co., San Francisco, Calif., 12 pp., illus.

Dort, Wakefield.
    1964. *Laboratory Studies in Physical Geology.* 2nd ed. Burgess Publishing Co., Minneapolis, Minn. 226 pp., illus.

El-Ashry, M. R., and Wanless, H. R.
    1967. Shoreline features and their changes. Photogram. Engineering 33:184-189, illus.

Emmons, W. H., Allison, I. S., Stauffer, C. R., and Thiel, G. A.
    1960. *Geology: Principles and Processes,* 5th ed. McGraw Hill Book Co., New York, N. Y., 491 pp., illus.

Feinberg, Arnold S.
    1964. *Airphoto Interpretation of Illinois Soils.* Civil Engineering Studies, Series NP-3, Univ. of Illinois, Urbana, 307 pp., illus.

Fischer, William A.
    1962. Color aerial photography in geologic investigations. Photogram. Engineering 28:133-139, illus.

Gimbarzevsky, Philip.
    1966. Land inventory interpretation. Photogram. Engineering 32:967-976, illus.

Howe, Robert H.
    1958. Procedures of applying air photo interpretation in the location of ground water. Photogram. Engineering 24:35-49, illus.

Kiefer, Ralph W.
    1967. Landform features in the United States. Photogram. Engineering 33:174-182, illus.

Lueder, Donald R.
1959. *Aerial Photographic Interpretation.* McGraw-Hill Book Co., New York, N.Y., 462 pp., illus.

Ray, Richard G.
1960. *Aerial Photographs in Geologic Interpretation and Mapping.* U.S. Geological Survey, Prof. Paper 373. Government Printing Office, Washington, D.C., 230 pp., illus.

_____ and Fischer, William A.
1960. Quantitative photography — a geologic research tool. Photogram. Engineering 26:143-150, illus.

Smith, H. T. U.
1967. Photogeologic interpretation in Antarctica. Photogram. Engineering 33: 297-304, illus.

Thoren, Ragnar.
1959. Frost problems and photo interpretation of patterned ground. Photogram. Engineering 25:779-786, illus.

Thornbury, William D.
1965. *Regional Geomorphology of the United States.* John Wiley and Sons, Inc., New York, N.Y., 609 pp., illus.

von Bandat, Horst F.
1962. *Aerogeology.* Gulf Publishing Co., Houston, Tex., 350 pp., illus.

U.S. Department of Commerce.
1960. The identification of rock types. Government Printing Office, Washington D.C., 17 pp., illus.

U.S. Naval Photographic Interpretation Center.
1956. *Military Geology.* Government Printing Office, Washington D.C., 174 pp., illus.

Wanless, Harold R.
1965. *Aerial Stereo Photographs.* Hubbard Scientific Co., Northbrook, Ill., 92 pp., illus.

CHAPTER 13

Engineering Applications

The Construction Engineer

Today almost all major highways, railroads, airfields, canals, and pipelines are planned and constructed on the basis of information derived through aerial surveys. Construction engineers rely on photogrammetric techniques to evaluate alternative locations for levees, dams, and hydroelectric structures, to conduct water-pollution and stream-siltation studies, to search for construction materials such as sand or gravel, and to measure stockpiles of raw materials. Aerial photographs are also one of the principal tools of engineering geologists in prospecting for new deposits of petroleum and minerals. In the sections that follow, emphasis is placed on highway location techniques, dams and reservoirs, water pollution, surface mining patterns, and stockpile inventories.

Highway Location Studies

In spite of global problems of overpopulation, there are still many regions of the world that are almost undeveloped. To make such areas suitable for exploitation, economic development, and human habitation, highways, railroads, and other access routes must be developed and maintained. In addition, new or enlarged transportation arteries are being designed and built each year in advanced countries, and photogrammetric surveys are playing an increasingly important role in these projects *(Figure 13-1)*.

Although there are notable differences, photographic interpretation techniques used in route location studies are similar to those employed for other engineering projects. The scientific evaluation of alternative routes requires studies of rather large areas, with emphasis on the analysis of surface soils, drainage characteristics, and searches for aggregate materials. It is, therefore, advantageous to have such projects staffed by engineers with geological training or by engineering geologists with a working knowledge of soils.

The uses of aerial photographs for the development of a new highway or railroad route may be conveniently organized into three distinct stages or phases, viz., (1) reconnaissance surveys and regional exploration, (2) preconstruction studies and comparisons of feasible routes, and (3) intensive study of the best route. Each phase refines the route location to a higher degree than the preceding stage. The basic task in location is the fitting of the road or railroad structure to the natural features of an area in a manner that will be most economical in construction and operation. This demands that natural features be effectively assessed, and aerial photographs provide an efficient means of meeting this objective. Natural features to be evaluated in a location study are topography, drainage, property values, soils and geology, borrow sources, vegetation, and special trouble areas. Imposed

"P & P" sheets are widely used in connection with pipeline location, highway design, transmission lines, microwave tower location, and many other engineering problems. The scale and the order of vertical accuracy are individually designed to meet the requirements of the specific project.

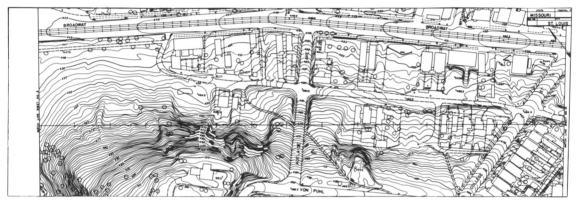

This plan sheet, with one-foot contours, covers the same area as the aerial photograph shown above.

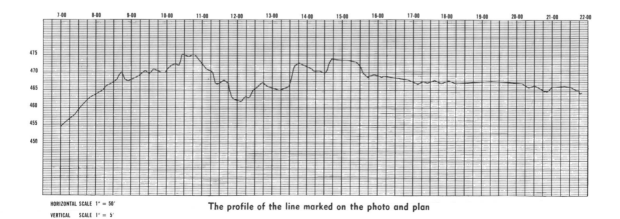

HORIZONTAL SCALE 1" = 50'

VERTICAL   SCALE 1" = 5'

The profile of the line marked on the photo and plan

FIGURE 13-1. Example of a plan-and-profile sheet compiled for an engineering survey. Courtesy of Jack Ammann Photogrammetric Engineers, Inc.

upon this information about the natural features of the area is the engineer's competence in determining the length, grade, and alignment of the route and the type of structures needed.

The Reconnaissance Survey

The primary objective of a reconnaissance survey is to choose several corridors between the terminals which appear to be technically feasible routes. An area having a width of 30 to 50 percent of the distance between terminals is studied on available maps and aerial photographs. If recent stereoscopic coverage of a suitable scale is not available, special photographic flights may be required. Depending on local topographic relief and intensity of land use, photographic scales may range from 800 to 5,000 feet per inch. It is desirable to use the smallest scale practical, because fewer stereoscopic setups are needed to encompass a given corridor area — with commensurate savings in time and money.

Where topographic maps have not been previously compiled for an area, the land surface may be evaluated solely through stereoscopic study of photographs. Spot elevations can be obtained by parallax measurements, followed by form line sketches of terrain. Form lines on individual contact prints may then be transferred to photo index sheets for a composite view of the various corridors in terms of drainage, broad soil groupings, land-use patterns, and rough comparisons of property values.

Comparisons of Feasible Routes

In this second stage, the small-scale photographs used for reconnaissance may be unsuitable, because the principal corridors should be covered by recent mapping photography that will produce contour intervals of five or ten feet. Print scales may range from 200 feet per inch in heavily populated urban areas to about 1,000 feet per inch in rural areas where land use is less intensive and right-of-way costs are likely to be lower.

From this large-scale photography, topographic maps are prepared of each corridor; single-strip maps at a scale of 200 to 400 feet per inch have often proved suitable in the United States. Such maps are commonly tied to existing horizontal and vertical control for refinement and reliability in evaluating alternate routes; whenever possible, state systems of plane coordinates are used in plotting the base maps. Preconstruction studies of alternative routes also require a close scrutiny of soil types, aggregate materials sources, vegetation obstacles such as muskeg or large timber reserves, and engineering problems such as hard rock cuts, tunnels, or landslides.

Plan-and-profile sheets are plotted, and proposed highway cross-sections are computed at stations established along each feasible route. Every route location is examined with regard to drainage, intersections, right-of-way costs, and road-user benefits; this procedure narrows the choice of locations to perhaps two or three alignments. These remaining alignments are then replotted to show traffic lanes, along with the profiles and grades of primary intersections. Positions and sizes of culverts are determined, and the extent of channel work is shown. Preliminary design work on large structures, e.g., bridges, may also be initiated.

To make final cost comparisons, grading contours of the highway-to-be, based on the recommended grade, are superimposed on the map. Amounts of cut and fill are determined by planimetering areas of horizontal sections (defined by each grading contour and the original ground contour) and multiplying by the contour interval. This method gives a graphic picture of the finished highway from which work limits, lengths of structures, extent of seeding, as well as right-of-way and grading, are determined.

Survey of the Best Route

In phase three, the photo interpretation task involves a more detailed study of drainage, soils, geology, and property values for the selected construction route. Large-scale photography of the chosen corridor is used to prepare topographic strip maps one-tenth to one mile wide along the path of the proposed highway. Maps, scales, and contour intervals required in this engineering stage range from 40 to 50 feet per inch with one-foot intervals to 500 feet per inch with 10-foot intervals. The highway centerline is located on the strip maps and then staked out on the ground for preliminary grading. This sets the stage for actual road construction to begin *(Figure 13-2)*.

Through the combination of aerial photographs and reliable strip maps, the construction engineer can be confident that all feasible routes have been given due consideration. Such assurances were acquired only via tedious and time-consuming ground survey methods prior to the adoption of photogrammetric surveys by highway designers and engineers.

Bridge Construction

Bridges for highways and railroads assume a wide variety of shapes and designs in accordance with cost considerations, type and intensity of traffic, load limits, availability of local construction materials, and considerations of minimum spans or clearances for

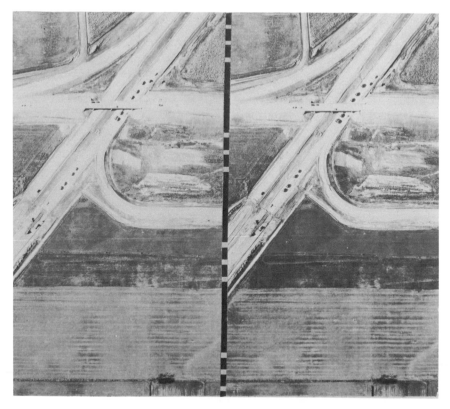

FIGURE 13-2. Construction of a divided, limited-access highway in Michigan. Several loaded dump trucks and grading equipment are discernible. Note that bridges or overpasses are usually completed prior to road surfacing. Scale is 500 feet per inch.

underpassing automobiles, trains, or ships. Oblique views of six different types of bridge construction are pictured in *Figure 13-3,* and a vertical stereogram of parallel highway and railroad bridges is shown in *Figure 13-4.*

In regions of steep topography, bridging costs may constitute the largest single expenditure for new railroad or highway routes. Once they are constructed and placed in service, the replacement or modification of heavily traversed spans becomes a major engineering problem. As indicated earlier, bridges are normally completed first in the construction of new transportation arteries. The logic of this established procedure is illustrated by the construction of limited-access highways through populated regions; overpasses must be built at an early stage to avoid interference with existing traffic on intersecting roads and to permit uninhibited work on the new right-of-way.

When new highway bypasses are planned through urbanized or industrial areas, existing spans or trestles may require modification because of insufficient clearances. *Figure 13-5* provides an apt example. Stereoscopic study of this photograph reveals that the old railroad trestle is supported by very closely spaced piers that will not permit the passage of automobile traffic underneath. Thus the construction of the new roadway requires that a wide-span railroad trestle be built to replace the older structure.

FIGURE 13-3. Six different types of bridges used for railroads and highways in Anglo-America.

FIGURE 13-4. Steel truss-frame railroad bridge (A) and dual-lane concrete highway bridge at Toledo, Ohio. Note that supporting piers for all three spans are aligned to allow easy passage of small craft underneath. Power transmission towers are circled on opposite river banks (C, D). Scale is 660 feet per inch.

FIGURE 13-5. Railroad passenger station (A) and construction of a highway overpass for trains (B). Note planned extension of new highway through residential area. Scale is 660 feet per inch.

Hydroelectric Dams and Reservoirs

The distribution of hydroelectric facilities in conterminous United States is governed largely by topography and amount of rainfall. The greatest water power potential is to be found in mountainous regions where stream gradients are high and precipitation is heavy *(Figure 13-6)*. In dry climates, especially where stream gradients are low, hydroelectric capacities are minimal; in fact, the impoundment of sufficient water supplies for human consumption is often a matter of grave concern to inhabitants *(Figure 13-7)*. To assist the neophyte interpreter in recognizing the components of hydroelectric installations, the basic nomenclature of a low-pressure dam is presented in *Figure 13-8*.

In many instances, human and industrial needs for clean water supplies are most critical in regions where ground and surface water sources are inadequate. The State of California with its rapidly expanding economy and population is a case in point. Several large urban centers, notably Los Angeles, receive a large proportion of their water supply via aqueducts from sources hundreds of miles away. Still, the basic problem of obtaining increasing quantities of unpolluted water for persons residing in precipitation-deficient regions remains largely unsolved.

To increase supplies of surface water, reservoirs have been constructed near urban communities by impounding rivers and streams. Unfortunately, watershed conservation practices have often lagged far behind engineering construction, with the consequence that hastily conceived reservoirs often have a short, finite life expectancy due to rapid sedimentation. As a general rule, large reservoirs should not be constructed unless administrative controls over the entire watershed can be exercised; only in this way can vegetative cover be maintained properly for intercepting precipitation, reducing surface erosion, and minimizing sedimentation. Aerial photography obtained at regularly scheduled time intervals offers an efficient means of monitoring water levels and checking periodic fluctuations in reservoirs *(Figure 13-9)*. Panchromatic photographs usually provide the most information on siltation levels, while shorelines and small tributaries are more distinctive on infrared prints.

Aerial Detection of Water Pollution

Water pollution studies are concerned with the changing characteristics of water that render it unfit or undesirable for human consumption, aquatic life, and industrial needs. Among the principal sources of water pollution are sewage and oxygen-consuming wastes, industrial by-products dumped into streams and lakes, radioactive substances, and agricultural pesticides. Increases in the temperature of water as a result of its use for industrial cooling purposes may also be regarded as a form of pollution when aquatic environment is endangered as a result *(Figure 13-10)*.

Aerial photographs provide a means of detecting and assessing the extent of some forms of water pollution. Although new infrared color films and image-producing thermal sensors are often desirable for making detailed lake and stream surveys, several types of water pollutants can be discerned on black-and-white panchromatic film exposed through a minus-blue filter (Strandberg, 1964). Under most circumstances, stream pollutants enter bodies of water from man-made "point sources" or from diffused sources that may be either natural or man-made. Point sources such as sewage outfalls are easier to find on aerial photographs because of sharp tonal contrasts between concentrated effluents and the receiving waters *(Figures 13-11 and 13-12)*.

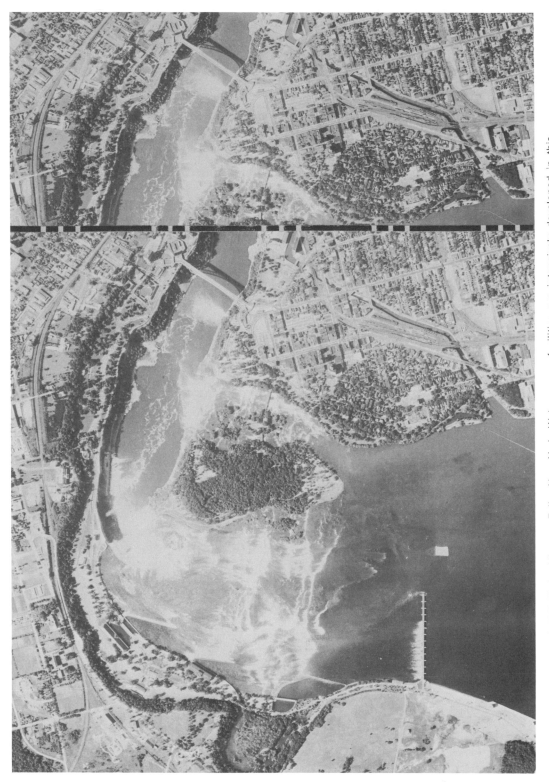

FIGURE 13-6. Niagara Falls, New York. Water power facilities are intensively developed in this region. Scale is 1,667 feet per inch.

FIGURE 13-7. Low-pressure dam on the Rio Grande in New Mexico. In this dry area, stream gradients are low, precipitation is meager, and occasional flash floods result in severe soil erosion. The problem of siltation behind the dam is evident here. Scale is 500 feet per inch. Courtesy of Abrams Aerial Survey Corp.

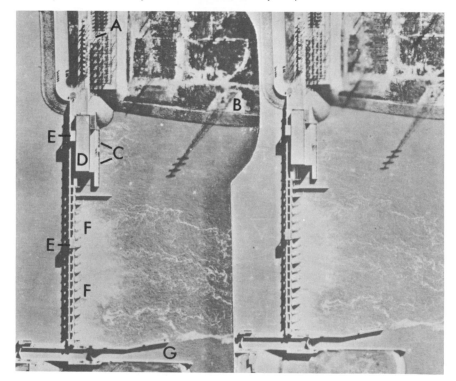

FIGURE 13-8. Features easily recognized in this stereogram of a low pressure dam include the transformer and switching yard (A), transmission tower (B), tail races (C), generator hall (D), traveling gate cranes (E), dam gates (F), and a lock for ships (G). Courtesy of U.S. Air Force.

Organic and inorganic industrial effluents include vegetable processing wastes, pulp and paper residues, sulfuric acid, metallic salts, and petrochemical wastes. As industrial effluents are commonly discharged into streams and estuaries through piped outlets, the concentrated pollution trouble spots are easily seen on aerial photographs. In the vicinity of seacoasts, these wastes may be responsible for huge areas of foul-smelling water that extend into the ocean for several miles. Oil slicks and petroleum effluents, which are not easily dissipated, are extremely detrimental to waterfowl populations *(Figure 13-13).*

Various types of surface mines also constitute sources of water pollution; not only are harmful acids and metallic salts discharged from some mines, but the movement or alteration of overlying surficial soils causes an increase in the sedimentation of adjacent bodies of water. Most types of stream sediments are readily detectable on panchromatic photographs or color films. Characteristic patterns of surface mines are summarized in the next section.

Surface Mining Patterns

An illustration of an open-pit iron mine in Minnesota and an oil field in Pennsylvania were presented in earlier chapters. Both surface and underground mining operations exhibit characteristic patterns or telltale signatures that may permit their identification on photographs of moderate scales. Several more or less typical mining operations are pictured in *Figures 13-14* through *13-21;* minerals involved are sulfur, phosphates, bauxite, lead and zinc, copper, gold, coal, and petroleum. All of these stereograms are on panchromatic film at scales of about 1,700 to 1,800 feet per inch, and they were selected from standard U.S. Department of Agriculture contact prints.

Almost all domestic sulfur is mined from deposits in Texas or Louisiana. Sulfur may be found in nearly pure form as crystals and powders, or it may occur in combination with metals, e.g., iron sulfide or pyrite. Most of the industrial production in the United States is consumed in the form of sulfuric acid. Phosphates are mined in southeastern and western states; more than three-fourths of the total production is used for commercial fertilizers. The distinctive pattern of open-pit phosphate mines is easily recognized on aerial photographs.

Bauxite mining in the United States is concentrated in central Arkansas, although commercial deposits are also exploited in Alabama, Georgia, and Virginia. Imports of bauxite (aluminum ore) largely come from Jamaica and South America. The deposits in this country occur near the surface, so open-pit mining is common; resulting photographic patterns are somewhat similar to those produced by the extraction of sand, gravel, and limestone. Lead and zinc ores are found in a number of states, but United States deposits are rapidly becoming depleted. Copper is also in short supply, and most of this country's consumption of this important metal is imported. Open-pit copper mines exhibit surface patterns of the type illustrated earlier for iron mines. In this chapter, surface characteristics for deep-shaft mining of copper, lead, and zinc are pictured.

Gold may be found in underground deposits in association with quartz or combined with copper, silver, lead, or zinc. It also occurs in gravel deposits near the surface and may be placer-mined as free gold by using dredges and hydraulic techniques to wash through large quantities of coarse, granular materials.

Deep, underground deposits of coal are tapped by vertical shafts or through bedding exposures in side hills that make horizontal extraction feasible. Coal deposits found nearer the surface are strip-mined by removal of the overburden with large power shovels;

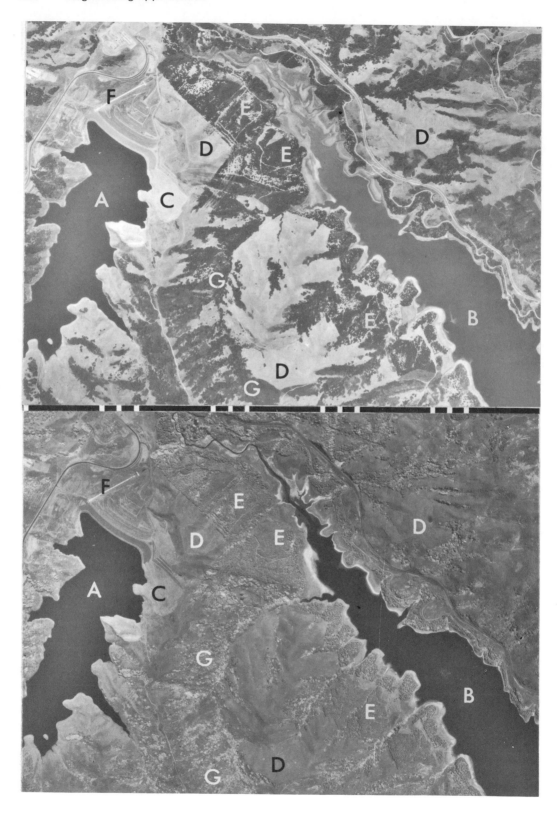

FIGURE 13-9. Panchromatic (above) and infrared (below) photographs of the Briones (A) and San Pablo (B) reservoirs in Contra Costa County, California. The Briones reservoir has a new earth dam and a low degree of sedimentation; the San Pablo reservoir has a much higher degree of sedimentation. Also discernible is exposed soil (C), annual grasslands (D), Monterey pine (E), spillway (F), and mixed hardwoods (G). Scale is about 2,800 feet per inch. Courtesy of U.S. Forest Service Remote Sensing Project, Berkeley, California.

thus the reclamation of strip-mined lands and re-establishment of vegetative cover are difficult and costly undertakings. Coal resources are widely distributed throughout the United States, and the locations of steel-production plants are normally governed by the proximity of coal, limestone, and iron ore deposits. Baltimore, Birmingham, Cleveland, Detroit, and Pittsburgh are among the larger steel manufacturing centers.

Petroleum exploration may produce a variety of surface patterns as seen on vertical aerial photographs; two such variations are illustrated in this volume. In forested regions, a patchwork mosaic of small clearings connected by a grid system of access roads is a common indicator. Shadows of drilling rigs, oil derricks, and pumping stations aid in the identification process. As successful wells are brought into production, small dark-toned sludge ponds may be seen, along with oil storage tanks. The leading oil-producing fields in the United States are found in the mid-continent region which includes such states as Kansas, Oklahoma, Texas, and Louisiana.

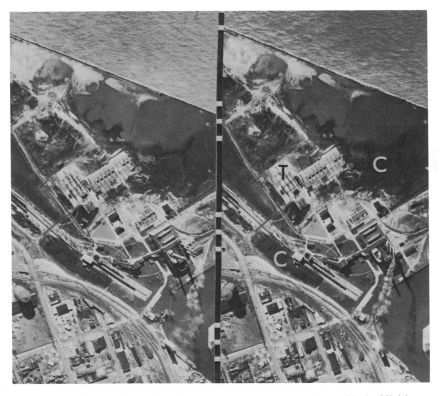

FIGURE 13-10. Thermal electric power plant along the shore of Lake Michigan. Piles of coal (C) and the transformer unit (T) are easily picked out. Such plants are the largest single users of water for cooling purposes. The water used for cooling is returned to the lake at a higher temperature than it originally possessed. Scale is 1,320 feet per inch.

Stockpile Inventories

Huge stockpiles of raw materials such as coal, limestone, mineral ores, fertilizers, and pulpwood chips must be periodically measured for inventory and cost-accounting purposes. In earlier days, such inventories were accomplished by laborious plane-table surveys or ground cross-sectioning; today, cubic volumes of materials 80 feet or more in height and covering 50 acres may be determined accurately and efficiently by photogrammetric methods (Massa, 1958).

In using the photographic approach, piles are contoured at one-foot intervals on the slopes and a ½-foot auxiliary on the tops. This is accomplished photogrammetrically by stereoscopic plotting of the contours of each pile from large-scale aerial photographs, e.g., 40 feet per inch. After contouring, the area of each contoured layer or slice is determined by planimetry and the cubic volume is computed.

When weight conversions per cubic foot or per cubic yard are known, volumes of piles may be converted to weight values in pounds or tons *(Table 13-1)*. Corrections should be made for variations in density for different piles of the same materials, because settling or compression will result in significant changes in volume-weight ratios. In summary, the photogrammetric method of stockpile inventory has these advantages:

1. It is more accurate, economical, and convenient.

2. The cut-off time for inventories can be set for one date, because all pictures can be obtained in one day.

3. Ground control need be established only once.

4. The method provides a permanent record of the size of the pile at the time the picture was taken, and volume can be checked at any future time if any question arises as to the accuracy of the record.

5. No bulldozing or pile dressing is required as is usually done for the cross-section method.

TABLE 13-1.   Approximate weights of material in pounds per cubic yard[1]

Cement, Portland, loose	2,538
Concrete, 1:2:4 mixture	
(Trap rock)	4,020
(Gravel)	3,945
(Limestone)	3,890
(Sandstone)	3,770
(Cinder)	2,860
Clay, dry, loose	1,700
Clay, damp, plastic	2,850
Clay and gravel, dry	2,700
Earth, dry, loose	1,975
Earth, moist, loose	2,110
Earth, moist, packed	2,590
Earth, mud, flowing	2,916
Earth, mud, packed	3,100
Garbage	675-1,350
Riprap, limestone	2,600-3,295
Riprap, sandstone	2,430
Riprap, shale	2,830
Rubbish, incl. ashes	216
Sand, gravel, dry, loose	2,430-2,830
Sand, gravel, dry, packed	2,700-3,240
Sand, gravel, wet	3,400
Snow, fresh-fallen	135-325
Snow, wet	405-540
Coal, anthracite, natural	2,620
Coal, bituminous, natural	2,270
Coal, lignite, natural	2,110
Coal, anthracite, piled	1,270-1,567
Coal, bituminous, piled	1,080-1,460

[1]Source: International Harvester Company.

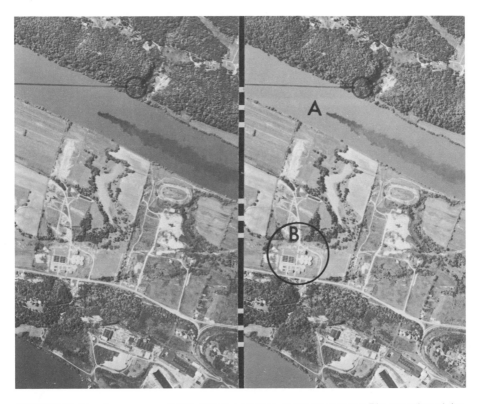

FIGURE 13-11. A sewage outfall below the surface of the Tennessee River produced the dark pollution pattern (A) on this photograph taken near Chattanooga; the sewage treatment plant is encircled (B). The dark coloration of the effluent is an indication of low dissolved oxygen levels, a situation detrimental to fish and other aquatic life. Scale is about 1,667 feet per inch. Courtesy of U.S. Department of Agriculture.

FIGURE 13-12. Sewage treatment plant (A) and eventual discharge of effluent into stream (B) in Monroe County, New York. The desirability of the new residential area (lower left) is probably questionable on certain days when wind currents are unfavorable. Scale is 500 feet per inch.

FIGURE 13-13. Discharge of petrochemical wastes into a large river near the Charleston, South Carolina naval shipyard. Scale is 1,667 feet per inch.

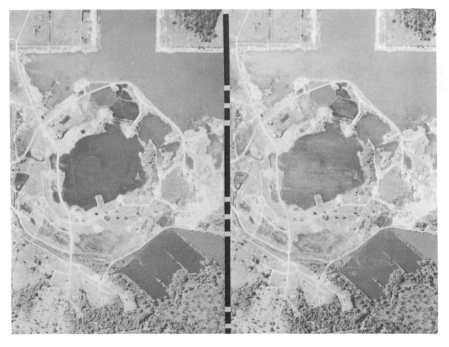

FIGURE 13-14. Mining of sulfur in Calcasieu Parish, Louisiana. Deposits are underground here, so the surface features remain relatively undisturbed around the structural dome.

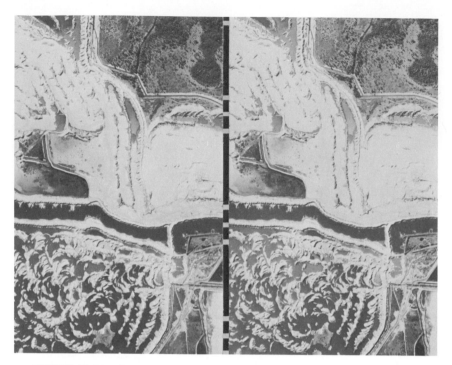

FIGURE 13-15. Open-pit phosphate mine in Polk County, Florida. Unless drastic land reclamation measures are taken here, these scars will blot the landscape for years.

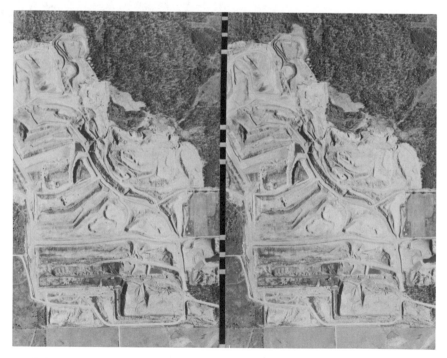

FIGURE 13-16. Bauxite surface mine in Saline County, Arkansas. Note the light tones produced by aluminum ore.

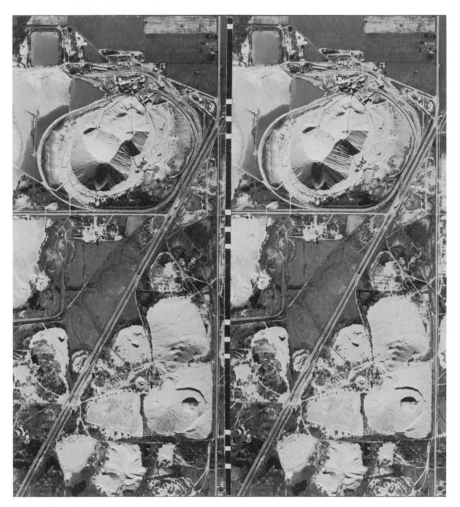

FIGURE 13-17. Lead-zinc extraction in Ottawa County, Oklahoma. Underground deposits are being brought to the smelter shown at the top of the photograph.

FIGURE 13-18. Deep-shaft copper mining in the Keweenaw Peninsula of Michigan. Copper ore and tailings dot the landscape here.

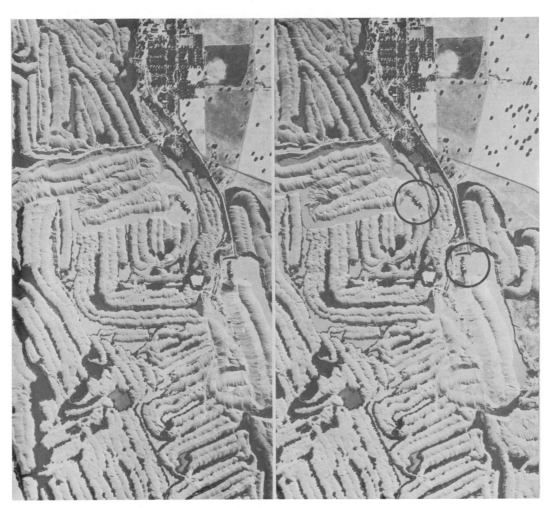

FIGURE 13-19. Placer-mining of gold in Yuba County, California. Dredges may be seen in the circled areas.

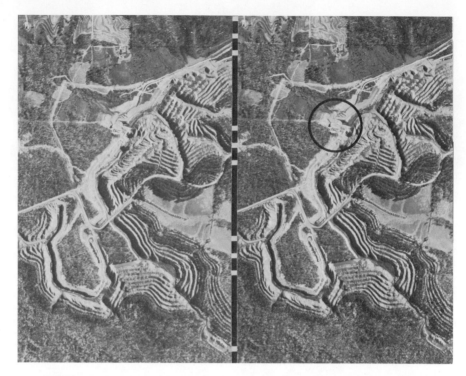

FIGURE 13-20. Strip mining of coal in Walker County, Alabama. A power shovel working a seam of coal is encircled.

FIGURE 13-21. Oil extraction in Lafayette Parish, Louisiana. Pictured here are a floating drilling rig (A) and oil storage tanks (B). In areas where canals are common, drilling equipment is easily moved from one location to another.

References

Blesch, Robert R., and Liang, Ta.
1962. Application of photo interpretation in route location. Proceedings of International Symposium on Photo Interpretation, Delft, The Netherlands, 477-486, illus.

Deacon, John H.
1962. Applications of photogrammetry to the design and construction of the Quebec Cartier Mining Railway. Photogram. Engineering 28:154-157.

Gill, Edward A.
1967. Coal exploration. Photogram. Engineering 33:157-161, illus.

Herd, Lloyd.
1957. Special measurements by photogrammetric methods. Photogram. Engineering 23:749-754.

Massa, William S.
1958. Inventory of large coal piles. Photogram. Engineering 24:77-81.

McLerran, James H.
1957. Photographic interpretation—its significance in the highway program. Photogram. Engineering 23:755-762, illus.

Schneider, William J.
1966. Airphoto interpretation of the water resources of the Florida Everglades. Paper presented to the American Society of Photogrammetry, Washington, D.C., 10 pp., illus.

Seestrom, William R.
1966. Highway routes in undeveloped areas. Photogram. Engineering 32:121-125, illus.

Sternberg, Irwin.
1961. Drainage studies from aerial surveys. Photogram. Engineering 27:638-644. illus.

Stoeckeler, E. G., and Gorrill, W. R.
1959. Airphoto analysis of terrain for highway location studies in Maine. Photogram. Engineering 25:85-97, illus.

Strandberg, Carl H.
1966. Water quality analysis. Photogram. Engineering 32:234-248, illus.

——————.
1963. Analysis of thermal pollution from the air. Photogram. Engineering 29:656-671, illus.

Wright, C. Robert.
1957. Aerial surveys and photogrammetric methods for highways. Photogram. Engineering 23:927-930.

CHAPTER 14

Urban-Industrial Patterns

The Airphoto Approach to Urban Planning

Urban planning may be defined as the orderly regulation of the physical facilities of a city to meet the changing economic and social needs of a community, including the development of plans for future industrial expansion. Although city managers have long relied upon large-scale maps for zoning and urban-renewal projects, the widespread use of photo interpretation techniques by municipal organizations represents a comparatively recent trend. It is now recognized, however, that properly timed aerial photography offers a unique and efficient means of studying such critical municipal problems as population growth, transportation networks, real estate assessment, and recreational needs. Aerial photographs provide the administrator with a complete perspective view of his city and surrounding environs. As a result, he is better equipped to analyze socio-economic patterns, residential distributions, industrial requirements, and the need for extension of public utilities and services.

The intense competition for space between residential, industrial, recreational, agricultural, and transportation interests presents a continual series of problems to the urban planner. Whenever any portion of a city's limited environment is allocated to one of these uses, careful consideration must be given to the probable impact of that allocation on each of the other competing uses and thus on the residents of the area.

Sequential aerial photography is now available for many cities in Anglo-America *(Figure 14-1)*. By studying comparative photographs taken at intervals of several years, it is possible to determine the effects of major decisions made by previous municipal managers during the growth of a city. Accordingly, an excellent file of case histories is made available to incumbent urban planners who wish to capitalize on both the good and bad decisions of their predecessors. A procedure for measuring land-use changes adjacent to interchanges on limited-access highways has been developed by Wagner (1963).

A Systematic Guide to Urban Analysis

A series of 11 topical guides designed to aid geographers in the systematic study of aerial photographs has been prepared by Stone (1964). These guides are postulated on the theory that photo interpretation is largely a deductive rather than an inductive process and, therefore, analyses should proceed from the known parts of a topic to the unknown. If interpretation activities are organized for working from general patterns toward specific identifications or inferences, stereoscopic study should begin with the smallest scale of photography and end with prints of the largest scale available. A topical outline for the interpretation of urban features is presented here. In using prepared guides of this type,

FIGURE 14-1. Oblique views of downtown Ottawa, Canada, in 1928 (above) and in 1964 (below). Parliament buildings are near top center of each photograph. Courtesy of Surveys and Mapping Branch, Canada Department of Energy, Mines and Resources.

the interpreter must realize that positive identifications are rarely feasible for all urban patterns; thus listings of uncertain areas should be accompanied by several possible identifications based on the concept of associated features.

1. Outline built-up areas having urban characteristics.
2. Mark the major land and water transportation lines passing through the city *(Figure 14-2)*.
3. Mark the principal commercial airports *(Figure 14-3)*.
4. For the built-up area, outline subareas to show types of water bodies, drainage systems, terrain configuration, and natural vegetation.
5. Divide the built-up area into subareas with differing street patterns.
6. Outline the older and newer parts of the city.
7. Identify the principal transportation lines within the city.
8. Mark the minor land and water transportation lines passing through the city.
9. Circle the places where there is a change in the type of transportation.
10. Outline the primary commercial subareas in the central business district and in the suburbs.
11. Outline principal industrial subareas, including municipal utilities.

FIGURE 14-2. Interstate highway bypassing the central business district of Chattanooga, Tennessee. Although some added parking areas are evident between the highway interchanges and the downtown section, new shopping centers such as the one circled pose an economic threat to downtown merchants. This type of problem confronts many cities in America. Scale is about 1,667 feet per inch.

12. Outline subareas of warehouses and open storage.

13. Mark the recreational areas.

14. Mark the cemeteries.

15. Outline sections of the residential subareas by differing characteristics of the residences and lots and their relative locations to other functional subareas.

16. Mark the principal administrative and government buildings.

17. Mark the secondary commercial centers.

18. Mark the isolated industrial plants.

19. Mark the probable locations of light industrial establishments.

FIGURE 14-3. Portion of the Miami, Florida International Airport. Since commercial airports are rarely connected to downtown and residential sections by efficient mass transportation systems, almost as much space is required to park automobiles here as is needed for airplanes. Scale is about 800 feet per inch.

Information accumulated for a given urban area comprises the basis for more detailed studies. For example, in planning for future expansion of public facilities, correlations might be established between information on population density, number of automobiles per dwelling unit, or water use per capita and such planning multiplier factors as roadway capacity or acreage of recreational land per thousand persons.

Parking and Transportation Studies

Special photographic flights made during peak traffic periods are ideal for discovering bottlenecks in automobile flow patterns. Similarly, coverage of congested business districts can quickly reveal diurnal parking patterns and the locations of districts having shortages or surpluses of parking spaces during each hour of the day. Law enforcement officers have also found sequential, low-altitude photographs to be of assistance in pinpointing areas where cars are habitually parked in restricted zones.

Individually painted parking spaces can be easily discerned and counted at photographic scales of 600 feet per inch; at larger scales, the size and type of vehicle can also be assessed *(Figure 14-4)*. In a few cities, aerial surveys of parking facilities have revealed that there is sufficient unused space in vacant backyards and alleys within the business district to make available more than double the existing parking capacity. Photographs also revealed that traffic would be able to reach parking lots behind shops by merely opening a few new

FIGURE 14-4. Large-scale view of parking lots in Youngstown, Ohio, about 11 a.m. Note concentrations of vehicles in some lots and surplus spaces in others. Busses, trucks, and compact cars can be distinguished from standard-sized automobiles here. Scale is about 330 feet per inch.

access streets to handle the traffic flow. In other urban areas, aerial photographs have indicated that more parking facilities than originally presumed will have to be provided; additional spaces are often needed to supply legal parking for vehicles that previously utilized loading zones and other nonallocated spaces.

When the time interval between successive, overlapping aerial exposures is known, speeds of vehicles imaged on adjacent prints can be computed (*Figure 14-5*). Such information can be of considerable utility in analyzing traffic flows during rush-hour periods. In some European countries, close-range terrestrial photographs made with stereometric cameras are used to obtain permanent pictorial records of traffic accidents. The precision of photogrammetric determinations of such items as tire marks, vehicle positions, and collision damage has been firmly established, so that photographic evaluations are com-

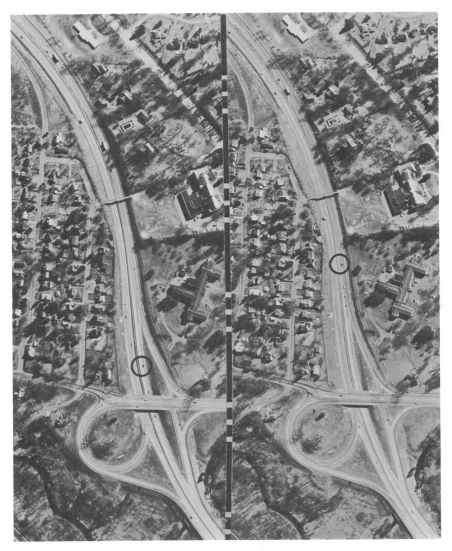

FIGURE 14-5. The speed of the circled vehicle may be easily computed from a knowledge of the time interval between photo exposures. Scale is about 500 feet per inch. What would be the auto speed in miles per hour if the exposure interval were 12 seconds?

monly admissible as court evidence (Salley, 1964). The photogrammetric technique provides more reliable measurements than ground taping of distances, and the accident scene can be re-examined over and over from files of four or five carefully oriented stereopairs. Furthermore, the stereometric process shortens the investigation time at the accident scene, with the result that roadways can be cleared for regular traffic with a minimum of delay.

Patterns of Residential Development

Many urban planners believe that the only answer to the control of haphazard "urban sprawl" is a rigidly administered property zoning system *(Figure 14-6)*. Certainly there are valid arguments favoring the orderly regulation of community development; otherwise smoky industrial plants may force down property values in exclusive suburbs, and taverns might be constructed adjacent to school buildings.

The suburbanite who wishes to reside in an area free from polluted air, speeding automobiles, or supersonic aircraft may be hard-pressed to find solace in today's metropolis.

FIGURE 14-6. The problem of urban sprawl and inadequate zoning has produced a conglomeration of residential structures in this section of Monroe County, New York. Former agricultural lands and a greenhouse area (A) are confined by a shopping center (B). Older, single-family homes (C) have given way to multiple-family apartments (D), and new single-family dwellings (E). Scale is about 500 feet per inch.

Nevertheless, interpreters of urban features have found that residential property is one of the key indicators of a family's socio-economic status, and that a person's "address" often reveals much more about an individual than just where he lives. One might, for example, reflect upon the social or economic status associated with a residence on San Francisco's Nob Hill around 1900. Residence location has meaning not only in terms of real estate cost or rental, but also in terms of occupation, educational level, income class, nationality group, cultural attributes, and even religious preferences.

In a study of the residential patterns of several American cities (Green, 1957), four items derived through airphoto interpretation were shown to be valid indicators of residential desirability and social structural characteristics. These indicators were:

1. Location of the residential area relative to three, concentric zones centered at the main business district.

2. Description of the residential area in terms of internal and adjacent land use.

3. Prevalence of single-family dwelling units.

4. Housing density in terms of average number of dwellings per block. When translated into population densities, extremes in one study area ranged from about 85 to 250 persons per block.

Even though the typical single-family dwelling in America has grown larger and more luxurious, the high cost and scarcity of building sites results in more and more houses being built on smaller parcels of real estate. The confining atmosphere and unimaginative landscaping that results are painfully illustrated by *Figures 14-7* and *14-8*.

FIGURE 14-7. Large "ranch-style" residences being constructed close together on small lots in Milwaukee, Wisconsin. As is commonly seen in new subdivisions, sod, topsoil, and trees have been scraped away to make for more efficient materials handling. The monotony of this scoured landscape will remain for years to come. Scale is about 400 feet per inch.

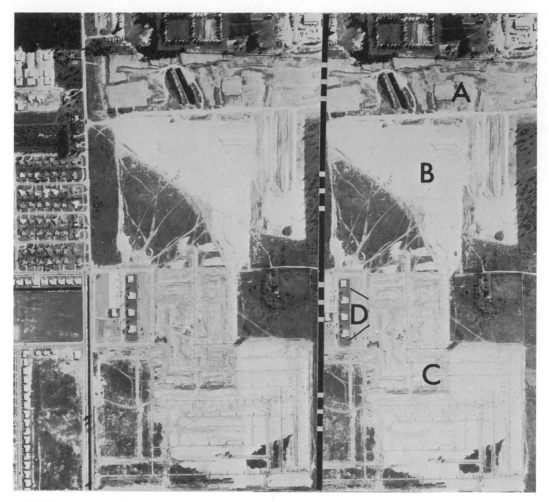

FIGURE 14-8. In many seacoast areas, one may dig a canal, use excavated materials to fill in low-lands, and create a subdivision with waterfront residences. Here in Dade County, Florida, excavated sand (A) is transported to adjacent development areas (B, C). In anticipation of advance residential sales, four model homes are already open to customers (D). The final result will seemingly appear somewhat similar to the mill-town arrangement at the extreme left edge of the picture. Scale is about 800 feet per inch.

Recreational Planning

The failure of many large cities to make early provision for parks, golf courses, and other outdoor recreational facilities has resulted in tremendous pressures on existing lands as populations have increased. Notable examples of foresight by city planners would include such urban oases as Central Park in Manhattan, Rock Creek Park in Washington, D. C., and City Park in New Orleans. In other heavily populated regions, however, carefully maintained havens of grass and trees may be sorely inadequate or wholly lacking.

When open areas are not reserved for public usage at an early stage in a city's growth, rising real estate values may effectively block the establishment of large municipal parks and athletic facilities at a later date. As a result, private country clubs, concentrated tourist attractions, or spectator sports may offer the only alternatives to local residents *(Figures*

14-9 through *14-12).* Surveys of population pressures on existing recreational areas and inventories of potential recreational sites are often aided by intensive study of large-scale aerial photographs.

Aerial Assessment of Taxable Property

To illustrate the usefulness of aerial photographs in the discovery and assessment of taxable property, a procedure developed by Rex (1963) is summarized here. This methodology was followed in making an aerial survey of property improvements in a suburban township of 33 square miles within the Chicago metropolitan area. The survey area was primarily a single-family residential locale with a population density of about 4,000 persons per square mile; population growth amounted to approximately 150 percent in the decade preceding the aerial survey.

Contract aerial photography at a scale of 1,000 feet per inch was obtained for the selected township; then copies of property record cards for the 45,000 ownerships involved were procured from the county assessor's office. Photographic enlargements, rectified to fit

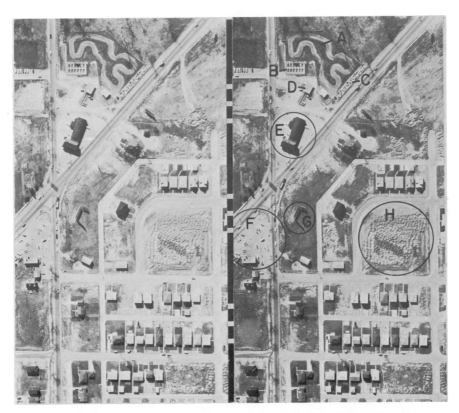

FIGURE 14-9. Recreational facilities near new residential development in Milwaukee, Wisconsin. Items designated are a "go-kart" track (A), trampoline pits (B), miniature golf (C), drive-in restaurant (D), roller rink or dance hall (E), gas station (F), and billboards (G). The dumped fill material (H) possibly came from basements excavated for new houses. Note that lots in the lower part of the picture are so narrow that many homes are of the "shotgun design" with no space for driveways. Scale is about 450 feet per inch.

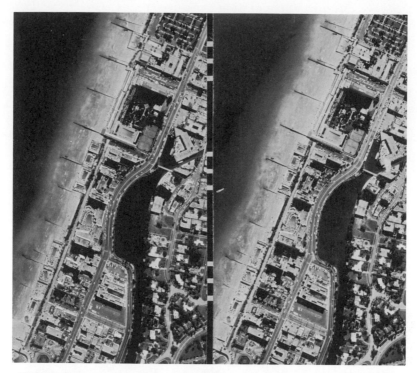

FIGURE 14-10. Hotels along Miami Beach, Florida represent intensively developed recreational facilities for tourists. Scale is about 800 feet per inch.

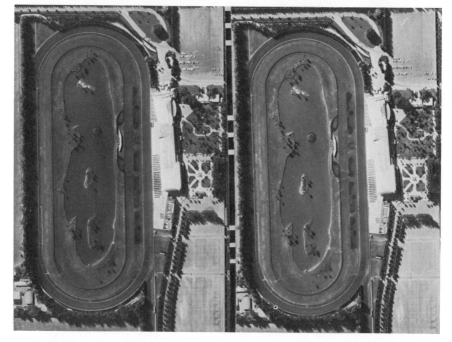

FIGURE 14-11. Horse racing, one of America's leading spectator sports, attracts many thousands to Hialeah Park in Miami, Florida each year. Palm trees and a central lake add to the esthetic value of the location. Scale is about 800 feet per inch.

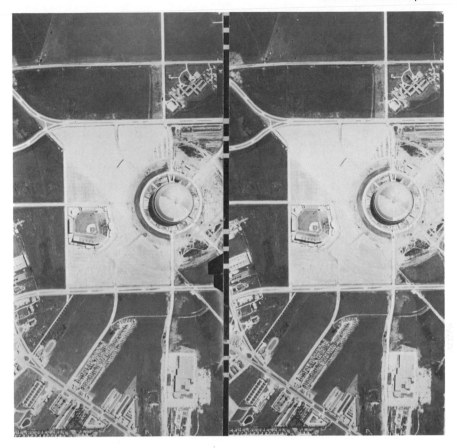

FIGURE 14-12. The covered Astrodome and adjacent baseball park in Houston, Texas are internationally known centers for spectator sports. This view was made in October, 1964 before landscaping was completed. Scale is about 1,700 feet per inch.

existing parcel identification maps, were ordered at a scale of 100 feet per inch; a total of about 250 enlargements were required to cover the survey area. Finally, transparent overlays were prepared from existing tax maps at the same scale as the enlarged photographs. The property record cards, print enlargements, and map overlays comprised the basic working tools on which photographic interpretation was based.

Current improvements listed on each of the 45,000 property record cards were checked against apparent improvements as interpreted from the enlarged photographs, and notations were made of each irregularity. Apparent discrepancies were then cross-checked against building permit files; irregularities that could not be reconciled were earmarked for field checking and ground appraisal of the improvement. The types of improvements readily found on aerial photographs included new residences, additions to existing residences, garages, private swimming pools, apartment buildings, commercial buildings, and commercial black-top areas.

As a result of this aerial survey procedure, more than 800 new improvements were picked up, of which about 230 were reappraised. For a total survey cost of about $26,000 (excluding field checks and appraisals made by the county assessor's office), property valuations amounting to several million dollars were added to the tax rolls. The total tax revenue derived from the survey was estimated as being in excess of $400,000.

Recognition of Industrial Features

The general classification or specific identification of certain industrial features is of vital concern to photo interpreters engaged in urban planning, control of water and air pollution, or military target analysis. In a few instances, unique structures or rooftop signs can make the task exceedingly simple *(Figures 14-13* and *14-14)*. In other cases, however, the correct categorization may require a sound background knowledge of industrial components, a high degree of deductive reasoning, and one or more photo interpretation keys. The more a person knows about industrial processing methods, the more success he will have in recognizing those same activities on vertical aerial photographs.

As pointed out by Chisnell and Cole (1958), each type of industrial complex has a unique sequence of raw materials, buildings, equipment, end products, and waste that typify the industry. Many of these components may be seen directly on aerial photographs; others that are obscured or inside structures must be detected by inference from the images of minor associated components. By studying the distinctive shapes, patterns, or tones of raw materials, for example, one may frequently deduce the kinds of processes or equipment that are hidden from view. Arrangements of chimneys, stacks, boilers, tanks, conveyors, and overhead cranes may also provide essential identification clues. And finally, the finished product can occasionally be seen as it emerges from an assembly line or is stored in open yards awaiting shipment.

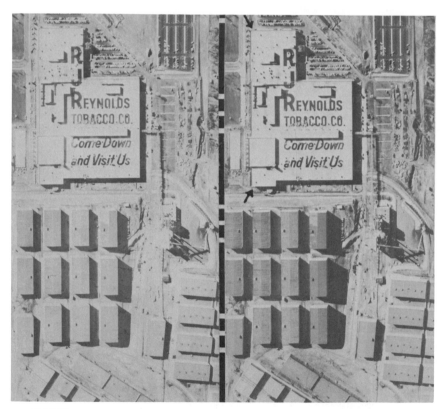

FIGURE 14-13. Cigarette manufacturing plant (above) and tobacco warehouses (below) in Winston-Salem, North Carolina. The name of the city provides a clue to the brands of cigarettes produced by this light manufacturing plant. Scale is 660 feet per inch.

FIGURE 14-14. If one can recognize a railroad turntable (A) and locomotives (B), then it can be deduced that the engines are being shunted into a repair or maintenance shop (C). This heavy fabrication industry is located at New Haven, Indiana. Scale is 660 feet per inch.

A number of photo interpretation guides for use in identifying general classes of industries have been compiled by or for various military agencies. One of these selective keys, based on general industrial categorizations of extraction, processing, and fabrication, is reproduced here by permission of Thomas C. Chisnell of Photogrammetry, Inc. If industries are imaged on photographs at a scale of 1,500 feet per inch or larger, it has been shown that relatively unskilled interpreters can use such a key to categorize various industries, even though a specific identification may not be feasible. Because industrial components tend to exhibit common images irrespective of geographic location, this key is applicable in many parts of the world.

In using the various recognition features to categorize an industry from its image components, the following procedure is recommended:

1. Decide whether it is an extraction, processing, or fabrication industry.

2. If it is a processing industry, decide whether it is chemical, heat, or mechanical processing — in that order.

3. If it is a fabrication industry, decide whether it is light or heavy fabrication.

Industrial Classification Key

Extraction industries are characterized by these features: excavations, mine headframes, ponds and derricks; piles of waste; bulk materials stored in piles, ponds or tanks; handling equipment, e.g., conveyors, pipelines, bulldozers, cranes, power shovels or mine cars; buildings that are few and small.

Processing industries are characterized by these features: facilities for storage of large quantities of bulk materials in piles, ponds, silos, tanks, hoppers and bunkers; facilities for handling bulk materials, e.g., conveyors, pipelines, cranes and mobile equipment; large outdoor processing equipment, e.g., blast furnaces, cooling towers, kilns and chemical processing towers; provision for large quantities of heat or power as evidenced by boiler houses; oil tanks, coal piles, large chimneys, many stacks or transformer yards; large or complex buildings; piles or ponds of waste. Three types of processing industries may be recognized:

1. Mechanical processing is typified by few pipelines or closed tanks, little fuel in evidence, few stacks, and no kilns.

2. Chemical processing is typified by many closed or tall tanks, gasholders, pipelines, and much large, outdoor processing equipment.

3. Heat processing is typified by few pipelines or tanks, large chimneys or many stacks, large quantities of fuel, and the presence of kilns.

Fabrication industries are characterized by these features: facilities for storing or handling bulk materials are rare; a minimum of outdoor equipment except for cranes; little or no waste; buildings may be large or small and of almost any structural design.

1. Heavy fabrication plants are typified by heavy steel-frame, one-story buildings, storage yards with heavy lifting equipment, and rail lines entering buildings.

2. Light fabrication plants are typified by light steel-frame or wood-frame buildings and wall-bearing, multi-story structures, lack of heavy lifting equipment, and open storage of raw materials is rare.

Examples of Industrial Categories

Extraction industries, typified by oil drilling, rock quarries, gravel pits, and mining operations, are among the easiest types of industries to classify. They may be recognized by the presence of excavations, ponds, mine shafts, and earth-moving equipment; buildings are usually small and often of temporary construction. Frequently, such operations appear to be rather disorganized as viewed on aerial photographs, even though extracted materials are mechanically handled by conveyors or stored in ponds, tanks, or bins. In some cases, the interpreter must exericse special care in distinguishing waste piles from usable materials. The numerous surface mining patterns that were illustrated in Chapter 13 provide appropriate examples of the extraction industries.

Processing industries are divided into three subclasses: mechanical, chemical, and heat processing. Mechanical processing industries are those that size, sort, separate, or change the physical form or appearance of raw materials. Industries that are typical of this category are sawmills, grain mills, and ore concentration plants; utilities in the same grouping would include hydroelectric power plants, water purification, and sewage disposal installations. Several of these types of industries were also illustrated in Chapter 13.

Chemical processing industries are those that employ chemicals to separate, treat, or rearrange the constituents of raw materials. Among representative chemical processing industries are sulfuric acid production, alumina plants, petroleum refining, wood pressure-treatment installations, and by-products coke production *(Figures 14-15* through *14-17).*

Heat-processing industries utilize heat to refine, divide, or reshape raw materials, or to produce energy from raw materials through the use of heat. Large quantities of fuel are

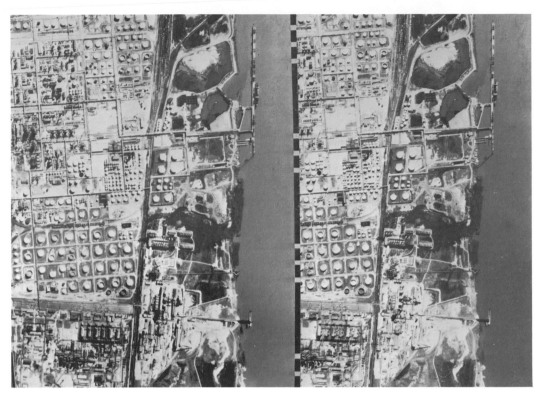

FIGURE 14-15. Petroleum refinery along the Mississippi River at Baton Rouge, Louisiana. Although this chemical processing industry is pictured at a scale of 2,000 feet per inch, it is a sufficiently distinctive complex to be categorized by use of the industrial classification key.

required, waste piles are common, and blast furnaces or kilns are often in evidence. Thermal electric power plants are included in this category, along with cement production, clay products manufacturing, iron blast furnaces, and copper smelters *(Figures 14-18 through 14-20)*.

Fabrication industries are those that utilize the output of processing plants to form or assemble finished products. Although a majority of all industries are of the fabrication type, they are the most difficult to specifically identify, because most of the activities are hidden from view by well-constructed buildings and enclosures. There is little outdoor equipment in evidence except for large cranes; bulk materials, waste piles, and storage ponds are usually absent. Heavy fabrication industries include structural steel plants, shipbuilding, and the manufacture or repair of railroad cars and locomotives *(Figure 14-21)*. Typical of the light fabrication industries are aircraft assembly plants, canning and meatpacking, small boat factories, and the manufacture of plastics products *(Figure 14-22)*.

Most interpreters find that the best way to identify an industrial complex is by looking for components that are key recognition features of the classification in which the industry falls. While one or two components may not provide a specific identification, associations with other features will usually provide the missing link in the recognition chain. Knowledge of the photographic scale and the exact geographic locale of photography are additional factors that are of primary importance in recognizing industries. When available, current sets of county maps, topographic quadrangle sheets, stereogram files of representative industries, and a recent commercial atlas are valuable reference aids to photo interpreters.

FIGURE 14-16. This chemical processing plant near Milwaukee, Wisconsin is engaged in the preservative treatment of wood materials with creosote. Both untreated stacks of wood (light tones) and treated materials (dark tones) are visible in the storage yard. Tram cars of untreated materials (A) may be seen lined up for movement into the pressure cylinder (B). Liquid preservatives are stored in cylindrical tanks (C). Scale is about 400 feet per inch.

FIGURE 14-17. By-products coke production in Youngstown, Ohio. Components labeled are: pushing rams to move coke from ovens into quenching cars (A), long coke ovens (B), tank storage of tars and other coal by-products (C), buildings where coal is washed (D), and towers where coal is fed into coke ovens (E). Scale is about 330 feet per inch. Although this would usually be classed as a chemical processing industry, heat processes are also in evidence at such installations.

FIGURE 14-18. Both extraction and heat processing industries are pictured in this stereo-triplet of a Michigan cement plant.

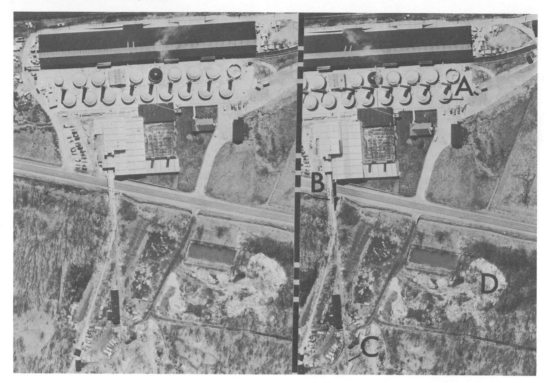

FIGURE 14-19. Clay products constitute the output of this heat processing industry at Newcomerstown, Ohio. Key components include clay kilns (A), tram cars of raw materials (B), hillside tunnel to clay mine (C), and waste materials (D). Scale is about 250 feet per inch. Courtesy of Abrams Aerial Survey Corp.

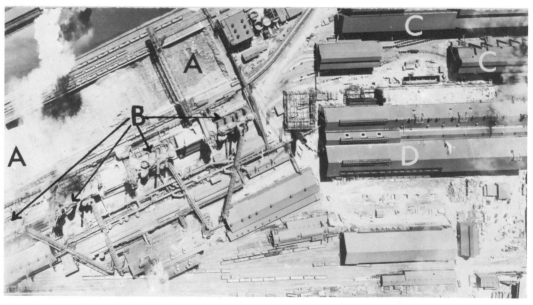

FIGURE 14-20. Heat processing industry at Youngstown, Ohio. Designated here are limestone and iron ore storage bins (A), blast furnaces that use coke, iron ore, and limestone to produce pig iron (B), buildings housing open-hearth furnaces (C), and iron rolling mills (D). Scale is about 330 feet per inch.

FIGURE 14-21. Railroad Pullman cars are manufactured at this heavy fabrication plant in Michigan City, Indiana. Visible are storage yards with overhead cranes (A), and rail lines entering the building (B). Painted on the roof is the name of the city and its longitude and latitude. Scale is 1,320 feet per inch.

Capacities of Storage Tanks

The capacity of any cylindrical storage tank may be easily determined from measurements of its inside diameter (D) and height (H). When these two values are measured in feet, the cubic-foot volume is computed by:

$$\text{Volume (cu. ft.)} = \frac{\pi \, D^2}{4} \, (H) \text{ or } 0.7854D^2 \, (H)$$

Depending on whether stored materials are in solid or liquid form, cubic volumes may then be converted to cubic yards, weight units (see Chapter 13), or to liquid measure. The following factors may be useful in converting cubic feet to other units of measurement:

To obtain	Multiply cu. ft. by
Cubic meters	0.02832
Cubic yards	0.03704
Gallons, British	6.229
Gallons, U.S.	7.481
Liters	28.316

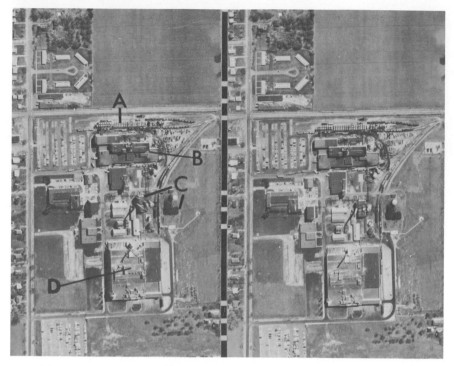

FIGURE 14-22. This plastics plant in Toledo, Ohio apparently combines both chemical processing and light fabrication activities. Identified are liquid chemical storage tanks (A), chemical processing building (B), power plant and coal piles (C), and multi-story fabrication building (D). Scale is 660 feet per inch.

References

Chisnell, Thomas C., and Cole, Gordon E.
  1958. Industrial components — a photo interpretation key on industry. Photogram. Engineering 24:590-602, illus.

Cissna, Volney J.
  1963. Photogrammetry and comprehensive city planning for the small community. Photogram. Engineering 29:681-684.

Green, Norman E.
  1957. Aerial photographic interpretation and the social structure of the city. Photogram. Engineering 23:89-96.

——————————— and Monier, Robert B.
  1959. Aerial photographic interpretation and the human ecology of the city. Photogram. Engineering 25:770-773.

Rex, R. L.
  1963. Evaluation and conclusions of assessing and improvement control by aerial assessment and interpretation methods: a case history. Sidwell Studio, Inc., Chicago, Ill., 15 pp., illus.

Salley, James R.
  1964. Close range photogrammetry — a useful tool in traffic accident investigation. Photogram. Engineering 30:568-573, illus.

Stone, Kirk H.
  1964. A guide to the interpretation and analysis of aerial photos. Annals of the Association of American Geographers 54:318-328.

Wagner, Robert R.
  1963. Using airphotos to measure changes in land use around highway interchanges. Photogram. Engineering 29:645-649, illus.

Witenstein, Matthew M.
  1956. A report on application of aerial photography to urban land-use inventory, analysis and planning. Photogram. Engineering 22:656-663, illus.

———————————
  1955. Uses and limitations of aerial photography in urban analysis and planning. Photogram. Engineering 21:566-572, illus.

CHAPTER 15

Air Intelligence and Military Target Analysis

The Need For Intelligence Systems

Intelligence activities may be defined as the process of gathering a myriad of facts and bits of information, making a coherent pattern of them, and drawing inferences from that pattern. In the American concept of intelligence, emphasis is on the use of overt or open sources of data, i.e., information that is legitimately available from foreign newspapers, military and scientific journals, foreign political discussions or debates, encyclopedias, radio broadcasts, and statistical compilations (Orlov, 1963). By contrast, certain other nations place primary reliance on covert sources of intelligence information. Such tactics may involve undercover agents, spies, and paid informants who employ the more direct approach of infiltrating a key facility with the singular purpose of stealing or copying documents of high strategic value. From a purely objective viewpoint, both approaches have obvious advantages and limitations.

In international affairs, intelligence is foreknowledge, and foreknowledge is a powerful peacetime tool for making advance predictions of a hostile nation's reactions to varying political, economic, and military crises. In times of all-out war, a superior intelligence system may hold the balance of power and the key to ultimate victory. As an illustration, skillful photo reconnaissance work by British interpreters during World War II led to the destruction of launching sites for German V-bombs on the continent; as a result, a long-range attack which might have been catastrophic was averted *(Figure 15-1)*.

The gathering of intelligence information is a cyclic and continuing process. It begins with a listing of data requirements, followed by the location and exploitation of information sources, and leads finally to the dissemination of the intelligence report or estimate. National security interests require that United States intelligence agencies maintain an alert and flexible aerial reconnaissance posture at all times. A strong reconnaissance capability can inhibit the outbreak of hostilities if the aggressor knows that his actions are fully seen, analyzed, and understood, because he has thus been denied the singular advantage of surprise. During wartime operations, an established capability in intelligence and photo reconnaissance can help to assure an early victory by supplying up-to-date information on enemy forces, terrain factors, communications systems, weaponry installations, and weather conditions.

The U.S. Central Intelligence Agency

The inadequacy of early intelligence systems in the United States was revealed by the 1941 Japanese attack at Pearl Harbor. The critical intelligence requirements of World War II led to the creation of the Office of Strategic Services, an organization which later

FIGURE 15-1. Top view, taken in 1944 at Peenemunde, Germany, shows elliptical earthwork feature where rockets were tested. Shown are V-2 rockets (A), cranes (B), and assembly shop (C). Lower view shows the same installation after an air strike. Courtesy of U.S. Air Force.

evolved as the present U.S. Central Intelligence Agency. An excellent book summarizing CIA activities has been written by former Director Allen Dulles (1963). The following description of CIA functions is quoted from a brochure on employment opportunities issued by the Agency:

"Established by Congress as an independent civilian agency of the United States Government through passage of the National Security Act of 1947, the Agency was placed under the National Security Council and made accountable to the President, with Congressional review to be exercised through select committees.

"The Director of Central Intelligence, head of the Central Intelligence Agency, is also coordinator of the total American intelligence effort and intelligence advisor to the President. The principal functions of the Central Intelligence Agency can be summarized as follows: (1) to perform the specialized intelligence collection and analysis functions that the National Security Council determines can best be performed centrally; (2) to correlate and evaluate all intelligence pertaining to the national security; and (3) to perform such other functions as the National Security Council may from time to time direct.

"Overseas, CIA has responsibilities for the collection of intelligence. Just as one dimension of intelligence is collection, so is another research and analysis. Major contributions to the foreign intelligence effort are made by CIA in the fields of economic research, geographic research, and scientific and technical research. Reports, monographs, and studies are regularly produced by CIA and other analysts in the intelligence community in support of the integrated political, military, and economic estimates and surveys prepared for the President and National Security Council."

The Nature of Military Intelligence

The technique of obtaining military intelligence by use of aircraft equipped with cameras and other remote-sensing devices is termed "photo reconnaissance." Military photo reconnaissance differs from other forms of interpretation in two important respects. First, reconnaissance photography is usually obtained without the consent of those who control the target areas — in fact, reconnaissance efforts are likely to be systematically obstructed by those who risk being exposed by overflights. Also, camouflage may be employed to hide critical targets, and dummy constructions may be thrown up to confuse image interpreters. Secondly, aerial photo reconnaissance and interpretation must be fitted into their military place. They must be accommodated to each phase of warfare. The practical value of the interpretation is heavily dependent on rapid results; the time factor is so important that photographic coverage must often be scheduled without regard to optimum exposure conditions.

Camouflage experts regard photo reconnaissance efforts as a personal challenge, and continued improvements in camouflage techniques make target detection increasingly more difficult for the military interpreter. Consequently, images of higher resolution are demanded by interpreters, and larger negative scales are required, thus entailing a significant increase in the number of photographs to be studied. Furthermore, when a given target is covered by ordinary film exposures as well as a camouflage-detection emulsion, the number of photographs to be examined is again greatly increased.

With low-altitude reconnaissance, each photograph spans such a small area that large numbers of prints are required to cover a given target. Nevertheless, the advantages of low-level imagery produced from supersonic photo reconnaissance flights have been clearly demonstrated. The 1962 detection of medium-range ballistic missiles on the Island of Cuba constitutes a prime example of precision, low-altitude photo reconnaissance. High-flying U-2 aircraft first discovered the presence of Soviet missiles in Cuba, watched their emplacement, and confirmed their hurried departure. However, the bulk of the detailed photography made available to military interpreters was obtained from tactical, fighter-type jet aircraft that operated at tree-top levels to avoid enemy radar detection and various forms of anti-aircraft fire. The clarity and sharpness of such photographs is shown by *Figures 15-2* through *15-5*.

In the best of the Cuban photographs, missiles and launching devices can be recognized by untrained observers. However, highly skilled personnel are required to identify minor components of such installations and to make rational inferences from the various stages of construction pictured. Military interpreters are trained to look for subtle hints that lead indirectly to important hidden information, e.g., vehicle tracks leading into apparently impenetrable swamps, trucks assembled where no roads are visible, or oil slicks on remote lagoons. A careful analysis of such clues will sometimes reveal skillfully camouflaged strongpoints such as radar installations, cave storage of missiles, revetted gun emplacements, or underground ammunition dumps. When recent or unusual patterns are spotted, their ages can be estimated by reference to earlier photographic coverage of the same area.

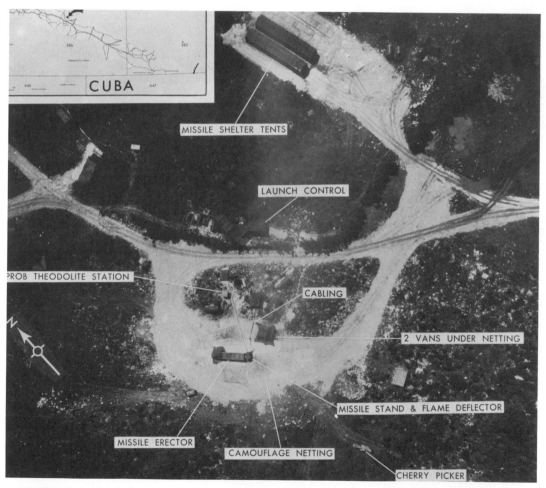

FIGURE 15-2. Vertical photograph of a medium-range ballistic missile site taken over Cuba on October 23, 1962. All elements necessary to launch a MRBM with a range up to 1,100 nautical miles are present. A special effort is being made to camouflage activities; all major components are under canvas, and camouflage netting is stretched out near the missile erector prior to being strung across the site. Courtesy of U.S. Air Force.

FIGURE 15-3. Oblique view covering the same area shown in Figure 15-2. Courtesy of U.S. Air Force.

FIGURE 15-4. Oblique view of a Cuban MRBM site following removal of launch erectors and a missile transporter. On this date, launch stands were still in place and construction was still underway on the nuclear warhead storage facility at the left. Courtesy of U.S. Air Force.

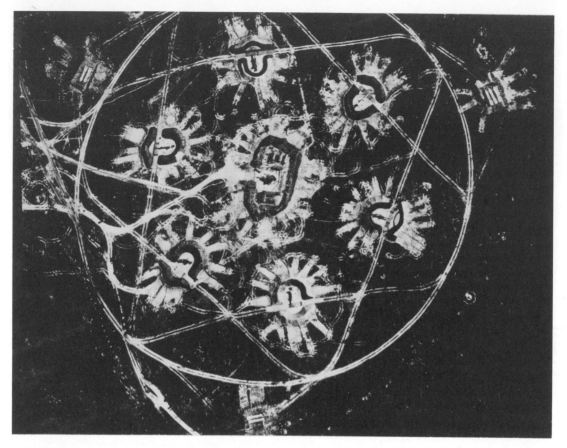

FIGURE 15-5. Surface-to-air missile site at La Coloma, Cuba in November 1962. Courtesy of U.S. Air Force.

Photo reconnaissance of Cuba and other potential "hotspots" around the globe is a continuing process. Though sometimes labeled as overt espionage, aerial reconnaissance is a vital contributor to national security in peace as well as in war. As outlined earlier, foreknowledge comprises the foundation of sound political and military decisions in the free world.

Selecting and Training Interpreters

Military photo intelligence work is the responsibility of a relatively small group of highly trained specialists. They must be able to seek out or recognize significant intelligence information and be able to collate, evaluate, and report their findings within a minimum time period. The range of required background knowledge makes photo intelligence work both interesting and exceedingly complex. Because the prime objectives of aerial reconnaissance missions may be unattained unless interpreters are adept, mentally alert, and properly motivated, only the most promising candidates are selected for extensive photo intelligence training. The question is, "How does one distinguish the most promising candidates?"

It is generally agreed that candidates to be trained as photo interpretation specialists should possess such attributes as good visual acuity, a sound educational background, imagination, patience, judgment, high perceptual or learning capacity, and proper motivation. Reliable and objective techniques are available for evaluating stereoscopic vision and color perception, but only a few attempts have been made to evaluate the potential interpretation ability of trainees prior to specialized instruction.

In a research study conducted by the author and involving 99 university students, relatively high correlations were established between scores on screening tests administered at the onset of training and "final performance ratings" based on visual search ability and recognition of urban-industrial features. Results of this experiment have been reported in *Photogrammetric Engineering*. Further attention should be devoted to the matter of personnel selection and training; the importance of the interpreter's role in the overall intelligence picture is emphasized by the following passage extracted from the *Military Photographic Interpretation Handbook* (1954):

"In the last analysis it is the skill and experience of the interpreter that determines to a very large degree the success or failure of the work. The interpreter must know what to look for; he must be able to identify what he finds; he must know the significance of an object in its location; he must be able to utilize effectively information from other sources; he must know how to use comparative photo coverage; and he must know the enemy, his equipment, and his order of battle. To these general requirements may be added many more specific ones, depending on the particular kind of interpretation involved. For example, an interpreter preparing detailed reports on industrial installations should have experience in important industries significant to a war economy. He should have an understanding of industrial processes, common industrial components, and the principles of industrial organization and management. With a good background for his work, an interpreter will, by induction and deduction, accurately associate visible features with others that do not appear on the photography. The skill of a photo interpreter arises not only from his capability for reading aerial photos but also from his background experience. This factor cannot be overemphasized, for an interpreter cannot be expected to analyze correctly a small-scale, plan-view photo image of an object he could not recognize even if he were on the site."

As examples of somewhat unfamiliar aerial views, the reader is referred to *Figures 15-6* and *15-7*.

Airborne Sensors For Photo Reconnaissance

To reduce the risk from anti-aircraft fire and surface-to-air missiles, today's photo reconnaissance planes are usually modified fighter-type aircraft that are operated at extremely fast speeds. As a rule, they are either restricted to very high altitudes where interception is less likely or to very low altitudes where detection by enemy radar and other tracking devices is more difficult. Because these altitude restrictions present problems beyond the capability of a single camera, newer aircraft are designed for all-weather, multi-sensor reconnaissance. In addition to carrying several conventional optical sensors of varying formats and angles of coverage, planes are also equipped with infrared and electronic sensors that permit successful missions during daylight or night flights.

As an illustration of the reconnaissance capability of military aircraft, the McDonnell RF-4C Phantom (see Frontispiece) features automatic in-flight film processing for all cameras, film ejection from a low-altitude panoramic camera station, and in-flight data recording on all film frames. Typical bits of information recorded on each exposure are date, time, radar and barometric altitude, latitude, longitude, heading, pitch, roll, drift angle, squadron or detachment, and mission number.

Oblique and vertical photographs may be obtained simultaneously with the Phantom, and illumination for night photography is provided by photo flash cartridges that are ejected upward from each side of the aircraft. In addition, the aircraft is equipped with both forward-looking and side-looking radar systems, infrared thermal mapping device, and an

FIGURE 15-6. Does this X-shaped pattern indicate a buried ammunition dump, intersecting rights-of-way for electrical power lines, or a dummy target constructed by enemy forces? Actually, it is simply a grass airstrip no longer in use. Scale is about 800 feet per inch. Courtesy of Abrams Aerial Survey Corp.

FIGURE 15-7. Although easily identified on the ground, the vertical aerial view of this complex might confuse the neophyte interpreter. It pictures the U.S. Coast Guard Station located at the mouth of Biscayne Bay in Dade County, Florida. Scale is about 800 feet per inch.

inertial navigation set used to compute such essential sensor data as groundspeed, ground track angle, drift angle, automatic ground-track hold provisions, groundspeed/altitude ratio, and angle of attack.

Looking ahead toward future developments, laser technology will undoubtedly produce applications in aerial reconnaissance such as ranging/velocity devices or special light sources. A revolution in night reconnaissance utilizing lasers is a distinct possibility.

Target Priorities

On any given wartime operation, there is a tremendous number of possible targets in relationship to the available striking force. Accordingly, the enemy's total resources must be very carefully analyzed in developing target priorities. Specialists known as target analysts study all aspects of the opposition's war economy and industrial potential, so that available air power can be directed toward destroying those targets that will cripple or impair the military offensive of enemy forces. The rapidity with which bombed installations can be repaired or rebuilt determines how often strikes must be rescheduled in a specific theater of operations. Although the photo interpreter may not participate directly in rating the importance or vulnerability of specific targets, he must be constantly aware of the existing priority system and capable of identifying primary and secondary targets even when they are poorly imaged or camouflaged.

From a purely military view, the logistics of rating targets are elemental. The enemy's military forces and installations capable of retaliation should be hit first, followed by attacks on armament storage and essential industries, and transportation-communications networks. In keeping with this line of reasoning, possible targets are grouped here under three major headings. No relative ranking within groups is implied, because such priorities will obviously change with time, place, operational objectives, and political considerations.

1. **Military targets with retaliatory power**
   Missile-launching sites *(Figures 15-8* and *15-9)*
   Anti-aircraft emplacements
   Bomber bases and military airfields
   Shipyards and submarine bases
   Military posts and troop concentrations
   Supply trucks and convoys

2. **Armament storage and industries producing war materials**
   Ammunition dumps and supply depots
   Armament manufacture, including nuclear materials
   Ship repair facilities (drydocks) and barge manufacture
   Aircraft factories
   Vehicle assembly plants
   Petroleum, oil, and lubricants (POL) refining and storage
   Steel mills and machine-tool plants
   Other metals industries
   Chemical production
   Cement plants
   Food production and water supplies

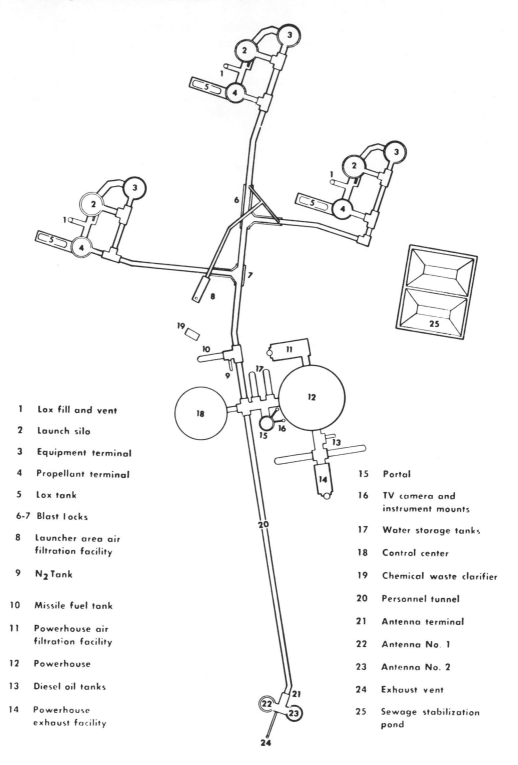

1	Lox fill and vent
2	Launch silo
3	Equipment terminal
4	Propellant terminal
5	Lox tank
6-7	Blast locks
8	Launcher area air filtration facility
9	N_2 Tank
10	Missile fuel tank
11	Powerhouse air filtration facility
12	Powerhouse
13	Diesel oil tanks
14	Powerhouse exhaust facility
15	Portal
16	TV camera and instrument mounts
17	Water storage tanks
18	Control center
19	Chemical waste clarifier
20	Personnel tunnel
21	Antenna terminal
22	Antenna No. 1
23	Antenna No. 2
24	Exhaust vent
25	Sewage stabilization pond

FIGURE 15-8. Schematic diagram of underground silo complex and missile-launching center. Courtesy of U.S. Air Force.

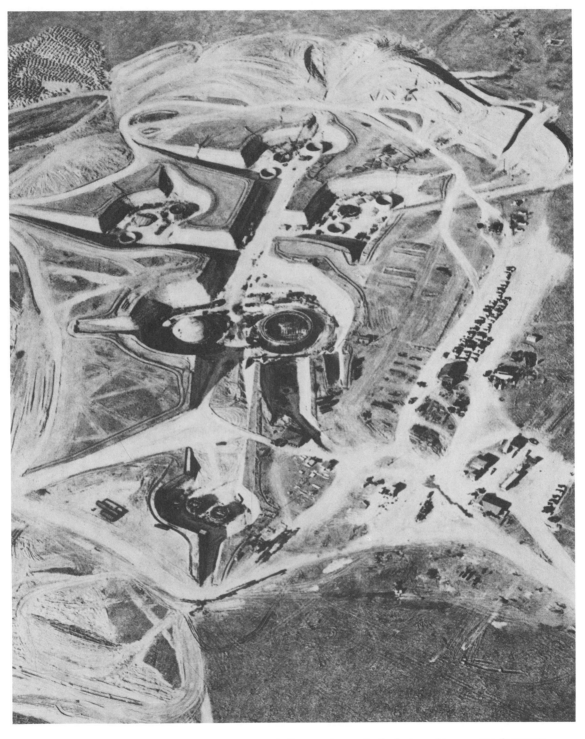

FIGURE 15-9. Construction of an underground silo complex and missile-launching center. Compare with Figure 15-8. Courtesy of U.S. Air Force.

3. **Transportation-communications networks**
   Highways, railroads, bridges, tunnels, and ferries
   Shipping lanes and harbor facilities
   Canals and locks
   Electrical power plants and hydroelectric dams
   Radio and radar installations
   Telephone lines and underground cables
   Power transmission lines and transformers

The Photo Reconnaissance Mission

The two basic requirements of a successful photo reconnaissance mission are (1) to obtain desired coverage of terrain and target areas, and (2) to assure the safe return of the reconnaissance aircraft. Therefore, penetration aids are used where appropriate, and routes to and from the target area are planned to avoid known air defense detection devices and weapons *(Figure 15-10)*. The choice of high or low-altitude regimes and type of aircraft used for a given mission is determined by such items as the specific purpose of photography, location and distance to the target, enemy defenses, terrain, weather, day or night coverage, aircraft performance, and navigation capability. The size and shape of target areas also have an influence on the type and number of aircraft deployed.

Whenever feasible, flight lines are oriented parallel to the long dimension of the target area, and flights are made downwind to shorten the time over the target and to minimize drift. Such recommended procedures may be altered in the event of extremely heavy enemy resistance or partial cloud cover over the target. High-speed vertical or oblique camera runs at low altitude over heavily defended areas are referred to as dicing runs; these are usually made by supersonic fighter-type aircraft for obvious reasons of safety *(Figure 15-11)*.

With conventional camera coverage, the time of photography depends on the amount of available light and special considerations, e.g., the need for photographing potential beach-landing sites at low tide levels. Ideally, most visible-light photography is obtained at least two hours after sunrise and two hours before sunset. Color films are preferably exposed during midday hours for best tonal renditions.

The time of photography is also dependent on the exact objectives of the sortie or mission. For enemy terrain not previously covered, pre-strike sorties must be timed to obtain maximum information on both primary and secondary targets as well as data on the intensity and distribution of target defenses. Camouflage detection may require sequential coverage at different hours so that target shadows can be analyzed. Damage-assessment missions should be scheduled as soon as smoke clears following a bombing run or strike.

For each roll of film exposed during a mission, a photo intelligence data card should be completed to show the following types of information:

1. Geographic region and specific location of target area
2. User's file number and security classification of film
3. Date and time of photography
4. Sortie number and designation of film processing unit
5. Map references to photographic coverage
6. Camera designation and focal length
7. Camera position, e.g., vertical or oblique angle
8. Flight altitude above mean sea level
9. Inclusive print numbers
10. Notes on photographic quality or missing coverage

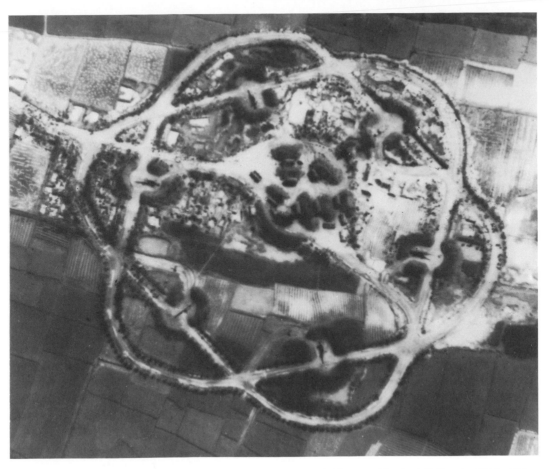

FIGURE 15-10. Surface-to-air missile site near Hanoi, North Vietnam. The installation is 450 by 700 feet in size and contains six launching pads. Five SAM's are visible. Courtesy of U.S. Department of Defense.

FIGURE 15-11. Low oblique view of communist MIG fighter planes parked in protective revetments near Hanoi, North Vietnam. Such imagery is necessarily obtained on high-speed "dicing runs"; hence there is some loss of photographic sharpness. Courtesy of U.S. Department of Defense.

Terrain Analysis and Trafficability

The military interpreter's primary task begins with the successful completion of the photo reconnaissance mission. He may be called upon to evaluate terrain conditions, identify key military or industrial targets, detect camouflaged installations, or recognize warships and military aircraft. Finally, his analyses must be summarized in clear, concise photo intelligence reports. Accordingly, these activities are discussed in the sections that follow.

The primary objective of military terrain analyses is that of predicting trafficability, i.e., the effects of terrain factors on the movements of land-based military troops and vehicles. In addition to slopes that are too steep to be readily climbed, there are four principal elements of the landscape that produce obstacles to movement. These are surface irregularities or microrelief, vegetation, hydrologic features, and cultural phenomena. A surface irregularity is considered to be a configuration of the terrain that is of such magnitude as to interfere with troop or vehicular movement. Examples include boulders that are found in many deserts and glaciated regions, potholes, streambeds, and hummocks such as those occurring in arctic regions.

In many parts of the world, plants grow so large and close together as to make vehicular movement impossible. However, even when trees are so spaced that movement between them is feasible, the necessary maneuvering may severely impede forward progress, not only because of the increased path length, but also because turning forces exert a higher load on the soil than those generated in a straight-line movement. Thus the soil strength requirements for a given vehicle are greater when the vehicle is maneuvering than when it is moving forward on a straight path.

Hydrologic occurrences include all bodies of water that impede military movement. Such features constitute obstacles whenever the water becomes deep enough or turbulent enough to threaten the safety or operation of military vehicles. Cultural features of the terrain that would restrict vehicle travel or necessitate maneuvering include items such as walls, hedgerows, ditches, dikes, embankments, and deep gullies.

The major problem in forecasting terrain trafficability by use of aerial photographs is the determination of the soil type. This cannot be done directly; instead, the soil type must be deduced from photographic evidence of the type, together with drainage, vegetation, topography, climate, and geological history. While this knowledge does not result in a direct inference of the soil type, it produces estimates of fundamental soil properties such as texture, soil moisture, plasticity, density, and internal drainage. With such information, the soil can then be fitted into an existing classification. Evidence must therefore be sought on aerial photographs that will permit reliable evaluations of fundamental soil properties.

Target Identification and Analysis

The identification of various physical, cultural, and industrial features has been stressed in several previous chapters of this volume. It should be obvious that the military interpreter requires a knowledge of economic and industrial geography and must also be prepared to work closely with intelligence specialists in these and other fields. Industrial analysts can be especially helpful in functional appraisals, i.e., determining "what goes on" inside a large factory or a group of innocuous-looking buildings. Without their assistance, the interpreter might be able only to guess at the purpose and importance of certain structures; with special help, the "possible" or "probable" presence of a given target may be translated into a positive identification. A complete functional analysis not only provides target identification; it also results in a detailed report that includes a numerical referencing system for the target components. One of the key features of such reports is a building-by-building survey of all facilities identified, e.g., the listing of industrial components as described and illustrated in Chapter 14.

Following the identification and functional analysis of a target complex, it is often necessary to make a structural analysis of features involved. Structural analyses are especially valuable when the target is a substantial engineering structure or a well-buttressed building that houses an industrial operation. The purpose of a structural analysis is to determine the relative vulnerability of the target, the type and tonnage of explosives needed to destroy it, and the most effective "aiming point" for pilots and bombardiers. For large industrial targets, the center of a circle having a radius of 500 to 1,000 feet might be selected as the aiming point; the exact size of the circle would be based on the area of the target complex and the expected pattern and precision of bomb drops. For small or linear targets such as bridges or canal locks, the "circle of error" must be much smaller to inflict significant damage.

Referring to *Figure 15-12*, for instance, highly precise bomb drops would be necessary to incapacitate the canal locks pictured; near misses here would do only limited damage

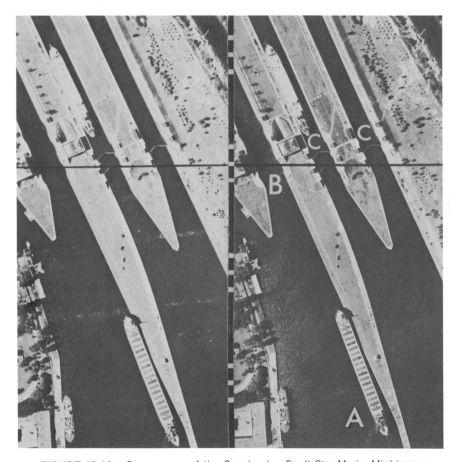

FIGURE 15-12. Stereogram of the Soo Locks, Sault Ste. Marie, Michigan. The ore boat (A) is moving toward the open lock (B). Two closed locks are also clearly visible (C). Scale is about 400 feet per inch. Courtesy of Abrams Aerial Survey Corp.

to this seaway installation. A different kind of target problem is presented by the ammunition dump shown in *Figure 15-13*. The underground storage of explosives in scattered, underground bunkers would probably require either pinpoint bombing of each storage cell or the use of incendiaries that might trigger a chain of explosions fed by the stored munitions. An example of a bomb-drop pattern around a radar installation is illustrated by *Figure 15-14*. Although the walls of all four structures are still in evidence, apparent direct hits were scored on the center building at "A" and the large building at "B". Differences in the diameters of craters are some indication of the various sizes of bombs that were dropped.

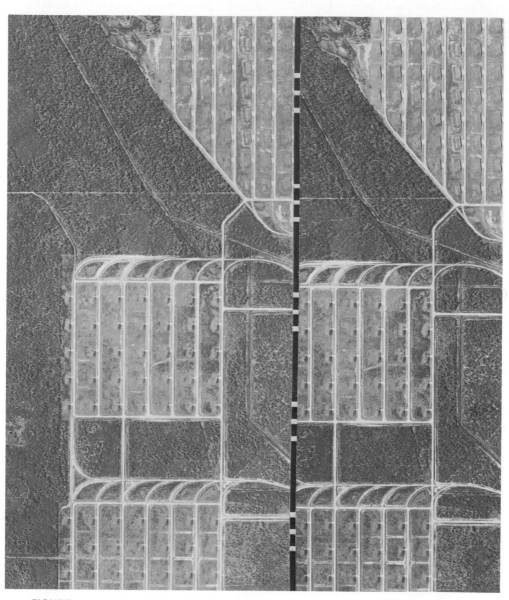

FIGURE 15-13. Ammunition storage in Calhoun County, Arkansas. Each storage cell is covered by several feet of earth material. Scale is about 1,667 feet per inch. Courtesy of U.S. Department of Agriculture.

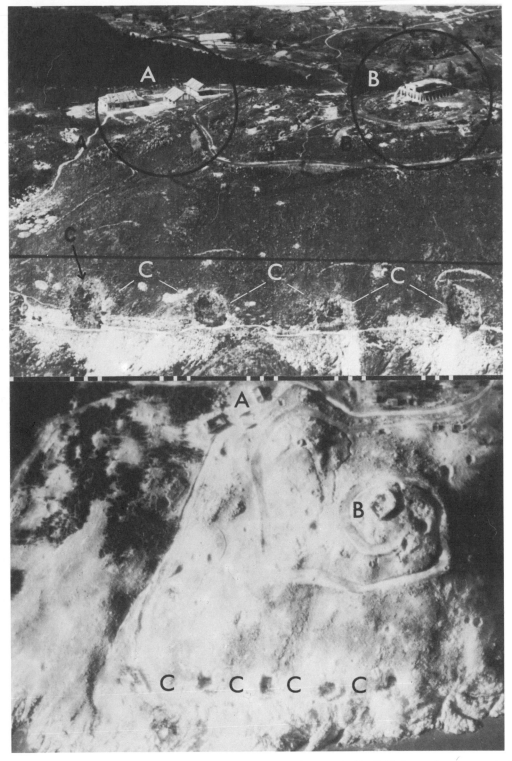

FIGURE 15-14. Oblique pre-strike view (above) of radar site area in North Vietnam showing control buildings (A), "Parthenon" support building (B), and coastal gun emplacements (C). The lower vertical view was made following an air strike on the installation. Courtesy of U.S. Department of the Navy.

Camouflage Detection

Camouflage is a means of protecting important targets by concealing or disguising various activities and installations. Within the broad spectrum of camouflage techniques are also included the use of decoys and dummy targets that are intended to confuse or mislead the photo interpreter, the aerial observer, or the bombardier. The rapid detection of camouflaged objects is vital to the interpreter, because air strikes cannot be directed against targets that pass unnoticed. Undetected targets can cause field commanders to misdirect troop movements and possibly lead to an enemy ambush. The interpreter should also realize that the more elaborate the camouflage, the more important is the hidden facility, because extensive and detailed concealment efforts are necessarily limited to the most critical installations.

Diversified concealment techniques may utilize natural cover, cut vegetation, bombed-out structures, or artificial "blending devices" such as nets, drapes, paints, and artificial toning schemes *(Figure 15-15)*. In other instances, bridges that have been destroyed by air strikes may be rebuilt one or two feet beneath the surface of a river to escape aerial detection, or dummy anti-aircraft emplacements may be set up to confuse and divert pilots on bombing missions.

Dummies or decoy targets are often cleverly constructed so that pilots and bombardiers will be lured into wasting their efforts by striking these unimportant installations. In other cases, dummies may be made obviously asymmetrical so that the opposition will

FIGURE 15-15. Camouflaged railway rolling stock in North Vietnam. While such crude attempts at concealment may be scorned by a skilled interpreter, they can be quite effective against visual observation from fast-moving aircraft. Courtesy of U.S. Air Force.

recognize them as decoys and will therefore carefully avoid bombing or strafing the pseudo-target. It then becomes feasible to store vital supplies of petroleum or ammunition underground beneath such dummies, with a reasonable assurance that they will remain safe from air strikes *(Figure 15-16)*.

For detecting buildings concealed by camouflage, the stereoscopic study of shadows is an important tool of the photo interpreter. Although carefully disguised features may not be readily discernible on a single print, the three-dimensional view quickly separates real buildings from two-dimensional shadows or camouflage. This technique is especially effective for picking out such items as false roads painted across buildings or camouflage that is designed to simulate roof damage on intact structures.

Whenever it is available, stereoscopic coverage should always be used in searching for camouflaged targets. Sequential photography is also of considerable value for making comparisons of terrain at different points in time. In areas where cut vegetation or infrared-absorbing paints are utilized for concealing installations, photographic coverage with camouflage-detection or infrared color film may be used to advantage (see Chapter 6).

FIGURE 15-16. To an untrained observer, this wagon-wheel pattern might appear to be a dummy or decoy target laid out by a diabolical camouflage expert. Actually, it is a multi-runway airfield used by carrier-based pilots for practicing short takeoffs and landings. Location is Broward County, Florida. Scale is about 1,667 feet per inch.

Interpreters of camouflage must constantly look for subtle changes in terrain features such as harmless-appearing clearings, excavations or debris piles that denote new construction, or vehicle tracks that seemingly lead nowhere. If certain installations are unusually conspicuous, they may be recognized as dummy targets; hence they must be carefully studied to determine whether they were purposely designed to be recognized or whether they merely represent unskilled attempts at disguise.

Finally, searches should be made continually in the vicinity of heavy defense installations. When anti-aircraft batteries or surface-to-air missiles are heavily concentrated in areas that seem to have no need for such protection, it may be an indication of a skillfully camouflaged industry or a troop concentration center. Or, it could be a carefully set trap to lead pilots over a worthless target and into a ring of flak. The task of the camouflage interpreter obviously entails responsibilities that cannot be minimized.

Recognition of Warships and Aircraft

Activities in the vicinity of shipyards, drydocks, and military airfields can be regularly monitored by the photo interpreter who receives frequent comparative coverage of such facilities. It is therefore important that he be able to recognize the main types of warships and airplanes that are apt to come under his surveillance. A full and comprehensive treatment of this subject is beyond the scope of this volume, because coverage here is limited to unclassified information and illustrations of United States vessels and aircraft. Nevertheless, a brief introduction should serve to familiarize the nonmilitary interpreter with elementary principles of ship and aircraft recognition.

Drawings that illustrate ship nomenclature and four general types of United States vessels are reproduced in *Figures 15-17* and *15-18*. The fastest means of identifying the type of ship being studied is by use of the discriminating length-to-beam ratio. Overall size and hull shape are also important clues to recognition. To identify specific classes of ships, characteristics such as the number and position of gun turrets, masts, stacks, type of superstructure, and aircraft-launching catapults are salient features to be considered. Military interpreters are supplied with reference manuals and up-to-date photo interpretation keys that permit rapid identification of ships and aircraft carriers; a portion of such a key is presented in *Table 15-1* as an example.

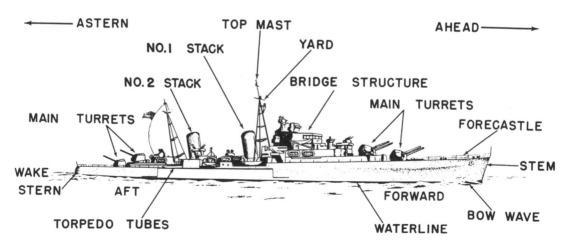

FIGURE 15-17. Ship nomenclature for battleships, cruisers, and destroyers. Courtesy of U.S. Department of the Navy.

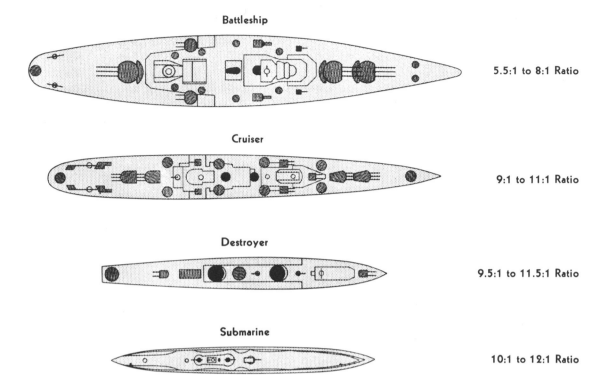

FIGURE 15-18. Four general types of United States vessels. Numbers indicate length-to-beam ratios for each type. The number and arrangements of gun turrets, stacks, and the superstructure design are useful clues in recognizing types of warships. Courtesy of U.S. Department of the Navy.

TABLE 15-1. Sample portion of a dichotomous key for identifying naval vessels[1]

A. Flight deck . . . . See B

A. No flight deck . . . . See D

B. Flight deck has no taper aft (square end); 1 large gun tube forward of flight deck; both forward and aft aircraft elevators square . . . . CVE Commencement Bay

B. Flight deck has slight taper aft; no large gun tube forward of flight deck; either forward or aft aircraft elevator rectangular . . . . See C

C. 1 large gun tube aft of flight deck (only half visible on vertical photos); aft aircraft elevator square . . . . CVE Casablanca

C. 2 large gun tubes aft of flight deck; aft aircraft elevator rectangular . . . . CVE Bogue

D. Wide beam in relation to length; pyramidal superstructure . . . . BB South Dakota

D. Narrow beam in relation to length . . . . See E

E. 3 main turrets—2 forward, 1 aft . . . . See F

E. 5, 4, 2, or no main turrets . . . . See I

(continued)

[1] Source: U.S. Department of the Navy.

Most United States vessels, with the exception of new super carriers, have a beam (width) that does not exceed 108 feet. This limitation has been historically imposed upon shipbuilders because of the 110-foot width of locks in the Panama Canal. Stereograms from three different United States shipyards are presented in *Figures 15-19* through *15-21*. A wide array of warships and aircraft carriers are pictured in these views.

Proficiency in aircraft recognition requires the photo interpreter to stay constantly aware of new designs and modifications that are rapidly made operational, especially during times of war. In essence, aircraft types are differentiated on the basis of fuselage length, wing span, wing shape, stabilizer design, and number and position of engines. Inasmuch as most military aircraft are now powered by jet engines, the fundamental differences between jet and propeller-driven planes will be briefed here. Descriptions are by permission of the U.S. Department of the Navy.

In the case of single-engine aircraft, jet planes will usually display one or more of the following recognition features as compared to propeller types:

1. The wing is farther back from the nose.
2. The widest part of the fuselage is near the center.
3. The wing is usually angled (tapered, swept, or delta) back inboard to outboard.

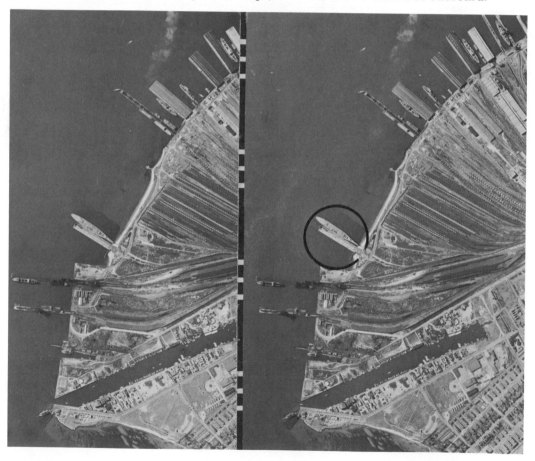

FIGURE 15-19. This 1953 stereogram from Newport News, Virginia shows a battleship of the Missouri class. At an assumed photo scale of 1,667 feet per inch, this "mothballed" vessel measures over 850 feet in length. Courtesy of U.S. Department of Agriculture.

FIGURE 15-20. A 1956 view of the U.S. Naval Shipyard at Hunter's Point in San Francisco County, California. Several classes of aircraft carriers, along with other naval warships, are shown. Scale is about 1,667 feet per inch.

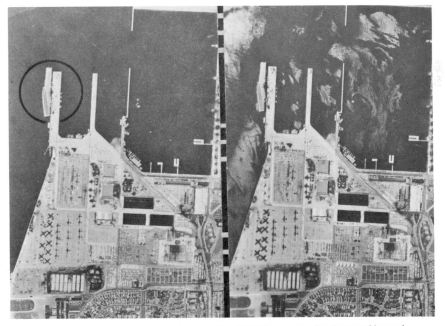

FIGURE 15-21. This 1959 view of the U.S. Naval Air Station at Alameda, California, shows a modern, canted-deck aircraft carrier that measures over 800 feet in length. Note also the variety of propeller-type aircraft in this view. Scale is about 1,667 feet per inch.

4. The wing usually has less surface area.
5. The distance from the wing to the horizontal stabilizer is less than that from the wing to the nose.
6. The horizontal stabilizer is well above the fuselage.

In distinguishing twin and multi-engine jets from their propeller-driven counterparts, fewer differences are apparent. However, jet types will usually have one or more of these characteristics:

1. The wing is usually angled (tapered, swept, or delta) back inboard to outboard (*Figure 15-22*).
2. The engines are usually suspended from the wing, whereas the engine nacelle is usually *in* the wing on propeller types.
3. The wing has less surface area.
4. The horizontal stabilizer is well above the fuselage.

Photo Intelligence Reports

Because photo intelligence reports may assume a wide range of formats under varying operational requirements, only three general types will be briefed here. These are flash reports, immediate reports, and mission review reports. As a general rule, all intelligence

FIGURE 15-22. Military jet bombers pictured here (swept wings) include 30 B-47's and one B-52 (circled). The straight-winged planes below the dashed line are older, propeller-type aircraft. This stereogram from Dade County, Florida is shown at a scale of about 800 feet per inch.

reports include certain basic data such as the name of the reporting interpretation unit, date of report, exact geographic description of the target area, the organizational unit which exposed the photography, and map references.

Flash reports are made after rapid study of new photographic coverage. A standard format is not required for flash reports; the interpreter makes notes of the obvious intelligence elements and immedately summarizes these by voice to the designated intelligence unit. Immediate reports are similar to flash reports in purpose, but they are prepared in written form and may contain additional details. Immediate reports represent the first careful analysis of photo reconnaissance imagery, and prescribed formats are frequently used. For maximum utility, they may be prepared directly on photographic prints for mass distribution *(Figure 15-23)*.

Mission review reports are prepared following further and more detailed analysis of reconnaissance imagery. As a rule, there are no time limitations on such reports, because their value lies in their overall intelligence content rather than their use by a specific requesting unit. A standardized format is commonly required, and the reports are widely distributed. A portion of a mission review report, based on a photo reconnaissance exercise over Hunter Air Force Base, follows:

1. Base located about 3.5 nautical miles SSW of Savannah, Georgia.

2. One hard-surfaced runway, east-west, 11,375 feet by 200 feet. An overrun of approximately 1,250 feet is under construction at the east end of the runway. Hard-surfaced taxiways connect the runway with a very large concrete parking apron and with an alert parking area containing 11 ramps.

3. Major buildings and facilities: two very large and four medium hangers, 19 wing hangers, two POL areas (one with five large, revetted pontoon tanks and one containing approximately 15 underground tanks), two ammo storage areas (one with 17 earth-covered bunkers and one with three earth-covered bunkers plus two more under construction), one control tower, one GCA radar, 17 operations and administration buildings, three

FIGURE 15-23. An immediate photo intelligence report based on this pre-strike and post-strike photography would include the mission or sortie number, dates of photography, photo scales or flight altitudes, and the extent of damage to the North Vietnam railroad bridge pictured. In this instance, photographs were made just five days apart. Courtesy of U.S. Department of Defense.

large administration buildings, 98 barracks units, one hospital with 23 interconnected wards, 320 family-housing units, and 16 large warehouses. Served by two secondary roads and one railroad.

4. Aircraft activity: 61 B-47's, 32 KC-97's, four C-130's, one C-121, two C-54's, one C-123, two F-80's, and three utility aircraft.

5. General activity: Airfield is operational, with moderate activity.

Post-Strike Damage Assessment

The principal objectives of post-strike damage asessment are (1) to estimate the amount of production loss to industries or the degree of destruction to structures, (2) to determine the need for additional strikes on certain targets, and (3) to analyze the effectiveness of various types of bombs and weapons used in aerial attacks. By necessity, appraisal of damage from post-strike aerial photographs is based on average ratios between visible damage and actual damage for different classes of targets.

Damage to structures such as bridges, ammunition dumps, and airport runways can be quickly and reliably assessed from various types of aerial imagery, whereas the effects on an industrial production line can only be estimated from an analysis of damage to the building which houses the industrial operation. Pre-strike and post-strike photographs, a simulated damage appraisal form, and standard damage symbols are shown in *Figures 15-24* through *15-27*. Last of all, the complete destruction of a target area is revealed by comparative vertical photography of Hiroshima, Japan, in *Figures 15-28* and *15-29*.

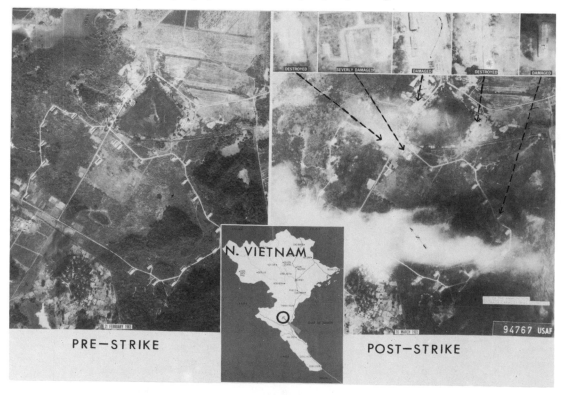

FIGURE 15-24. Pre-strike and post-strike views of an ammunition depot in North Vietnam. Damages can be more easily assessed on exposed targets of this type than for operations housed inside substantial industrial buildings. Courtesy of U.S. Department of Defense.

COVER USED				AC/AS INTELLIGENCE PHOTOGRAPHIC DIVISION PHOTO-INTELLIGENCE SECTION		D/P

COVER USED
- MISSION: *23 SKIDOO*
- PRINTS: *94767 USAF*
- DATE: *16 MARCH 1965*
- QUALITY: *GOOD*
- SCALE: *1:20,000*
- DATE OF ATTACK: *16 MARCH 1965*

AC/AS INTELLIGENCE PHOTOGRAPHIC DIVISION PHOTO-INTELLIGENCE SECTION

LIMITED DAMAGE INTERPRETATION

NO. *007*

D/P
- DATE: *20 MARCH 1965*
- INTERPRETER: *I. C. SMOKE*
- SHEET NO. *1* OF *1*
- AREA NO. *VICTOR* / TARGET NO. *CHARLIE*

TARGET: *AMMUNITION DEPOT*   LOCATION: *NORTH VIETNAM*

This Limited Damage Interpretation has been undertaken in accordance with the condiiions as checked below:

- [ ] Photography is inadequate in scale
- [ ] Photography is indequate in quality
- [X] Stereo coverage is lacking or incomplete
- [ ] Detailed interpretation is not required
- [ ] Damage is below 10% of built-up area
- [ ] Total damage is less than 50,000 sq. ft.
- [ ] Excessive time between attack and photography
- [ ] Other factors as noted below

BUILDING		VISIBLE DAMAGE		DESCRIPTION OF DAMAGE
REF. NO.	AREA	STRUCT'L	SUPERF'L	
30 TO 40 BUILDINGS IN DEPOT	*1,024 ACRES*	*SEE PHOTOS (FIG. 15-24)*		*21 % OF AMMUNITION STORAGE CAPACITY WAS DESTROYED*

SAMPLE ONLY

TOTALS			APPROVED BY:
SITE	SITE AREA	*APPROX. 1,024 ACRES*	*John D. Facsimile Cdr., U.S.N.*
	BUILT-UP AREA	*SAME*	
	% OF SITE BUILT-UP	*100 %*	
DAMAGE	AREA OF DAMAGE	*400-500 ACRES*	
	% OF BUILT-UP AREA	*21 %*	

ALL AREAS ARE PLAN AREAS IN THOUSANDS OF SQUARE FEET

FIGURE 15-25. Assessment of air strike damage based on Figure 15-24. Simulated data were supplied by the author. The damage interpretation form is reproduced by permission of the U.S. Department of the Navy.

FIGURE 15-26. Pre-strike and post-strike views of a European aircraft factory during World War II. Component shop (1) is largely destroyed, and subassembly shop (2) is heavily damaged. Small buildings (3) and hanger (4) are demolished. Construction of other hangers (5, 6) was never completed. Courtesy of U.S. Department of Defense.

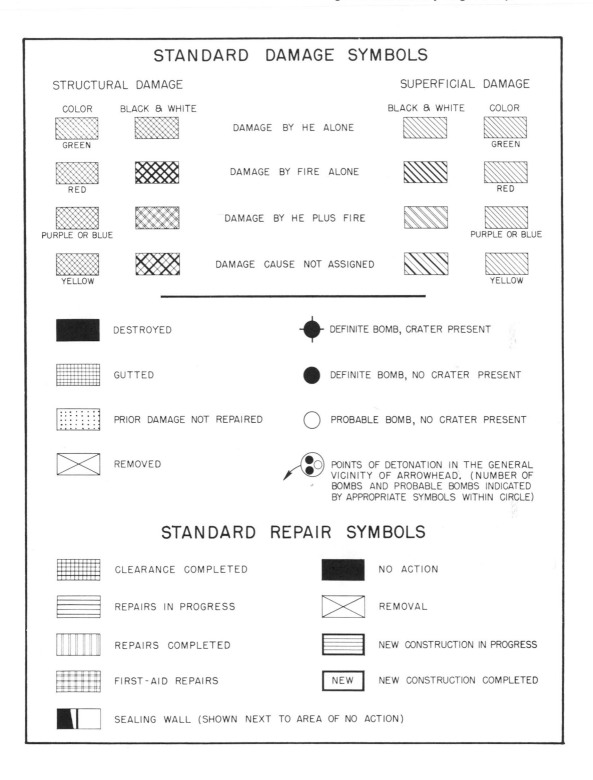

FIGURE 15-27. Symbols for photo reconnaissance damage assessment. Courtesy of U.S. Department of the Navy.

FIGURE 15-28. Pre-strike view of Hiroshima, Japan, showing the high density of the built-up areas. Fire lanes cleared by the Japanese are clearly discernible. Courtesy of U.S. Air Force.

FIGURE 15-29. View of Hiroshima following the dropping of an atomic bomb. Courtesy of U.S. Air Force.

References

Avery, T. Eugene.
  1965. Evaluating the potential of photo interpreters. Photogram. Engineering 31: 1,051-1,059, illus.

Bigelow, George F.
  1955. A preferred approach to the military photo interpretation of industries. Photogram. Engineering 21:579-582.

Colwell, Robert N.
  1965. Aids for the selection and training of photo interpreters. Photogram. Engineering 31:327-339, illus.

Dulles, Allen.
  1963. *The Craft of Intelligence.* Harper and Row, Inc., New York, N.Y. 277 pp., illus.

Griffith, Samuel B.
  1963. *Sun Tzu: The Art of War.* Oxford-Clarendon Press, London, 197 pp.

Kalk, Michael, and Enoch, Jay M.
  1960. An objective test procedure designed to aid in selecting, training, and rating photo interpreters. Photogram. Engineering 26:228-237, illus.

Martinek, Harold, and Sadacca, Robert.
  1961. Human factors studies in image interpretation. Photogram. Engineering 27: 714-716.

Monier, Robert B., and Vent, Herbert J.
  1959. Photo interpretation: an application to radiation studies of survivors of the Hiroshima and Nagasaki nuclear explosions. Photogram. Engineering 25: 787-792, illus.

Orlov, Alexander.
  1963. *Handbook of Intelligence and Guerrilla Warfare.* University of Michigan Press, Ann Arbor, Michigan, 187 pp.

Sadacca, Robert.
  1963. Human factors in image interpretation. Photogram. Engineering 24:978-988.

Seacord, Daniel F., Jr.
  1959. Photography of nuclear detonation. Photogram. Engineering 25:367-372, illus.

Tully, Andrew.
  1962. *C.I.A.: The Inside Story.* William Morrow and Co., New York, N.Y., 276 pp.

U.S. Departments of Army, Navy, and Air Force.
  1954. Photographic interpretation handbook. Government Printing Office, Washington, D.C., 303 pp., illus.

Van Lopik, J. R.
  1962. Optimum utilization of airborne sensors in military geography. Photogram. Engineering 28:773-778, illus.

Whitmore, George D.
  1958. The role of photogrammetry in an "open skies" program. Photogram. Engineering 24:376-382, illus.

GLOSSARY OF PHOTOGRAMMETRIC TERMS[1]

Air base: The line joining two aerial camera stations. (MPI)

Altitude: Height above a datum. The datum is usually mean sea level. (MPI)

Anaglyph: A stereogram in which the two views are printed superimposed in complementary colors. A three-dimensional image is rendered when the stereogram is viewed through spectacles having filters of the same colors (usually red and green).

Angle of coverage: The apex of the cone of rays passing through the front nodal point of a lens. *Normal-angle lens* — a lens having an angle of coverage up to 75°; *wide-angle lens* — a lens having an angle of coverage of 75° to 100°; *ultra wide-angle lens* — a lens having an angle of coverage greater than 100°. (MP)

Aperture, relative: The ratio of the equivalent focal length to the diameter of the entrance "pupil" of a photographic lens. Expressed "f:4.5," etc. Also called "f-number," "stop," "aperture stop," "diaphragm stop," "speed". (MPI)

Base, film: A thin, flexible, transparent sheet of cellulose nitrate, acetate, or similar material which is coated with a light-sensitive emulsion and used for taking photographs. (MPI)

Base, photo: The distance between the principal points of two adjacent prints of a series of vertical aerial photographs. It is usually measured on one print after transferring the principal point of the other print. (MPI)

Camera calibration: The determination of the focal length, the lens distortion in the focal plane, and the location of the principal point with respect to the fiducial marks. The settings of the fiducial marks and the positioning of the lens are ordinarily considered as "adjustments," although they are sometimes performed during the calibration process. In a multiple-lens camera, the calibration also includes the determination of the angles between the component units. (MPI)

Camera magazine: The removable part of a camera in which the unexposed and exposed portions of film are contained. (MPI)

Camera station: The point in space, in the air, or on the ground, occupied by the camera lens at the moment of exposure. Also called the "exposure station." (MPI)

Contact print: A print made from a negative or a diapositive in direct contact with sensitized material. (MPI)

Contrast, subject: The difference in light intensity between the brightest highlights and the deepest shadow.

Control point: A reference point precisely located on a photograph and on the ground; used in assembly of photographs for map compilation.

Coverage: The ground area represented on aerial photographs, photomosaics or maps. (MPI)

---

[1]Source of the majority of terms: *Manual of Photogrammetry* and the *Manual of Photographic Interpretation*, by permission of the American Society of Photogrammetry. These terms are identified, respectively, as (MP and MPI).

Crab: 1. (Aerial photography) — The condition caused by failure to orient the camera with respect to the track of the airplane, indicated in vertical photography by the sides of the photographs not being parallel to the principal-point base line. See *drift*.

    2. (Air navigation) — Any turning of an airplane which causes its longitudinal axis to vary from the track of the plane. (MPI)

Datum: A reference element, such as a line or plane, in relation to which the positions of other elements are determined. Also called the "reference plane" or "datum plane". (MPI)

Density: The comparative amount of silver deposited by exposure and development in a given area. It is expressed in terms of the percentage of light passing through the area. (MPI)

Depth of field: The distance between the points nearest to and farthest from the camera that are in focus and acceptably "sharp".

Diapositive: A positive photographic print on a transparent medium — usually glass. Most commonly used in stereo-plotting instruments.

Displacement, relief: The difference in the position of a point above or below the datum, with respect to the datum position of that point, owing to the perspective of an aerial photograph. Relief displacement is radial from a point on the photograph corresponding to the ground position vertically beneath the camera. In vertical photography, relief displacement is radial from the principal point of the photograph. (MPI)

Distance, hyperfocal: The distance from the camera lens to the nearest object in focus, when the camera lens is focused at infinity.

Dodging: The process of holding back light from certain areas of the sensitized paper in making a print in order to avoid overprinting those areas. In projection printing, it is accomplished by inserting an opaque medium of proper shape and size between the lens and the easel, and in contact printing, either by varying the illumination in given areas of the negative or by inserting translucent or opaque paper between the light source and the negative. Dodging may also be performed automatically by means of specially designed electronic or fluorescent printers. (MPI)

Drift: 1. (Air navigation) — The horizontal displacement of an aircraft, under the action of the wind, from the track it would have followed in still air.

    2. (Aerial photography) — Sometimes used to indicate a special condition of crab wherein the photographer has continued to make exposures oriented to the predetermined line of flight while the airplane has drifted from that line. (MPI)

Effective area: For any aerial photograph that is one of a series in a flight strip, that central part of the photograph delimited by the bisectors of overlaps with adjacent photographs. On a vertical photograph, all images within the effective area have less displacement than their conjugate images on adjacent photographs. (MPI)

Emulsion: A suspension of light-sensitive silver salt, usually silver chloride or silver bromide, in a colloidal medium, usually gelatin, used for coating photographic films, plates, or paper. (MPI)

Ferrotype: To burnish photographic prints by squeegeeing wet upon a japanned sheet of iron or stainless plate and allowing to dry; this produces a harder, glossier surface on the photographic print. (MPI)

Fiducial marks: Index marks, rigidly connected with the camera lens through the camera body, which form images on the negative. The marks are adjusted so that the intersection of lines drawn between opposite fiducial marks defines the principal point. (MPI)

Filter: A transparent material used in the optical path of a camera lens to absorb a certain portion of the spectrum and prevent its reaching the sensitized photographic film. (MPI)

Focal length, equivalent: The distance measured along the lens axis from the rear nodal point to the plane of best average definition over the entire field used in the aerial camera. (MPI)

Focal plane: The plane (perpendicular to the axis of the lens) in which images of points in the object field of the lens are focused. (MPI)

Fog: A darkening of negatives or prints by a deposit of silver which does not form a part of the image. Fog tends to increase density and decrease contrast. It may be caused by exposure to unwanted light, exposure to air during development, forced development, impure chemicals, etc. (MPI)

Glossy print: Print made on photographic paper with a shiny surface. (MPI)

Hotspot (sunspot): The destruction of fine image detail on a portion of a wide-angle aerial photograph. It is caused by the absence of shadows and by halation near the prolongation of a line from the sun through the exposure station.

Index, photo: An index map made by assembling the individual photographs into their proper relative positions and copying the assembly photographically at a reduced scale. (MPI)

Intervalometer: A timing device for automatically operating the shutter of a camera at any predetermined interval. (MPI)

Isocenter: The point on a photograph intersected by the bisector of the angle between the plumb line and the photograph perpendicular. The isocenter is significant because it is the center of radiation for displacements of images owing to tilt. (MPI)

Line, flight: A line drawn on a map or chart to represent the track over which an aircraft has been flown or is to fly. The line connecting the principal points of vertical aerial photographs. (MPI)

Magazine: A container for protecting and holding film while the camera is in operation. It is usually detachable from the camera so that a new magazine or film roll may be introduced during flight. (MPI)

Map, flight: A map on which are indicated the desired lines of flight and/or positions of exposures for the taking of aerial photographs, or the map on which are plotted, after photography, selected air stations and the tracks between them. (MPI)

Map, planimetric: A map showing only the horizontal positions of drainage and cultural features.

Map, topographic: A map showing correct horizontal and vertical positions of features represented.

Marks, static: Marks on a negative caused by discharges of static electricity, particularly when the unexposed negatives are handled rapidly under dry conditions. The marks are of many different types. Some are easily recognized as branching or tree-like static, and some are distinctive, more or less sharply defined as dots. (MPI)

Matte print: Print made on photographic paper with a dull finish; more suitable for pencil or ink annotations than a glossy print. (MPI)

Mosaic: An assemblage of overlapping aerial photographs whose edges have been matched to form a continuous photographic representation of a portion of the earth's surface. (MPI)

Nadir, photograph: That point at which a vertical line through the perspective center of the camera lens pierces the plane of the photograph. Also referred to as the "nadir point". (MPI)

Negative, dense: A negative of which all parts have high opacity; the result of over-exposure. (MPI)

Negative titling: Information (e.g., sortie number, camera, date, height, etc.) recorded on the negative for identification. (MPI)

Overdevelopment: The result of permitting film or paper to remain in the developer too long, resulting in excessive contrast or fog. (MPI)

Overexposure: The result of too much light being permitted to act on a light-sensitive material, with either too great a lens aperture or too slow a shutter speed or both. Results in excessive image density. (MPI)

Overlap (photography): Amount by which one photograph overlaps the area covered by another, customarily expressed as a percentage. The overlap between aerial photographs in the same flight is distinguished as the *end lap,* and the overlap between photographs in adjacent parallel flights is called the *side lap.* (MP)

Parallax: The apparent displacement of the position of a body with respect to a reference point or system, caused by a shift in the point of observation. (MPI).

Photogrammetry: The science or art of obtaining reliable measurements by means of photography. (MPI)

Photographic day: One with good visibility, bright sunlight, and less than 10 percent cloud cover.

Photographic interpretation (photo interpretation): The act of examining photographic images for the purpose of identifying objects and judging their significance. (MPI)

Plate, pressure: A flat plate, usually of metal but frequently of glass or other substance which, by means of mechanical force, presses the film into contact with the focal plane plate of the camera. (MPI)

Print, semi-matte: A print intermediate in glossiness between a matte and a glossy print. (MPI)

Processing: The operation necessary to produce negatives, diapositives, or prints from exposed film, plates, or papers. (MPI)

Rectification: The process of converting a tilted or oblique photo to the plane of the vertical.

Representative fraction (R.F.): The relation between map or photo distance and ground distance, expressed as a fraction (1/25,000) or often as a ratio (1:25,000 or 1 inch on map = 25,000 inches on the ground). Also called "scale". (MPI)

Resolution: The ability of the entire photographic system, including lens, exposure, processing, and other factors, to render a sharply defined image. It is expressed in terms of lines per millimeter recorded by a particular film under specified conditions. (MPI)

Resolving power: A mathematical expression of lens definition, usually stated as the maximum number of lines per millimeter that can be resolved (that is, seen as separate lines) in the image (MPI)

Run: The line followed by a photographic aircraft in making a photo strip. (MPI)

Sensitivity, color: The sensitivity of a photographic emulsion to light of various wavelengths. (MPI)

Shrinkage, differential: The difference in unit contraction along the grain structure of the material as compared to the unit contraction across the grain structure; frequently applied to photographic film and papers and to mapping papers in general. (MPI)

Shutter, between-the-lens: A shutter located between the lens elements of a camera and usually consisting of thin metal leaves which open and close or revolve to make the exposure. (MPI)

Shutter, focal plane: A shutter located near the focal plane and consisting of a curtain with a slot which is pulled across the focal plane to make the exposure. (MPI)

Soft: A term applied to a print or negative of relatively low contrast; also applied to a picture which is not sharply focused. (MPI)

Strip: Any number of photos taken along a photo flight line, usually at an approximately constant altitude. (MPI)

Template (templet): A device used in radial triangulation to represent the aerial photograph; the template is a record of radial directions taken from the photographs.

Texture: In a photo image, the frequency of change and arrangement of tones. Some descriptive adjectives for textures are fine, medium, or coarse; and stippled or mottled. (MPI)

Tilt: The angle between the optical axis of the camera and the vertical. (MPI)

Tone: Each distinguishable shade variation from black to white. (MPI)

Underdevelopment: Insufficient development, due to developing either for too short a time or in a weakened developer, or occasionally at too low a temperature. (MPI)

Underexposure: The result of insufficient light being allowed to pass through the lens to produce all the tones of an image; or of sufficient light being allowed to pass for too short a period of time. (MPI)

Vignetting filter: A filter which gradually decreases in density from the center toward the edges. It is used in certain cases in photography or printing processes to produce a photograph of uniform density. (MPI)

Weight, double: Heavy-weight photographic paper. (MPI)

Weight, single: Light-weight photographic paper. (MPI)

INDEX

INDEX MOSAIC
OF
CHATTANOOGA, TENNESSEE

SCALE IN MILES

0   ¼   ½   ¾   1   2